INTERNAL SOURCES OF DEVELOPMENT FINANCE

INTERNAL SOURCES OF DEVELOPMENT FINANCE

Concepts, Issues, and Strategies

P. C. KUMAR

QUORUM BOOKS
Westport, Connecticut • London

Library of Congress Cataloging-in-Publication Data

Kumar, P. C.
    Internal sources of development finance : concepts, issues, and
strategies / P. C. Kumar.
        p.   cm.
    Includes bibliographical references and index.
    ISBN 0-89930-461-3 (alk. paper)
    1. Finance—Developing countries.   2. Economic development—
Finance.   3. Privatization—Developing countries.   I. Title.
HG195.K86   1994
332.2′8′091724—dc20   92-31838

British Library Cataloguing in Publication Data is available.

Library of Congress Catalog Card Number: 92–31838
ISBN: 0-89930-461-3

First published in 1994

Quorum Books, 88 Post Road West, Westport, CT 06881
An imprint of Greenwood Publishing Group, Inc.

Printed in the United States of America

∞™

The paper used in this book complies with the
Permanent Paper Standard issued by the National
Information Standards Organization (Z39.48-1984).

10 9 8 7 6 5 4 3 2 1

In Memory of
My Parents
KMP and SP

Contents

Illustrations

FIGURES

TABLES

Introduction

Global economic development has engaged the attention of policy makers and social scientists in the past four decades more than any other topic. Every nation has perceived a vested interest in the associated dialogue in the context of its own development and from geopolitical considerations. The developing countries have been motivated by the need to meet the aspirations of their peoples and to improve their living standards and quality of life. The developed nations of the western world have perceived global development as a means of meeting the need for ever-expanding markets for their products and factors of production. Doubtless, strategic considerations weigh heavily as well. Global development is one of those rare topics that is characterized by unqualified consensus, even though there may be disagreement on the means to reach the end.

In strictly economic terms, development includes, *inter alia*, the capacity of a national economy to embark upon and sustain a steady growth in its gross national product (GNP). A related measure is the rate of growth of per-capita GNP, implicit in which is the capacity to expand national output faster than the growth of population. A measure that adjusts the per-capita GNP for inflation, the growth in real GNP, is an indicator of goods and services available for consumption and investment to the average individual. An implication of planned or directed development is the alteration of the structure of production and employment among the various sectors of the economy. More recently, the accepted economic measures of development have been supplemented by noneconomic social indicators, such as education, housing, medical care, etc.

Given the widespead interest in economic development, it has spawned a variety of theories. Single-variable theories emphasize low level of investment, limited human resources and capital, or the intrinsic nature of societies replete with rigidities as the principal factors inhibiting their development. Multi-variable theories emphasize several simultaneous factors, such as the appropriate political and social framework together with incentives for saving and investment. It is generally agreed that economic development is a complex process.

However, a central residual question relates to the financing of the process of development. It remains at its core a consideration quite independent of the path taken to reach the goals of development. The primary purpose of this book is to attempt to answer questions such as: How can nations promote internal sources to finance their development? What are the underlying conceptual foundations for such processes? What are the related issues? How effective are their strategies? What general lessons are available for other nations from these experiences?

This book attempts to provide partial answers to these questions. It is organized as follows. Part I recognizes that economic growth is not the sole determinant, but remains an important element, *inter alia*, of economic development. Chapter 1 provides a broad survey of some aspects of economic development. Chapter 2 deals with a survey of the literature on economic growth.

Part II deals with the internal sources of finance available for development. Chapter 3 discusses tax policies as elements of development finance. Chapter 4 provides a detailed treatment of the conceptual foundations of financial intermediation, the role of capital markets in Chapter 5 and by specialized institutions, such as development banks, in Chapter 6. The growing trend towards privatization—the shift from public ownership to private ownership, which is another aspect of financial intermediation—is discussed in Chapter 7.

As in works of this nature, acknowledgements are due to several individuals. While they are too numerous to identify individually (I hope to be forgiven for this omission), two groups merit special mention. First, thanks are due to Eric Valentine, Publisher of Quorum Books, for his cooperation, patience and understanding. His gentle prodding was instrumental in no small measure in getting the manuscript into its final form. Second, my gratitude is due to the members of my family for their solicitous support during the various mutations of this project. They endured my constant absences from the family scene with tolerance.

I

ECONOMIC DEVELOPMENT AND GROWTH: SURVEY AND SYNTHESIS

Part I provides an overview of the theories of economic development and growth. Chapter 1 provides a survey of the theories of economic development. It begins with a distinction between economic growth and economic development. The chapter discusses the role of the state in the development process. It describes the neoclassical, Marxist, and structuralist–institutionalist perspectives on economic development. Chapter 2 surveys theories of economic growth, such as the classical Harrod–Domar model, sources-of-growth analysis, and the roles of technology, investment, exports, and manufacturing activity. Olson's behavioral theory of the influence of common interest groups on economic growth is described. The rekindled interest in supply-side economics and its implications for growth are pursued. The chapter examines a more recent development in the literature, namely, endogenous-growth theory. However, the principal conclusion that emerges from this survey is that finance has not been considered a major factor in the growth and development process. Developing nations need to stregthen their financial institutions and markets, both from the aspect of developing internal sources to finance their growth and development as well as integrating themselves into the global marketplace.

1

The Concept of
Economic Development

1. INTRODUCTION

The topic of economic development came into prominence in the post-World War II era. The reconstruction of Germany and Japan brought home the realization that several other nations were also candidates for development. The term economic development has a number of connotations. It includes a clinical description, such as "the study of the economic structure and behavior of poor countries," as well as an action-based definition: "growing capacity for poverty reduction." There is general agreement that economic development is a multidimensional concept, in the sense that it embraces not only growth in income but a broad transformation of the economy in all its aspects as well. The scope of the literature in this area is indeed broad. Bardhan (1988), Chakravarty (1987), Chenery and Bruno (1962), Gemell (1987) and Stern (1989), survey the conceptual foundations of economic development and its policy implications. Little (1982) and Todaro (1985) also provide extensive treatment of the topic in their books. Adelman (1975) and Lewis (1984) provide interesting commentaries on the current state of the art. Chenery and Srinivasan (1988, vols. 1 and 2) provide extensive and intensive treatment of specific aspects of the subject.

This chapter is organized as follows. The following section discusses various definitions and descriptions of the concept. Section 3 summarizes Bardhan's contrast of the three principal approaches to economic development, namely, neoclassical, Marxist, and institutionalist–structuralist. Section 4 provides a discussion of some conceptual issues and, in particular, the role of government intervention, which Lal (1985) terms *dirigiste* economics. These arguments are counterbalanced by Lewis (1984) who asserts that the resource-allocation process in developing nations is not an extrapolation of the experiences of the developed nations. Section 5 summarizes and concludes the chapter.

2. WHAT IS ECONOMIC DEVELOPMENT?

Lewis (1984) defines development economics as the study of the economic structure and behavior of poor (or less developed) countries.[1] This definition characterizes economic development in a multidimensional framework. The concept embraces growth in per-capita income, but also includes growth in productive capacity, and improvements in health and education levels of its citizens, as well as reduction in poverty. Growth in income is a necessary but not sufficient condition for economic development. The latter is the transformation of the economy to include greater capital accumulation, better development of human resources, and more extensive evolution of infrastructure, both physical and institutional, for example, markets. Little (1982) identifies economic development (economic progress or real economic growth) as the growth in present value of weighted average per-capita consumption.[2] The allocation of weights raises the issue of equity and implies a value judgment of some sort. Little (1982), therefore, concludes there can be no real objective definition of development. Chenery (1983) observes that the term economic development came into general use in the post-World War II period "to indicate that something more than increased output was required to raise the welfare of poor countries" (p. 854). Morris (1984) prefers a definition of economic development based on increases in productive capacity to one related to poverty reduction. She argues for a concept of economic development as growing capacity for eventual poverty reduction. A suggestion is made that there should be a distinction between growth of capacity and its distributional consequences. Morris claims that this definition provides a natural link between historical and contemporary experience. A purely poverty-reduction-based definition would suggest there was no economic development in Great Britain in the first three decades of the industrial revolution. By the same token, poverty reduction is not progressing today in Great Britain, France, or Belgium to the same extent as in the previous century. That observation should not lead to the conclusion of an absence of development in these nations. Furthermore, Morris argues that a production-capacity-motivated definition provides a conceptual basis for identifying and comparing the diversity of paths by which countries develop. She therefore prefers to focus on "the expansion of capacity, both technological and institutional, of an economic system to provide sustained reductions in the proportion of the population in poverty" (p. 147).

Hirschman (1982) provides an interesting taxonomy of development theories. He describes the development theories of the 1940s and '50s as sharing two basic ingredients, namely, the monoeconomics claim and the mutual-benefit claim. The former states that economic principles are basically the same when applied in different scenarios and function equally well in all of them. The mutual-benefit claim states that economic relations between countries can be shaped to yield benefits to both. Both the claims are jointly embedded in orthodox economics. For example, it is believed there is an unified body of economic theory that applies equally well to developing and developed nations. It is not necessary to modify the theory when applied to developing countries. It is also believed that trade benefits both nations as a result of the comparative advantages possible. Development economics, on the other hand, accepts the mutual-benefit claim but rejects the monoeconomics claim. This explains the plethora of definitions of economic development. Marxist economics accepts the monoeconomics claim but rejects the mutual-benefit claim. Finally, the neo-Marxist theories reject both claims.

Thus the concept of economic development is multidimensional. It not only includes economic growth but also how the benefits of that growth are to be distributed. It admits a variety of definitions and incorporates many goals. Therefore, it is not surprising that value judgments abound in this concept.

Sen (1988) refers to the problems of measuring economic development in terms of the growth in Gross National Product (GNP). Such a measurement abstracts from the distributional aspects of national income. Continued growth need not alleviate skewed income distributions across the population. In addition, there are problems of externalities and nonmarketability of certain outputs. GNP only includes those items for which a market exists and to which an equilibrium price may be assigned. Some items of output may be excluded in this aggregation; for example, consumption of agricultural output by peasants. Environmental externalities are also excluded. Furthermore, market prices used in computing GNP may be inherently biased. Relative prices for a commodity can vary in different parts of the world due to market imperfections and when equilibrium conditions do not obtain. Lastly, a criticizm extended by the proponents of the "basic needs" approach to development is that GNP is not an indicator of "quality of life."[3] GNP may be interpreted as the "means" for potential well-being available to a nation. It does not answer the question: "To what ends are these means directed?"

3. APPROACHES TO ECONOMIC DEVELOPMENT

Chenery and Srinivasan (1988, p. xi) discuss the conceptual foundations of development economics and refer to the existence of "competing paradigms, rather than a dominant orthodoxy." Bardhan (1988) elaborates on this theme by contrasting the three principal approaches to economic development, namely, neoclassical, Marxist, and institutionalist–structuralist, in five different contexts—the microeconomic theory of the household, institutions and resource allocation, income distribution and growth, trade and development, and the role of the state. The following subsections summarize the essence of this viewpoint.

3.1. Microeconomic Theory of the Household

Neoclassical analyses cast all economic agents (including peasants) as engaged in maximizing some objective function, such as utility, subject to some constraints, such as budgets. Within the constraint space, agents are free to pursue their objectives. The Marxist approach emphasizes the burdensome nature of the structural constraints, which do not permit flexibility in the pursuit of individual objectives. A key element of this approach is the unequal distribution of the constraints to various agent groups. The constraints may be less binding on high-income groups and more so on low income groups. The neoclassical paradigm of profit maximization in a competitive environment may thus apply only to high-income groups. In thin or imperfect markets, pure profit maximizers are likely to be absent and nonmaximizers may continue to survive for long periods. Neoclassical theory equates rationality with price responsiveness. Agents perceive price changes as opportunities for profit generation and respond accordingly, which behavior is considered synonymous with rationality. The Marxist approach recognizes the act of improving one's conditions given the constraints as rational behavior.[4] Thus, one may justify the peasant–patron relationship as a rational solution to the absence of complete and contingent markets. Finally, neoclassical analyses assume the separation of production and consumption decisions in perfect markets. The Marxist approach emphasizes that in imperfect markets such separation is not feasible and that these decisions are interdependent.

3.2. Institutions and Resource Allocation

The underpinning of neoclassical theory is the concept of well-defined property rights. A consequence is that efficient resource allocation is independent of any existing institutional arrangements. The emphasis has been on allocational efficiency and not necessarily on the resulting equity of the allocation process. But recent work on the economics of information, which focuses on adverse selection, moral hazard, incomplete markets, and market failures, concludes that efficient resource allocation does not necessarily follow. Furthermore, allocation is affected by asset distributions among agents.

3.3. Income Distribution and Economic Growth

The treatment of income distribution varies among the approaches. Neoclassical theory maintains that factor markets determine factor prices and implicitly affect income distribution. The Marxist approach emphasizes income distribution as the outcome of class struggle. The institutionalist–structuralist argument is that income distribution is an attribute of the specific institutional arrangement and is therefore an exogenous factor. What, then, is the relationship between income distribution and economic growth? Neoclassical theory asserts that economic growth determines income distribution. The assumption of concave savings functions implies that, in the long run, these will equalize for all individuals. Economic growth will result in eventual "trickle–down" benefits to individuals at the lower end of the income spectrum. The other two approaches emphasize a reverse direction of causality—income distribution affects the magnitude and pattern of economic growth. Income inequality and poverty affects the rate and quality of consumption and hence the demand for products. Institutional factors contribute to and perpetuate income inequalities, such as differential access to capital, unequal endowments and "connections," differential consumption propensities, application of inappropriate technology, and limited employment opportunities for marginal groups in the workforce. Such institutional biases limit or prevent all income groups from participating and benefiting from the growth process.

3.4. International Trade and Development

The discussion of the role of trade in economic development assumed significance in the 1980s following the phenomenal growth in the last three decades of the "Asian Tigers"—Hong Kong, Singapore, South Korea, and Taiwan—attributed to their outward-looking policies. These strategies and performances are being emulated and matched in the 1980s and '90s by China, Malaysia, and Thailand.

Neoclassical theory emphasizes the benefits from international trade driven by considerations of comparative advantage among nations. Circulating capital, which is an important determinant of comparative advantage, is deemed to be endogenous. The opposing viewpoints have taken the consistent view that trade contacts are disadvantageous and lead to unwanted foreign intrusions. Trade policies in the erstwhile colonies of Great Britain and France have undoubtedly been influenced by such considerations. Furthermore, the availability of circulating capital depends on historical and institutional forces.

While trade-based development may lead to uneven patterns of growth, Bardhan (1988) observes that ". . . the issue of unpleasant aspects of capitalist growth should be kept separate from that of viability of capitalism" (p. 59). The state has a signicant role, particularly in trade-based development, as witnessed by the successful strategies of Japan, South Korea, and Taiwan. Neoclassical theory offers the best justification on analytical grounds for international trade. Nevertheless, the structuralist distrust of imperfect and incomplete trading markets and the expensive acquisition of over-priced technology has valid bases.

3.5. The Role of the State in Development

The role of the state as the arbiter of economic development policy is fairly ubiquitous. Interventionists have justified an activist role for the state based on several considerations. First, markets may not exist for many products or services, for example, insurance and futures markets. Even if such markets do exist, their structure may not be competitive, but is more likely to be monopolistic or oligopolistic. Second, developing markets abound in externalities of various kinds that are not reflected in market prices. Furthermore, these markets exhibit increasing returns to scale. Third, developing markets tend to be inefficient in that their reactions to information are imprecise. Such reactions may be due to unsatisfactory generation or processing of information. Fourth, at the micro level, individuals and firms who are the recepients of information may take time to interpret price signals and hence adjust slowly. This reaction may be exacerbated by conditions of asymmetric information, as a result of which market participants are not equally informed about products, prices, and production possibilities.

The traditional arguments against state intervention have been based on skepticism of government omniscience or its benevolence. First, individuals are more acutely aware of their preferences and conscious of their welfare than governments can ever be. Second, government planning may not be a substitute for competitive markets, as governments may be more prone to misjudgments. Furthermore, government planning may be more rigid and less flexible and carry greater risks with fewer diversification possbilities. Third, the most fundamental consideration is that government controls result in "crowding out" of private initiatives. A corollary to this argument is that governments cannot motivate individuals, innovate, control costs, or allocate investments as efficiently as the private sector. Coordination by governments is poor, especially in situations where different groups or regions are involved. Fourth, market reactions to governmental actions may take the form of informal or "black" markets that constrain government objectives. Such instances are deemed "incentive incompatible." Fifth, a social cost, which is a by-product of government controls, is the expenditure of valuable resources by individuals and corporations to circumvent these controls. Sixth, government intervention creates common interest groups—bureaucrats and lobbying groups with specific agendas.

The neoclassical theory has focused on the importance of "getting prices right," whereas the other approaches insist on the importance of the historical and institutional environment. The cost-effectiveness of market and adminstrative decision systems are different. Market systems are more effective in reducing transaction, identification, and enforcement costs, whereas, administrative decision systems are more effective in reducing negotiation costs due to economies of scale.[5] This observation suggests a strategy based on eclecticism rather than mutual exclusivity. Markets may not be the appropriate medium to provide essential services and facilities, such as physical infrastructure, education, health, and social security, at least in the initial stages of development. Administrative action may be required to provide the legal and technological infrastructure for the effective functioning of markets. But after the markets have been installed, the role of government is confined to oversight and supervision to ensure their proper functioning.

4. CONCEPTUAL ISSUES IN ECONOMIC DEVELOPMENT

4.1. Dirigiste Economics

Lal (1985), in a powerful indictment of development economics, supports the role of orthodox economic analysis in the development of third world countries. He labels the form of development economics espousing government intervention as *dirigiste economics*.[6] The essential elements of the *dirigiste* dogma relate to concerns about the efficacy of price mechanisms, inattention to allocation of resources, rejection of free trade as expensive, and overwhelming reliance on government intervention (these elements have been discussed in the previous section).

There is a selective imbalance in the application of Keynesian economics by developing nations. First, the traditional Keynesian solution to counter mass unemployment in a depression—stoking demand—is considered irrelevant. The justification is that the root cause of underdevelopment is lack of capital to offer employment to those currently unemployed. However, other aspects of Keynesian economics are embraced enthusiastically. For example, developing nations share the Keynesian concern with the determinants of the level of economic activity and its focus on national income–expenditure analysis. Pricing of commodities and factors of production are considered to be of little importance. The emphasis is on increasing material resources and ensuring their best utilization. Second, developing countries focus on changes in income to equilibrate supply and demand (in the Keynesian tradition) and eschew changes in prices (in the neoclassical tradition). Prices are considered unimportant in developing countries, as consumption is at basic levels and hence characterized by "limited substitutability" of products (Lal, 1985, p. 8). Furthermore, the preoccupation with macroeconomics leads to neglect of microeconomic problems, with the consequent deemphasis on prices. These considerations promote direct controls on production, with the state undertaking the provision of certain goods deemed too important or which the private sector cannot supply.[7]

Lal (1985) argues that while laissez-faire policies may be inefficient and inequitable, it does not follow that government intervention will bring about welfare improvement. While market failure is an inherent risk in laissez-faire policies, bureaucratic failure is an implicit risk with government intervention. The author concludes that no *dirigiste* policy can do better.

Dirigiste policies, it is claimed, smack of paternalism. They stem from an arrogant belief that unsophisticated producers and consumers in developing nations rely on the paternalistic guidance of some government agency in making decisions. Lal (1985) concludes that the empirical evidence supports the following:

- Unsophisticated producers and consumers in developing countries respond to relative price changes and therefore can act effectively.
- The degree of substitution of input factors in the production of the national product is not much different in developing or developed countries.
- Institutional features peculiar to developing countries, such as particular social and agrarian structures or usurious informal credit systems, do not constitute a handicap to growth. They are neither irrational nor uneconomic as claimed by some proponents of the *dirigiste* dogma. On the contrary, they represent a second-best adaptation to the prevailing risks and uncertainties.

In conclusion, Lal (1985) asserts that imperfect planning is still no substitute for imperfect markets. Even in developing countries with imperfect markets, flexibility of prices is likely to be observed. Participants do not have "reserves" to fall back upon and hence need to adjust to changes in prices, whereas in developed nations participants can postpone adjustment on the strength of the "reserves" on hand.

4.2. Multidimensional Development Theory

Notwithstanding Lal's powerful indictment of development economics, a different perspective on the issues is presented by Lewis (1984). He addresses the fundamental question of whether developing countries differ in structure and behavior from the developed nations in ways that require different concepts or tools to understand their problems. In the short run, the resource allocation process in developing nations is not a straightforward extrapolation of the experiences of the market-oriented developed nations. Modifications are required and sociological implications cannot be ignored or assumed to be held constant while decisions are being made solely on economic considerations.

Lewis (1984) observes that in the long run "growth occurs wherever there is a gap between capability and opportunity" (p. 8). The opportunities are provided by the natural resource endowments and sizes of markets. Capabilities are generated by a skilled population, committed government institutions, adequate savings, and infusion of the appropriate technology. Thus, growth opportunities are created by a divergence between actual and potential accomplishment. Incentives and institutional structures are important to closing this gap. However, equally important are the intangible factors, such as, political security, quality of the infrastructure, entrepreneurial capabilities, cultural attitudes, work ethic, etc.

5. SUMMARY AND SYNTHESIS

The foregoing discussion exemplifies the controversies surrounding the concept of economic development. Given the fact that there is a variety of definitions of economic development, it is not surprising that there is absence of agreement on the strategies to be pursued. However, nations are free to identify the specific goals they perceive to be relevant within the context of their accepted definitions. They are equally free to design the strategies they understand to be most effective. These decisions are circumscribed by the particular political system prevailing in each country. Nevertheless, given the enormous disparities in the levels of development among nations, there is a sense of urgency to the development process. There is no time to permit the luxury of extensive debate and experimentation. But to the extent that the successful experiences of other nations are capable of being transplanted, there are advantages to replicating them. The cliche that it does not pay to reinvent the wheel is indeed most apt.

The concept that economic development is the growing capacity for eventual poverty reduction has some merit. This definition suggests the accumulation not only of real capital but also human capital; not only at the current point in time but in the future as well. Hence the imperative to promote the development of markets for real outputs, capital as well as labor. This need justifies the focus on various sectors—industrial, agricultural, and financial. Within this construct, economic growth is a necessary condition but not sufficient in itself. Absolute growth in GNP does not necessarily imply that the benefits of the increased output are available in the form of increased consumption opportunities for the entire population, especially those at the bottom end of the income distribution. Nor does it signify enhanced potential for individual self-actualization in a Maslowian sense, especially to those who have been denied. The proponents of the trickle-down theory would advocate that society should not even be concerned with such considerations. To those who accept the relevance of these goals, the crucial issue is whether their delivery can be entrusted to free markets. Lal (1985) and others subscribe to the viewpoint that free markets are the only medium for this purpose. The opposing viewpoint calls for an activist role for the government in this context.

Economic development is a multidimensional concept. It calls for growing capacity for poverty reduction. This implies the development of a variety of resources, both real and human, and the accumulation of diverse forms of capital. Any theory of development has, therefore, to be eclectic in its nature. The advantages of free markets have been described in detail. It suffices to indicate that their principal benefit is the generation of prices which determine efficient resource allocation. On the other hand, government intervention becomes necessary to give development a "human face." But bureaucratic failure very often has worse consequences than market failure. In an underdeveloped economy, government involvement in the provision of the necessary infrastructure for the functioning of markets may be necessary. Government intervention is largely supply-oriented to facilitate the creation of markets and, thereafter, to ensure their efficient functioning. As development in the economy evolves, active government involvement should be progressively reduced. The role of government should be confined to monitoring and regulation of markets and its intervention is justified only in the instance of market failure. The risk in this strategy is that a bureaucracy once created becomes self-perpetuating. It is loath to contribute to its own dismemberment or contraction. It acquires a life and purpose of its own and evolves into a common-interest group with its own agenda. In such situations, bureaucratic failure is a very real danger. The antidote lies in the political process, which should provide a system of checks and balances to discourage the emergence of any overly powerful constituency.[8]

The literature on development has largely ignored the importance of sociological and cultural factors. Lewis (1984) makes a brief reference to such effects. In development, as in other processes, the quality of inputs determine the outcomes. Particular endowments, such as geography and climatic conditions, place nations at a comparative advantage with respect to certain agricultural outputs. The same can be said about countries endowed with mineral or oil deposits. The quality of the human input is conditioned by sociological and cultural factors. Much has been written about the "economic miracle" in Japan. It is acknowledged that the cultural element in management has played no small part in the economic growth of this nation endowed with no natural resources. Yet it is the homogeneity of purpose and cohesion among its people that has contributed to its position as a major world power today. The work ethic, attention to detail, and commitment to excellence enabled Japan to dominate markets all over the world. This is an element of development for which neither free markets nor government intervention are effective substitutes. The presence of these qualities guarantees that the absence of other resources will not be an obstacle to development.

In conclusion, economic development is a complex area. The development of nations cannot be explained solely on the basis of economic or politico-economic factors. However, we will continue to focus on financial and economic factors, keeping in mind that there may well be anthropological, cultural, and sociological factors that contribute to and distinguish the development of nations.

The following chapter reviews and synthesizes theories of a particular aspect of development, namely, economic growth.

NOTES

1. Lewis qualifies these economies as having "output per head less than 1980 US $2,000" (p. 1).
2. See Little (1982), p. 6.
3. See Streeten (1977) and Stewart (1985) for this discussion.
4. In this context, neoclassical analyses assume optimizing behavior on the part of economic agents, whereas the Marxist approach emphasizes "satisficing" behavior.
5. Stern (1989) provides a taxonomy of the reasons for market failure and problems with state intervention. See Tables 3 and 4, p. 616.
6. Lal identifies proponents of this particular school to be Nurske (1953, 1961), Myrdal (1958), Hirschman (1958), Balogh (1963), Rosenstein-Rodan (1943), Chenery (1957), Prebisch (1950), Singer (1950), and Streeten (1972). Opposition to these views have been articulated by Haberler (1957), Viner (1953), Bauer and Yamey (1957), and Schultz (1964).
7. See Lal (1985), p. 10. Much of Lal's criticizms are directed against aspects of development discussed in Section 2.
8. In fairness it should be pointed out that even in the United States this has not been too successful.

2

Theories of Economic Growth

1. INTRODUCTION

This chapter provides a brief but relevant survey of the theories of economic growth. Section 2 starts with the classical Harrod–Domar model to show that economic growth is directly related to the savings rate and indirectly to the capital–output ratio. The Solow model, which details the "sources of growth" or "growth-accounting" approach, follows in the second subsection. Neoclassical models of economic growth stress the importance of technology, investments, and trade, each of which is discussed in turn. Technological change is a major determinant of economic growth. The catchup hypothesis states that the creators of technology invest time, effort and capital in research and development, whereas the borrowers can avail themselves of instant technology. Thus the technological gap between the two sets of nations narrows. Investment is another factor that contributes to economic growth. In the era of rapid economic growth, investment is the medium by which scientific discoveries and inventions result in enhanced output. International trade is important in promoting economic growth through economies of scale leading to better utilization of resources, reduction of balance of payments, and improved productivity. Recent empirical evidence suggests that there is a positive relationship between outward orientation and economic growth. Finally, manufacturing activity is considered important for economic growth, as it is believed that labor productivity increases only with more intense manufacturing.

The contributions of Olson (1971, 1982), who provides a behavioral element in the theory of economic growth, are discussed in subsection 2.8. He notes that organized groups pursuing their own agendas that are not consistent with national welfare can have adverse impacts on economic growth. The 1980s have witnessed the resurgence of the supply-side philosophy, and the implications for economic growth are discussed in subsection 2.9. The final topic of section 2 is endogenous-growth theory, which claims that the aggregate economy grows only through growth of the individual firm, which is determined by endogenous investment in the stock of knowledge rather than purely exogenous factors such as technical change.

Section 3 draws attention to the fact that a common element of the preceding models of economic growth is the absence of any role for finance. Finally, section 4 summarizes the chapter.

Good surveys of the theories of economic growth as well as recent developments in the field are discussed in Becker and Burmeister (1991), Burmeister and Dobell (1970), Britto (1973), Choi (1983), Dixit (1976), Eltis (1984), Haache (1979), Hamberg (1971), and Stern (1989). Scott (1989) presents a good survey of "orthodox and unorthodox" growth theories. Some of the classical works in this area include Hahn and Mathews (1964), Kuznets (1966), Meade (1961), Schmookler (1966), Solow (1970), and Stiglitz and Uzawa (1969).

2. THEORIES OF ECONOMIC GROWTH

2.1. Harrod–Domar Model

Consider a closed economy in which I is the planned investment, Y is the expected income, and s is the anticipated savings rate. Then the identity that planned investment equals planned savings is expressed as

$$I = sY \tag{2.1}$$

If K is the capital stock, then recognizing that investment is the change in capital stock, it follows that $I = K' = (dK/dt)$.

Define $c = K/Y$, the capital–output ratio, which measures input capital per unit output and is therefore an efficiency measure. Dividing eq. 2.1 by K yields

$$\frac{I}{K} = \frac{sY}{K}, \quad \text{or} \quad g = \frac{s}{c} \tag{2.2}$$

where $g = I/K = K'/K$ = growth in capital.

It follows from eq. 2.2 that growth is directly related to the savings rate and indirectly to the capital–output ratio. If the capital–output ratio is constant, the growth rate is determined by the savings rate. However, if the capital–output ratio increases in the long run at a rate greater than the rate of savings, growth will decline.

2.2. Solow Model

Solow (1956) demonstrates with an aggregate production function that long-term growth (s/c) will be in equilibrium with the labor growth rate (n) by the adjustment of the capital–output ratio. What happens if the savings rate increases? In the short run, the growth rate will increase, but in the long run growth will decline to the labor-growth rate with the increase in the capital–output ratio. If technical progress leads to augmentation of labor at a rate a, then per-capita output will grow at the rate a and long-term growth $s/c = a + n$.

Solow (1957) demonstrates that technical progress may be broken down into factor contributions and growth in factor productivity. Consider an aggregate production function $Y = F(K, L, t)$, where L is labor and t is time. Then

$$\frac{dY}{dt} = \frac{\partial F}{\partial K} \cdot \frac{dK}{dt} + \frac{\partial F}{\partial L} \cdot \frac{dL}{dt} + \frac{\partial F}{\partial t} \tag{2.3}$$

Dividing eq. 2.3 by Y and defining

$$\frac{dY}{dt} = Y', \quad \frac{dK}{dt} = K', \quad \frac{dL}{dt} = L', \quad \text{and} \quad \frac{\partial F}{\partial t} = F_t$$

yields

$$\frac{Y'}{Y} = \frac{K}{Y} \cdot \frac{\partial F}{\partial K} \cdot \frac{K'}{K} + \frac{L}{Y} \cdot \frac{\partial F}{\partial L} \cdot \frac{L'}{L} + \frac{F_t}{Y}$$

or

$$\frac{Y'}{Y} = \frac{\theta K'}{K} + \frac{\beta L'}{L} + \frac{F_t}{Y} \tag{2.4}$$

Equation 2.4 states that output growth is determined by growth in capital, growth of labor, and growth in total factor productivity, and is the basis for the "sources-of-growth" or "growth-accounting" approach. Empirical estimations of eq. 2.4 and its variations have been performed by Solow (1957), Dennison (1962), and by Jorgenson and Grilliches (1967, 1972). Robinson (1971) finds that the growth of inputs is more critical for growth of national income in developing countries than in developed ones.

2.3. Technological Factors and Economic Growth

Technology may be defined as the knowledge base required for the production of goods and services. Technological change or improvement in technology is a major determinant of economic growth. Diffusion of technical changes through the economy in the form of improved processes and products leads to long-term growth in productivity. Technology gaps inevitably exist, as some nations are creators, leaders, and pioneers and others are adaptors or followers. It also follows that because developing nations borrow or use ready-made technology, their growth rates will be relatively higher. Whereas the creators of technology invest in research and development and undergo long gestation periods of trials and tests, the borrowers can avail themselves of instant technology. This observation is the basis for the catchup or the convergence (of technology) hypothesis.[1] Choi (1983) observes that "knowledge is expensive to produce but cheap to reproduce" (p. 70). This factor contributed in no small measure to the impressive growth rates of Hong Kong, Singapore, South Korea, and Taiwan in the 1970s and 1980s.

All technology is developed from some fundamental discovery, as depicted in Fig. 2.1. This fundamental discovery is translated into commercial feasibility through product development. The gap between the announcement of a fundamental discovery and the introduction of a commercially viable product in the market which follows it is rapidly decreasing. For example, Faradays's Laws of Electromagnetic Induction were enunciated in the nineteenth century, but they gave birth to the first electric motor about forty years later. On the other hand, Bardeen and Brittain announced the laws governing semiconduction in the late 1940s, but transistor applications followed only five years later. In the more recent past, the time lapse has been even less in the case of laser technology. Nevertheless, product development leads to mass production, as in the case of the induction motor.

With the experience gained from production, innovation generates improved and more efficient methods of production. As the production is accelerated, innovation also gives rise to new variations developed for specific applications. Thus, the induction motor gave birth to the synchronous and synchronous induction motors and other forms of electrical prime movers. Eventually, all this accumulated knowledge is packaged and made available as a subset of electrical technology through the process of diffusion. Developing nations can take advantage of the diffusion process to position themselves directly at the production stage bypassing the earlier stages, which are both expensive and risky. By absorbing the diffused technology directly, the developing nations exhibit higher growth rates.

If per-capita income is taken as a proxy for the level of technology (a higher

Figure 2.1
Technological Diffusion and Developing Nations

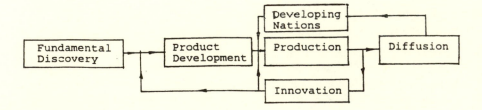

level of technology is associated with higher levels of income), then the catchup hypothesis would imply a negative correlation between the growth rate of the manufacturing sector (where, presumably, technological changes occurred) and per-capita income. Empirical studies generally support the catchup hypothesis. It is accepted that technological change is only one among many variables determining the growth rate of productivity.

2.4. Investment and Economic Growth

Two streams of opinion characterize the role of investment in the growth process. The classical theorists (Harrod, Domar) assert the overwhelming importance of investment for two reasons. First, investment has multiplier effects on income; and second, incremental investments enlarge the levels of capital stock. Furthermore, new investments promote increased efficiency in the form of higher productvity as well as improvements in management and organizational methods. In the aggregate, new investments result in technical progress.

On the other hand, neoclassical theory has downplayed the importance of investment. These models have stressed the growth of labor supply and technology as factors determining the growth of aggregate output. Over the business cycle, there have been cyclical variations in the levels of capital utilization. Furthermore, not all sectors in the economy may exhibit uniform levels of capital intensity. Finally, capital coefficients may shift as a result of technical progress and changes in patterns of aggregate demand.

In the modern era of rapid technological change, investment is the medium by which scientific discoveries and inventions result in enhanced output. Theory suggests that growth in productivity is a function of scientific discoveries or inventions. Schmookler (1966) provides empirical evidence to support the hypothesis that the rate of invention is determined by the rate of investment. Scientific discovery or invention is a function of the investment in research and development, which, analogous to any other form of investment, depends on the anticipated returns and risks. Investments in research and development beget more inventions.

In summary, increasing investments are necessary to hasten the process of economic development. This goal calls for investments in both real capital as well as human capital. The latter, investment in human capital, is essential if higher levels of technology are to be employed that will lead to enhanced productivity.

2.5. International Trade and Economic Growth

The historical basis for the importance of international trade is the notion of the "comparative advantage" of a nation. This proposition states that a country should produce and export a product as long as its internal cost of production is less than the cost of obtaining the product from another country. Conversely, a country should import a product if the cost of production is greater than the cost of obtaining the product from another country. The argument for exports being growth-promoting relies on cost reduction as a result of economies of scale, which in turn leads to better utilization of resources. Export promotion can lead to surpluses in the international balance of payments, which in turn spurs internal demand, leads to improvements in productivity, and enhances the competitive position of the country, which completes the cycle by placing greater emphasis on export promotion. A side benefit of international trade is that a prerequisite to entry into foreign markets is achievement of high quality standards, which promotes the introduction of new technology. The trade-oriented successes of Hong Kong, Singapore, South Korea, and Taiwan bear witness to these considerations. Thus the benefits of international trade stem from the fact that the traditional assumptions of the neoclassical model of perfect competition—full utilization of homogeneous and divisible resources and absence of economies of scale—do not obtain.[2]

Export-oriented policies may be detrimental to growth if they demand special and costly resources, and if the economic cost of protecting infant industries is high. There may be high uncertainties in activities relating to international trade with unstable prices and demand. Krugman (1987) suggests that free trade is "a useful target in the world of politics," and "its status has shifted from optimum to reasonable rule of thumb" (p. 132).

Developing nations in the 1950s evolved policies reflecting increased emphasis on import substitution. To some extent, these policies were influenced by "self-sufficiency" considerations in the Soviet Union and import substitution was perceived as the path to industrialization and growth. The rationale for such policies were based on the observation that the terms of trade for developing nations—the prices received for their exports relative to the prices paid for their imports—were being eroded.[3] The internal demand for the products imported by developing nations was highly inelastic. On the other hand, demand for their exports, being mostly primary products, was highly influenced by the availability of synthetic substitutes.[4] Such situations lent credibility to the self-reliance arguments and some developing nations adopted increasingly inward-looking policies.[5]

Nevertheless, recent empirical evidence (*World Development Report, 1989*) and casual observation (the examples of China, Malaysia, and Thailand in the 1980s) suggest that there is a positive relationship between outward orientation and economic growth.

2.6. Industrialization, Manufacturing Activity, and Economic Growth

Manufacturing has been the centerpiece in the plans of almost all developing nations. The scope of manufacturing activity has varied among these nations. Some have emphasized heavy industries (China, India, and Mexico), whereas others have focussed on medium-scale industries (Hong Kong and Singapore), and a third group have concentrated on agriculture-based industries. The attraction for manufacturing activity stems from the belief that labor productivity can only increase with more intense manufacturing; further scientific discoveries lead to still higher levels of productivity, and secular increases in international prices of industrial goods would outpace the growth of prices of primary products. Manufacturing activity would be accompanied by synergistic benefits in other economic sectors, the accumulation of human capital, and the acquisition of skills and technology.[6] Finally, many developing nations may have perceived a vigorous manufacturing sector as an indicator of a break from their colonial past.[7]

The conceptual basis for industrialization is provided in Lewis (1954) and Fei and Ranis (1965). Rapid growth of the industrial sector results in migration of labor from agriculture with accompanying increases in productivity. Increases in the levels of manufactured output lead to growth in labor income which results in greater demand for agricultural products and other goods and services. Thus, industrialization induces balanced growth rates in all sectors.

The growth of the manufacturing sector is determined by several factors. The relative importance of this sector increases with the growth of per-capita income. But more specifically, a nation may have a natural comparative advantage in manufacturing with access to material inputs or highly educated labor. Import substitution programs may subsidize and protect infant industries (this aspect is discussed in later paragraphs). The income elasticity of demand for some manufactured goods is high and, through feedback effects, results in still higher levels of manufacturing activity. Chenery and Syrquin (1975) observe that the higher levels of value-addition in industries such as chemicals, heavy metals, and paper are more likely in larger countries than smaller countries. A plausible explanation is that the scope for economies of scale is higher in countries with larger domestic markets. Incentives for manufactured exports will be high if risks in foreign markets are perceived to be lower than the risks in domestic markets. Scale economies in marketing is another factor promoting manufactured exports.

Manufactured exports raise the question of the relationship between trade and industrial performance. The key element of this relationship is the rate of growth of productivity in the industrial sector. Productivity increases lead to reduced costs which make competitive prices in export markets possible. Two factors work to enhance the demand for industrial goods and thereby the growth of this sector. First, income elasticity of the demand for industrial products is greater than the value for agricultural goods. Thus, growth of the manufacturing sector leads to increased demand for industrial products. Second, prices of industrial products decline with increasing productivity in this sector. High price elasticity of demand generates additional demand for industrial products. A side benefit is that the income effect associated with declining prices for industrial products relative to agricultural product prices leads to increased demand for agricultural products and thereby promotes growth of this sector as well. However, the productivity growth in the industrial sector has had negative effects on other sectors. The growth of industrial incomes has an effect equivalent to a tax on other sectors. For example, labor is not easily attracted to employment in other sectors as the opportunity cost of employment in the industrial sector becomes a substantial deterrent.

Developing nations are susceptible to adopting industrial policies based on import-substitution strategies. Such strategies are based on the belief that "infant industries" require protection. Protection promotes the creation of human capital as new skills are acquired and modern technology is familiarized. There is optimism that the human capital generated would be adequate to sustain future growth when protection is dismantled. It should be noted that this strategy is based on a "learning-by-doing" approach, which emphasizes self-reliance, as opposed to one based on massive importation of technology. It is fair to state that the experiences of most developing nations has been that the optimism has not been warranted.[8]

Pack (1988, p. 348) refers to an interesting perspective on the costs associated with protection of the manufacturing sector. The explicit cost arises since the protected sector is receiving in subsidies more than it's earning or saving in foreign exchange. This subsidy needs to be financed by some other sector that earns or saves the requisite foreign exchange. Such a requirement is a tax imposed on the financing sector. In addition, there is an implicit cost to protection. The growth of the manufacturing sector, which is not attributable to productivity gains, implies that the subsidy grows over time at the same rate. Thus, the financing sector that produces the compensating earnings or savings in foreign exchange is required to have minimum growth equal to the growth rate of the subsidy. This requirement represents an implicit cost on the financing sector.

Two types of inefficiencies may be associated with protection. *Allocative* inefficiency arises as a result of the inability of the protected sector to function in a competitive market when barriers to imports are lifted. This condition may be described as a "survivability test" and provides the usual justification for developing nations not lifting the barriers to imports. Quality improvement and absorption of new technology, which are the benefits of facing the competitive challenges of imports, are not considered. *Technical* inefficiency arises when an industry that has the potential to compete against imports employs or consumes more resources under protection. The subsidies implicit in a protected environment reduce the explicit cost of resources and lead to a "slackening" of management cost controls.

While considering the costs of protection and the associated inefficiencies, it is useful to consider the advantages of neutral trade policies. A manufacturing subsector that operates in competitive export markets experiences forced improvements in productivity levels. Better utilization of capacity leads to reduction of costs. Product ranges tend to get more specialized. Quality improvements and absorption of new technology (mentioned above) are natural benefits. At the same time there is more "learning-by-doing," which leads to adaptation and synthesis of new technology. Finally, the synergistic benefits of a neutral trade regime that promotes international competition are manifested in reduced prices and improved quality.

The experiences of developing nations indicate that industrialization policies have not produced the expected benefits. Productivity improvements have not been pervasive but limited to small pockets of the manufacturing sector. Even the observed productivity improvements are not in all instances attributable to total factor productivity but to more capital-intensive technology (increased capital–labor ratios) and the protection afforded to the sector. The burden of the associated inefficiencies have been borne by the consumers and not by employers or employees of the manufacturing sector.

2.7. Olson's Model of Comparative Economic Growth

Olson (1971, 1982) provides an insightful perspective on the impact of groups, whose members are united by common goals, on national economic growth.[9] His analysis introduces a behavioral element into the theory of economic growth. Conventional wisdom dictates that if members of a group were united in a common purpose, then the group would act to further its collective interest. This notion is predicated on the presence of members motivated by self-interest; if all members shared the common self-interest, then they would join in group action to further their interest. Olson identifies a fallacy in the conventional wisdom. Membership in the group is granted with the payment of a membership fee or with the investment of some kind of effort. But the benefits of group action take on the nature of a "public good"—a benefit available freely to all the members. Individuals who seek to maximize the benefit–cost ratio of their membership are likely to find such an arrangement unappealing. They would prefer an arrangement by which their benefits could be large in relation to their costs. The inevitable conclusion is that without special arrangements, large groups will not act in their self-interest.[10]

Common interest groups (CIGs) provide benefits for their members through political action (as in the case of consumers, farmers, and other producers) or market action (as in cartels). These CIGs are supported not for the collective benefits they offer but their "selective incentives"—benefits applied selectively to individuals depending on whether they contribute to the specific benefits. Selective benefits may be positive (for example, frequent flier programs initiated by airlines) or negative (for example, coercion to join trade unions or special taxes and penalties).[11]

Can collective action occur without selective incentives? Yes, if the group that benefits from collective action is small, so that intensity (per-capita distribution) of benefits is large; in addition, benefits should be greater than the costs involved. If a large number of individuals benefit from the collective action, intensity of gains will be small. Thus without any selective incentives, motivation for group action diminishes as the group size increases. Thus, large groups are less likely to act in their common interest than small groups.[12]

What are the implications of CIGs for economic growth of nations? On balance, such institutions affect aggregate income and efficiency of the economy adversely. In general, the performance of the economy has systematic effects on benefits accruing to CIGs. Such benefits will increase or decrease depending on whether aggregate economic activity expands or contracts. The CIG is more concerned with the distributional aspects of aggregate income rather than its growth-enhancing considerations.[13] Extending the argument in the preceding paragraph, even if the CIG could have positive effects on aggregate economic activity, the benefits it accrues after distribution to other claimants would be less than the costs incurred or only marginally greater. Thus, incentives for the CIG to pursue aggregate growth-enhancing policies are virtually nonexistent.

The CIG can employ specific mechanisms to increase the benefits to its members that adversely affect economic efficiency or aggregate output. By lobbying for legislation to increase product prices or wages or the differential application of taxes, resources are diverted to the benefit of the CIG, which results in a cost borne by the rest of society. The formation of a cartel is an alternate strategy available to the CIG, which results in output reduction with concomitant increases in prices. However the net loss to society arising from the collective actions of CIGs is mitigated by diversification. These effects are not always mutually reinforcing and some effects may neutralize or reduce the impacts of other effects.

Three corollaries follow from the previous discussion.[14] The first is that the prevalence of CIGs is greater in longer-lived societies. This assertion follows from the fact that the organization of CIGs is a time-consuming process. Agreements may coalesce in small groups only after much discussion and negotiation. There are also large search costs and identification costs associated with organizing selective incentives in large groups. For example, coercive actions are difficult to organize, inasmuch as the design of social rewards and social pressures take time. There should be a logical connection between "the activity that produces the collective good" and "activity that produces income." For example, the organization of a trade union should be justified by its ability to negotiate benefits for its members. The establishment of causal linkages between goals or aspirations and their realizations is a time-consuming process. After all the efforts invested in creating and organizing the CIG, it will not "fade away into the sunset" with time. On the contrary, CIGs will ensure the perpetuation of their survival. As Olson (1982) aptly observes, "selective incentives make indefinite survival feasible" (p. 40). Thus with the passage of time, a stable society will witness the proliferation of CIGs.

The second corollary suggests that the small, compact groups have superior organizational capabilities. Furthermore, with the evolution of stable societies, such organizational power may be diluted marginally but will not be eliminated completely. Thus the impact of small groups that are sharply focused on limited objectives will be disproportionately large.

Finally, CIGs can adversely affect the rate of innovation or technical change. They can also affect the allocation of resources and thus adversely affect the rate of economic growth. For example, labor unions have vested interests in maximizing labor income and opposing or at least minimizing the impact of labor-saving technology.[15] Similarly, oligopolies have resisted technical change. Industries have lobbied for special tax allowances or benefits to provide safety nets for failing firms. In addition, when there are effective barriers to entry, reduction in economic growth can be exacerbated. The cumulative loss to society through these actions is greater than the benefits experienced by CIGs.[16]

2.8. The Supply-Side Revolution

While Say's law, the basic tenet of supply-side economics, has been discussed in the earliest textbooks an economics, it has only served as the intellectual basis for policies since the 1980s.[17] Its proponents believe that entrepreneurs and producers of goods and services remain the source of all economic development (Fink, 1982, p. xiv). The implication is that economic development may be defined as the creation of that environment which encourages risk-taking behavior in entrepreneurs and the supply of goods and services by producers. Gilder (1982, p. 14) encapsulates the basis of all capitalism in "the awareness that one must give in order to get, supply in order to demand." Economic theory downplays supply by forcing equalization with demand in equilibrium models to determine prices and quantities. Furthermore, demand is nothing but some vague, amorphous concept in the minds of consumers. It is only supply that actualizes demand.

Some key analytical differences between the Keynesian approach and the supply-side philosophy may be identified. First, the bedrock of the Keynesian approach is aggregate demand; the related strategy calls for stoking demand to pull an economy out of recessionary conditions. Supply-siders prefer to focus not on aggregate demand but on decisions made by individuals to consume, save, and invest. Consider the implications of an increase in the marginal tax rate. Two tradeoffs are identified as crucial to any tax-structure design. The first tradeoff is in the relationship between leisure and work. With increases in the marginal tax rate, the cost of leisure, measured by the opportunity cost of net after-tax income foregone, decreases. Thus, there is a disincentive to work and to save. On the other hand, with decreases in the marginal tax rate, net after-tax income increases, and thus the cost of leisure increases. The second tradeoff is in the relationship between current and future consumption. With increases in the marginal tax rate, monetary returns and the decreased investment base are low, and so is the cost of current consumption. This acts as a disincentive to save and to invest. But with lower marginal tax rates monetary returns on the increased investment base are higher, and so is the cost of current consumption. Thus, the incentive to save and to invest increases.[18] A reduction in the tax rate results in the transfer of resources from consumers to producers. Thus, it is argued that the Keynesian approach ignores supply-side feedback effects on work and investment.

Second, the Keynesian approach perceives the impacts of a tax in terms of its income effects; whereas the supply-side approach emphasizes the changes in relative prices associated with taxes—price effects. Third, the Keynesian approach focuses on the average tax rate, while the supply-side approach is more concerned with the marginal tax rate, which is seen to affect investment, resources employed, aggregate output, and thus income as well. Supply-siders base these effects on varying propensities to consume among individuals.

Hazlett (1982), as a representative of the Austrian school of economics, emphasizes the role of consumers in affecting aggregate economic activity. Prices are determined by consumers and not by "powerful producers." The entrepreneur has only one function and that is to determine consumer desires and to satisfy them. Hazlett criticizes the Keynesian approach for confusing aggregate demand with consumer demand. In aggregating demand across the population, the implications of demand by specific groups of consumers is lost. The Austrian school does not distinguish between supply-side stimulation of the economy by tax cuts and the Keynesian strategy of stimulating the economy by public works. Both aproaches ignore consumer demands and hence the indifference to the both of them. Hazlett (1982) points out that a strategy that favors the supply-side of the economy— entrepreneurs and producers—at the cost of consumers' choice cannot be successful.

On the other hand, market process economists such as Fink (1982) recognize the interdependencies existing among the various economic agents—consumers, savers, entrepreneurs, and investors. Economic growth entails the coordination of the individual plans of various groups of agents. This coordination becomes particularly necessary as an economy on an expansion path shifts from an internal point in the production possibility curve to a point on the curve. Such coordination is made possible by the signals contained in changes in market prices. Market-process economists charge that both Keynesians and supply-siders ignore the need for coordination and the important role of market signals.

Supply-side economics has gained prominence with the policies of the Reagan administration in the United States and those of the Thatcher government in the United Kingdom in the 1980s. It retains the flavor of an ideological approach to the management of political economy rather than an explicit theory of economic growth. The empirical evidence to support supply-side policies is limited at this point.

In conclusion, the supply-side revolution represents a frontal attack on traditional Keynesian policies. On the other hand, the Austrian school finds fault with the supply-side philosophy to the extent that it diminishes the importance of the consumer. The market-process economists are concerned that the supply-siders ignore the benefits of coordination provided by signals released by the market. As Fink appears to acknowledge, the distinction between the viewpoints of the supply-siders and the market-process economists is very fine. Once the former acknowledge that the market should remain unhampered and free to generate its coordinating signals, reconciliation between the two is easily reached. The focus of both the Keynesian approach and the Austrian school is on the importance of demand; the distinction is one of identifying the source. Whereas, the former relies upon fiscal policy to stimulate growth through governmental demand, the latter attaches importance to consumer rather than institutional demand. As each of these philosophies bears the kernel of truth, an eclectic approach to their relevance to economic growth is warranted.

The argument that the supply of inputs needs to be encouraged for aggregate output creation is irrefutable. Modern production technologies demand a variety of inputs, both direct and indirect. Whereas a well-nurtured market can supply the former, the latter, encompassing transportation systems, communication networks, education, and other infrastructural elements, require the active participation of the government. This requirement is particularly relevant to the problem of growth in a developing country. Once the authorities have provided the necessary infrastructure, the stage is set for the supply of direct inputs for output creation. The market processes must be allowed to take over to provide the coordinating signals. Total development has to evolve under the watchful eyes of the government to ensure protection against exploitation for the weaker sectors of society. As the evolution progresses, the authorities can distance themselves from the market to permit its efficient functioning. However, a complete "hands-off" approach is not advisable, for even in industrialized societies like the United States, governmental regulation becomes absolutely necessary in key areas such as consumer protection.

2.9. Endogenous-Growth Theory

The growth of the individual firm, and by extension the aggregate economy, is attributed to endogenous investment in the stock of knowledge, and, by implication, human capital, rather than exogenous factors such as technical change. This strand of thought has evolved from the early works of Arrow (1962) and Uzawa (1965). Scott (1989) presents a model in which the very process of investing creates and reveals new opportunities for further growth. Romer (1986) considers knowledge "as a basic form of capital." Three elements of the impact of knowledge on output need to be considered. First, there are decreasing returns to investment in research in the form of additional knowledge gained. For example, doubling of the level of knowledge is not the automatic result of doubling the level of investment. Second, output is an increasing function of the knowledge base; knowledge has an increasing marginal product. Finally, investment in knowledge is an externality in the sense that knowledge cannot be bottled or hermetically sealed. The permeation of knowledge across firms results in diffused human capital. Thus production possibilities of firm A are extended as a result of investment undertaken by firm B.

Romer (1990) asserts that technological change is the major determinant of economic growth. Technological changes are defined as improvements in the way that inputs are combined to produce a final product. Productivity improvements result from technological changes and incentives for continued capital accumulation. Market incentives play a major role in the creation of technological changes. Individuals, in responding to market incentives, endogenously generate technological changes. Market incentives are major vehicles by which fundamental knowledge results in consumable goods. Finally, there are continuing economies resulting from the fixed cost associated with the production of technological change. Once the process has been recreated, it may be recycled without additional costs. The returns to technological change directly increase with the size of markets. Thus, large markets justify increased investment in research, which eventually results in rapid economic growth. However, a large population is not a substitute for international trade. There is no justification for inward-looking trade policies that result in effectively sealed borders. A large population base assists economic growth; however, a broad base of human capital is a sufficient condition.[19]

The role of human capital in economic growth is explored extensively in Lucas (1988). He equates human capital with "general skill level," such that an individual with skill level h is twice as productive as another with skill level ($h/2$), or half as productive as one with skill level ($2h$) (p. 17). The current allocation of an individual's time among various activities affects the accumulation and level of human capital and thus determines the individual's future productivity. Over the life cycle of the individual, human capital is acquired rapidly in the early years, less rapidly in the middle years, and very little or perhaps not at all in the later years. The levels of human capital attained by members of a family affect the initial endowment of human capital in a young member of this family. Perhaps this explains why children of parents with advanced educational degrees are more likely to pursue graduate education. Lucas (1988) observes "human capital is a social *activity*, involving *groups* of people in a way that has no counterpart in the accumulation of physical capital" (p. 19). Both human and physical capital endowments determine the growth potential of a nation.

Human capital can be accumulated through formal education, such as schooling, or by "learning by doing." In the latter case, it is the effort devoted to producing a good that determines the accumulation of human capital. The dynamics of "learning by doing" exhibit declining returns over time, in the sense that human capital is accumulated rapidly in the initial stages, then more slowly in the intermediate stages, and still more slowly or not at all in the final stages. There are intergenerational as well as interproduct transfers of human capital. Skills acquired by earlier generations are easily transferred to and learned by succeeding generations. The skills acquired in the design and manufacture of a product can be applied to similar aspects of another product. Thus human capital permeates all activities and organizations and is an important element of endogenously generated growth. The emphasis given to education and training by the international lending institutions points to the importance of human capital in the development process.

3. THE ROLE OF FINANCE IN THE GROWTH PROCESS

The interesting feature of the literature surveyed in this chapter as well as the previous chapter is absence of any recognition accorded to finance. The Harrod–Domar model employs the savings rate but makes no reference to institutions and markets that intermediate between savers and investors. There need to be mechanisms by which the resources of savers are channeled through these institutions and markets to users who promise the best returns. None of the models of economic growth give explicit recognition to this need. Chandavarkar (1992, p. 134) observes that "... finance still remains very much the poor relation of mainstream development economics." The author further notes that "the two [i.e., finance and development] dwell in an uneasy intellectual apartheid, perhaps equal, but still very much separate." Lucas (1988, p. 6) acknowledges that "... the development of financial institutions is a limiting factor to development more broadly conceived. . . ."

The discussion in this chapter has focused on economic growth stimulated by changes in the assets side of the balance sheet of nations—investments, capital, etc. But the literature has been conspicuously short on the liabilities side of the balance sheet. Inasmuch as there are common strategies for economic development and growth that nations can pursue and share, there has not been much discussion of schemes for their financing. There are many tradeoffs and substitutions possible among the various factors contributing to economic development; but there is no substitute for good financial policies. The remaining chapters focus on two questions: How can nations finance their development? What can we learn from the experiences of other countries?

4. CONCLUSION

This chapter has provided a broad survey of theories of economic growth. The *sources-of-growth* approach attempts to explain the growth of output in terms of input growth. Empirical studies indicate that the influence of input growth on output growth is strong.

Economic growth has been explained in terms of *technological factors* as well. Technology is defined as the knowledge required for the production of goods and services demanded by society. It includes not only direct manufacturing, but also marketing, finance, and organization, etc. In general, technology is expected to contribute to growth in long-term productivity.

Exports are also deemed to have implications for economic growth; this is embodied in Kindleberger's concept of exports being the "engine of growth." Export-led growth is expected to have beneficial effects on supply and demand. International competition contributes to overall improvement of quality; higher-level technology is absorbed, resulting in enhanced output and leading to productivity increases. These developments coupled with increased demand contribute to overall growth of the economy. The empirical evidence is somewhat mixed on the importance of exports as the sole determinant of economic growth. Unilateral causation is difficult to spot. Only when demand conditions in export markets are conducive and the supply conditions in domestic markets improve to meet the challenge can growth really be export-led.

Olson (1982) describes economic growth in behavioral terms rather than in relation to economic factors such as input-factor growth, technology, exports, or manufacturing activity. In a free democratic society there is an abundance of *common-*

interest groups—associations of individuals or firms that have collective monopoly power, political power or both. Examples are labor unions, professional and trade unions, farm organizations, employers associations, lobbies, cartels, etc. According to Olson's concept of "selective incentive," an individual will be stimulated to act in a group-oriented manner, provided there are incentives that confer benefits on him in a selective fashion that exclude all or some of the other members of the group. Olson posits that size is an important factor in determining whether the pursuit of individual interest will result in group-oriented behavior. In general, broad-based CIs are sparsely distributed and their aggregate effect on growth is negligible, whereas narrowly based CIs are more common and affect growth adversely. The empirical evidence supports the existence of a significant relationship between the duration of stable freedom of association and growth rates. There is evidence that the accumulation of CIs has a negative influence on growth.

The 1970s and 1980s have witnessed resurgence of support for the *supply-side* position. Gilder (1981) contends that suppliers—producers and entrepreneurs—are the source of all economic growth. Roberts (1978) argues that tax structures based on the Keynesian philosophy overlook impacts on individual tradeoffs between leisure and work and between consumption and investment. His concern is that Keynesian policies ignore supply-side feedback effects—incentives from higher after-tax rewards for work and investment. Ture (1982) provides a contrast of the supply-side position with the Keynesian analysis. Whereas the former is concerned with relative price effects and marginal tax rates, the latter is preoccupied with aggregate income and the average tax rates respectively.

Hazlett (1982) attacks the supply-siders for being so preoccupied with the supply curve that they ignore the primacy of consumers. Fink (1982), extending the case of the market-process economists, argues that supply-siders focus on incentives but not the informational problems associated with economic coordination. Individual plans and, by extension, aggregate economic growth are dependent on the degree of coordination available among consumers, savers, investors, and entrepreneurs. Signals for coordination, such as, prices, interest rates, and profits, are generated by markets. If supply-siders are only concerned with incentives, their approach is incomplete. If their perspectives are expanded to include information and plan coordination, their approach is not different from that of the market-process economists.

The salient feature of these theories of economic growth is the lack of recognition of financial factors—markets and institutions—in the growth process. The remaining chapters specifically address this issue.

NOTES

1. See Abramovitz (1979) for perspectives on the convergence of productivities of the United States and other nations in the post-World War II period. Ames and Rosenberg (1963) develop three versions of the catchup hypothesis that suggest that technological leadership will rotate among nations.

2. See Choi (1983) for an excellent survey of earlier empirical studies investigating the relationship between trade and economic growth.

3. Grilli and Yang (1988) provide some empirical support for this hypothesis, although it seems to be period-dependent.

4. Bond (1987) determines that the demand for developing nation commodity exports has high long-run price elasticity but relatively low short-run price elasticity.

5. China and India are examples that come to mind.

6. The benefits from manufacturing activity spread into other areas, such as education, birth rates, and overall health measures. Employment in this sector demands certain prerequisites in education, both general as well as technical. Manufacturing firms usually support vocational and technical training schools. They also provide basic health services, either directly or through some health insurance scheme. Better quality of life is usually accompanied by lower birth rates.

7. Many writers have provided intellectual support for industrialization policies. Kaldor (1978) believes manufacturing would continue to be the dominant sector even in mature economies. Verdoorn (1949) states that productivity growth stems from increased manufacturing output. [see also Sen (1983)]. Choi (1983) provides a summary of the major empirical studies. Scott (1989, Chapter 4) provides an interesting discussion on these and related issues.

8. Developing nations do not deal effectively with technical inefficiencies. For example, there is the inability of the political system to deal with divisive issues such as closure of inefficient plants or reduction of the labor force. There is also the inability of the bureaucratic system to deal with the dismantling of protection. There are positive disincentives to take such actions, as they diminish the control of the bureaucracy over the existing system of permits and licenses. These are examples of application of Olson's theory of common-interest groups discussed in more detail in the next section.

9. The analysis presented by Olson has wider implications. It can be applied to a variety of situations where members of a group are brought together to serve a common goal. Nevertheless, conflicts may arise when individual members pursue their personal goals, which may be at variance with group goals. At the most basic level, the family is one such group. While overall goals may be identified as collective welfare, financial security, and provision of the elements of good living, individual choice of action may run counter to family objectives. The corporate entity is another example. Bondholders and stockholders, as suppliers of capital, have different objectives from those of managers, who have control over the assets of the firm. The dichotomy between corporate ownership and control has spawned numerous papers in the area of principal–agent relationships. Jensen and Meckling (1976) pioneered this literature and interesting extensions are provided in Barnea, Haugen and Senbet (1985). Government bureaucracies constitute the third example. Bureaucrats are supposed to further the welfare of the populace and are subject to the control of the executive branch and the oversight of the legislative branch. More often than not, bureaucrats pursue individual goals, which may include empire building, widening the span of their control, financial gains, and other professional objectives. Some of these goals may be accomplished only at some cost to the interests of the populace. For an early analysis of this issue, see Niskanen (1971). However, there is a difference between corporate managers and bureaucrats in this context. While corporate managers are subject to the discipline of the market (product, labor, and financial considerations), there is no such restraint on

bureaucrats. For an attempt to outline such conflicts of interest in organizations, see Kumar and Tsetsekos (1989).

10. This problem may be characterized by a utility–theoretic framework. Consider an individual member having a utility function, whose arguments are benefits of membership in the group and uniqueness of the benefits. In this case, uniqueness implies exclusivity. The member prefers higher benefits but also prefers that the benefit accrue exclusively to him or her. For example, if there is a distribution of benefits across recepients, the individual prefers to be in, say, the upper five percentile. The extent of benefits is determined by a functional relationship with cost or initial effort, which is subject to a supply constraint.

11. Positive selective incentives also include psychological factors, such as psychic rewards, public recognition, reputation, etc. Such selective incentives are referred as "social selective incentives" (Olson, 1982, p. 23). Such incentives do not apply to large groups unless they consist of smaller groups capable of social interaction. A necessary condition for the efficacy of these incentives is social homogeniety, as little agreement could be reached among members of socially heterogeneous groups.

12. See Olson (1982), pp. 29–34.

13. The analogy in Olson (1982) relates to differential slicing of the pie rather than increasing its size (p. 42).

14. Olson (1982, Chapter 3) identifies a set of nine implications of the actions of CIGs. Three of these implications are relevant to this discussion.

15. In recent history, the introduction of computers in any part of the world encountered initial opposition. The opposition was quickly dissipated with the realization that this technology spawned new categories of employment.

16. See Choi (1983, Chapters 8–10) for extensive testing of Olson's theories. The difficulty in econometric tests has been suitable identification of measurable variables. In general, the theory appears to be supported by cross-sectional tests of a sample of industrialized nations as well as the 48 contiguous states in the United States.

17. See Canto et al. (1983), Evans (1983), Gilder (1982), Greenhut (1983), Hailstones (1982), and Meyer (1981) for the basis of the supply-side philosophy. A discussion of the conceptual background is provided in Roberts (1982) and Ture (1982). Hazlett (1982) provides a critique of the supply-side position from the perspective of the Austrian economics school. Fink (1982) discusses supply-side policies from the viewpoint of market-based economics.

18. See Roberts (1982), p. 4.

19. In the 1950s and 60s, China and India followed inward-looking policies that largely resulted in growth inconsistent with their potential. International trade can enhance human capital through technological change and knowledge acquisition.

II

INTERNAL SOURCES OF DEVELOPMENT FINANCE

Economic development is the concern of many nations in the world. The constant need to provide the basic necessities of life and to create the opportunities for economic growth as well as individual advancement engage the attention of authorities in these nations. The biggest challenge in deploying the available resources to meet these goals has been the availability of finance. Concepts, issues, and strategies in developing sources of finance internal to the nation are the topics of Part II. Chapter 3 discusses tax policies as one of these elements. It concludes by observing that tax policies are effective only if individuals are responsive to price changes. Furthermore, the adminstrative capacity to implement tax schemes should be available. Internal sources may be tapped effectively if the necessary institutional structure is present. Chapter 4 explores the conceptual foundations of financial intermediation—the process by which financial resources may be channeled from savers to entrepreneurs in need. The institution instrumental in this transfer—the financial intermediary—provides a variety of services to the advantage of both savers and entrepreneurs. One variety of such institutions is the capital market and its networks. Chapter 5 emphasizes that "infrastructure," in the form of a legal framework delineating and enforcing property rights, accounting standards and efficient communication systems, aid the functioning of securities markets. Chapter 6 examines another type of financial intermediary—the development bank. While the performances of these institutions have been far from satisfactory in the 1970s and 1980s, opportunities to diversify their activities into innovative provision of capital services are available. Such services include supply of working capital, leasing, and investment-banking services. The growing trend towards privatization of public ownership is the topic of Chapter 7. The discussion in this chapter emphasizes that a competitive environment is a necessary condition for the success of these strategies. Chapter 9 concludes Part II by examining the substitutions and complementarities that exist among these strategies.

3

Taxation as an Element of Development Finance

1. INTRODUCTION

Throughout the world, governments are being required to minimize their role in the management of their economies. The traditional functions of the state include national defense, administration of justice, and the provision of infrastructural facilities that may be beyond the scope of private individuals. In addition, government may be required to promote growth and development, stability, equitable distribution of income and wealth, as well as national independence or self-reliance. In the erstwhile centrally planned economies, this goal was mandated by the political system. In decentralized developing economies, the role of government may be either catalytic (indirect) or calls for active involvement in the promotion of growth and the distribution of income and wealth (direct). Even in developed market-oriented economies, given the complexities of modern problems, there is a definite role for government. It is therefore useful to consider the financial resources available to the state.

Financial transactions or fiscal instruments may be classified as government outlays or government receipts. These transactions have increased in their size and complexity over time. Outlays include purchase of goods and services (also called requited or exhaustive expenditures), transfer payments (nonrequited or nonexhaustive expenditures), and the acquisition of financial assets. Government receipts include taxes, fees, and income from state property and enterprises, proceeds from the sale of land and other capital assets, grants from other governments and international institutions, borrowing, and money creation. The focus of this chapter is on taxes, inasmuch as it is an important source of finance for development. The next section discusses some general aspects of taxes and the structure of taxation in developing countries. The conceptual foundations of taxation, including the basic intertemporal and simple life-cycle models and a model of tax design for developing countries are discussed in the third section.

Issues such as constraints on taxation in developing countries, tax structure and the stage of development, as well as the relevance of supply-side arguments relating to taxation in developing countries, are the topics of the fourth section. Strategies and policies for tax reform are presented in the fifth section. The sixth section summarizes the chapter.

2. GENERAL ASPECTS OF TAXATION

Taxes are compulsory contributions for which no explicit, reciprocal benefits are provided to the payer. The household or enterprise is forced to surrender purchasing power to the government for its own direct use or transfer to others. Taxes thus reduce the disposable income and wealth of those who bear them. They are therefore distinctly different from prices, which are voluntary payments for goods or services in exchange. The absence of a direct, counterbalancing benefit results in the tax being considered burdensome.

2.1. Purpose, Functions, and Necessity of Taxes

The primary *purpose* of taxation is to divert control of economic resources from taxpayers to the state for its own use or transfer to others. Taxes therefore restrain total spending by households and enterprises but influence the allocation of economic resources. Furthermore, taxes affect the distribution of income and wealth and recognize social costs that are not reflected in market prices. They are paid in cash by taxpayers who relinquish purchasing power in this process. However, some taxes may be paid in kind, such as taxes exacted on oil companies. Other taxes may be in the form of services to be rendered or goods delivered at less than full compensation. Examples of these are military service, or procurement prices at less than market value, or surrender of foreign exchange at less than the international exchange rate.

The *function* of taxes is seen most clearly in direct taxes, where the individual who pays taxes loses purchasing power. Excise duties, customs duties, and sales taxes are indirect taxes that are collected from producers or distributors with the expectation they will be passed on to consumers.

Taxation is *necessary* because it is not always feasible to finance government by charging for services provided. In the case of public goods, charges for services are infeasible. Whereas in the case of mixed public–private goods, prices cannot perform the allocative and distributive functions of taxation.

2.2. A Description of Tax Systems in Developing Countries

Tanzi (1987) provides an extensive survey of tax systems in developing countries. He finds a positive relationship between per-capita income and the tax ratio (total tax revenue/GDP). This finding lends support to the hypothesis that as countries develop, tax bases grow more than proportionately to the growth of income; the capacity to tax grows with the growth of income. Another feature is that there is a positive correlation between the degree of urbanization and growth in income. A relevant characteristic of urbanization is that it facilitates tax collection while generating demand for public services. Other studies have demonstrated that the total tax ratio may be influenced by factors such as monetization and openness of the economy, share of mining in GDP, an export ratio that excludes mineral exports, the literacy rate, and the urbanization rate.[1]

While the level of taxation is undoubtedly important, equally so is the structure of taxation. Income taxes, domestic taxes on goods and services, taxes on foreign trade, and other taxes, such as social security and wealth taxes, are considered in the following discussion.

2.2.1. Income Taxes. Individual income taxes account for 1.9% of GDP and 10.3% of total tax revenue for Tanzi's sample of 86 countries (Tanzi, 1987). He concludes from these data that income taxes (actually collected) are much less important in developing countries than in developed countries. Economic development, as measured by per-capita income, has a weak correlation with the proportion of these taxes to GDP. This observation is both surprising and disappointing, given that these taxes have been considered to be the traditional instruments for achieving income redistribution. The numerous requirements for an effective and efficient system of personal income taxation are rigorous and are satisfied only at high levels of development. With a large agricultural sector, poor accounting standards, low literacy levels, and most economic activity being concentrated in small establishments, the effective taxation of personal income is rendered difficult in developing countries. In developing countries, the higher concentration of income reduces the justification for a broad-based system of taxes. In effect, the incidence of taxes is directed at the wages of public sector employees and those of large corporations. With an increase in the proportion of personal income derived from work in the public sector and large corporations, the scope for taxing personal income also increases.[2]

2.2.2. Corporate Income Taxes. Economic development has a greater impact on corporate income taxes than on personal income taxes. There is a significantly high degree of correlation between the share of corporate income taxes in GDP and per-capita income.[3] The data also reveal that the share of corporate taxes increases with the level of development, reaches a maximum, and then declines. A partial explanation for this observation is that in the initial stages of development, mineral exports form a large share of total income and constitute an important tax handle. However, as development progresses, the importance of mineral exports declines, while the scope for other tax handles increases.

2.2.3. Domestic Taxes on Goods and Services. The data reveal that there is no correlation between the share of these taxes in GDP and per-capita income. This is generally true for aggregate domestic taxes on goods and services as well as general sales taxes and excise taxes considered independently. General sales tax in some form is levied in most countries. But these are qualified by numerous exemptions, so that the tax base consists predominantly of imports subject to these taxes. In many countries the share of general sales tax revenue collected from imports is more than half the total.[4] Not more than 20% of domestic value added is subject to this form of taxation. The high rate of base erosion explains the low tax revenue accompanying the high legal rates.

The contribution of excise taxes is about the same as general sales taxes. Among the many products on which excise taxes are levied, alcohol, tobacco, and petroleum are the most popular. The share of petroleum in total excise tax revenue is 43%. Alcohol accounts for 27% and tobacco's share is about 23%.

2.2.4. Foreign Trade Taxes. These taxes are seen to be more important than income taxes, accounting for 5% of GDP and 30.6% of total tax revenue of developing countries. Import duties, contributing 4.2% of GDP and 25% of total tax revenue, are the most important revenue source. Import duties, as a percentage of GDP, are most important for countries with per-capita income below $350 and least important for countries with per-capita incomes in excess of $1700. Total tax ratios increase with per-capita income, whereas the ratio of import taxes to GDP is negatively related to the level of income. The data reveal that there is some degree of substitution between import duties and domestic taxes on goods and services. Countries that make extensive use of import duties do not generally resort to taxes on domestic transactions, whereas those that broadly tax domestic goods and services make little use of import taxes. Empirical tests support this observation. Tanzi concludes that import duties are positively influenced by the openness of the economy and negatively influenced by the level of per-capita income and by the countries' reliance on domestic taxes on goods and services.[5] The foregoing is not meant to imply that the import tax base is free from tax erosion. The average proportion of exempted imports for a sample of eighteen countries is 45%.[6] The most important reasons for the erosion of the import duty tax base are: the public sector is exempt; embassies and other agents with diplomatic status are permitted duty-free imports; private enterprises benefiting from special legislation are exempt from import duties; imports for social reasons are free of taxes.

On the other hand, export taxes, while significant in many countries, have more limited importance than import duties. Tanzi (1987) argues it is easier to tax the exports of agricultural products than agricultural incomes. Export taxes should be more important to countries that export agricultural products. Thus there is some substitution between corporate income taxes and export taxes; countries that use corporate income taxes extensively should resort to limited use of export taxes and vice versa. This hypothesis is borne out, albeit with a limited sample.[7]

The statistical descriptions of these tax systems do not necessarily conform to their statutory specifications. The statutory specifications include information relating to rates, taxable bases, methods of payments, etc. Tanzi (1983) suggests that there are several reasons for these divergences. First, there is a distinction between explicit and intentional taxation; second, there is inadequate recording and accounting; and lastly, there is a lag between the actual receipt of a tax payment and the point in time when the liability was recognized. An international comparison of tax systems is vitiated by dynamic changes in the degree of tax evasion and lags described above, as well as the quality of accounting standards and their enforcement.

3. CONCEPTUAL FOUNDATIONS OF TAXATION

Increases in taxation on individuals are accompanied by income and substitution effects. A reduction in the after-tax return to capital is synonymous with making future consumption more expensive. If utility is held constant, this tends to favor current consumption by the *substitution effect*. Note that a person may be a net borrower (a demander of capital) or a net lender (a supplier). A reduction in the after-tax return results in a decline in the income of the lender and present consumption is reduced, assuming goods are normal. In the case of a net borrower, a reduction in the after-tax cost of borrowing has a positive *wealth effect* and present consumption is raised. Thus, in the case of the lender, the substitution and wealth effects are in opposition but it is not unambiguously clear which dominates.

Taxation also has its *financial effects*. In corporate entities, these effects influence the form in which savings occur, as a result of differential treatment of retained earnings and dividends. The liability to pay taxes arises only when returns on investment are distributed in the form of dividends. When different types of assets are taxed differently, there may also be a *capitalization effect*. In the case of assets in inelastic supply, market equilibrium results in the price of these assets adjusting to the point where the return per dollar invested is the same as on other assets. Thus if there are two assets, A and B, and the tax on one, say A, is increased, then the price of A is reduced to the point where the same after-tax return is still obtained.

Standard models in the theory of public finance are described in the following subsection. They are developed to provide a conceptual backdrop for the discussions that follow. Atkinson and Stiglitz (1980) and Sandmo (1985) are the principal sources for the models. Similar analyses are available in Hansen (1958).

3.1. The Basic Intertemporal Model

Let us assume an individual has a life expectancy of N years. From age j onwards, he receives wage income of w_j and consumes c_j. He receives bequests during his life with a present value of B and expects to leave a bequest of D on his death. Let us further assume a capital market in which he can borrow or lend any amount at a fixed rate of interest, k, through his time horizon. The intertemporal budget constraint is represented by the following identity:

$$\sum_{j=1}^{N} \frac{w_j}{(1+k)^{j-1}} + B = \sum_{j=1}^{N} \frac{c_j}{(1+k)^{j-1}} + \frac{D}{(1+k)^N} \tag{3.1}$$

If capital markets are absent, so that he cannot borrow, and if his inheritance is received at age K, the following additional constraints apply:

$$\sum_{j=1}^{J} \frac{w_j}{(1 + k)^{j-1}} \geq \sum_{j=1}^{J} \frac{c_j}{(1 + k)^{j-1}} \quad \text{for all } j < K \tag{3.2a}$$

$$\sum_{j=1}^{N} \frac{w_j}{(1 + k)^{j-1}} + B \geq \sum_{j=1}^{N} \frac{c_j}{(1 + k)^{j-1}} \quad \text{for all } N \geq j \geq K \tag{3.2b}$$

The following equivalence results from the budget constraint:

1. *A proportional tax t on wages plus inheritances is equivalent to a proportional tax t' on consumption plus bequests.*

The former is represented as

$$\left[\sum_{j=1}^{N} \frac{w_j}{(1 + k)^{j-1}} + B \right] (1 - t) = \sum_{j=1}^{N} \frac{c_j}{(1 + k)^{j-1}} + \frac{D}{(1 + k)^N} \tag{3.3a}$$

and the proportional tax on consumption plus bequests

$$\sum_{j=1}^{N} \frac{w_j}{(1 + k)^{j-1}} + B = \left[\sum_{j=1}^{N} \frac{c_j}{(1 + k)^{j-1}} + \frac{D}{(1 + k)^N} \right] (1 + t') \tag{3.3b}$$

Thus the effect on the budget constraint is identical where

$$(1 - t) = \frac{1}{1 + t'} \tag{3.4}$$

Eq. (3.4) indicates the equivalence between a tax-inclusive basis used for income tax and a tax-exclusive basis used for indirect taxes. Thus a wage tax of 25% is equivalent to a consumption tax of 33%.

Some aspects of this equivalence are worth noting:

1. Consider an individual with a life span of N years who is engaged in gainful employment for W years and is in retirement for the remaining period $(N - W)$ with no income. An income tax is applicable for W years, whereas the consumption tax is applicable for the entire life span of N years. If the government and individuals can borrow or lend at the same interest rate, there are no general equilibrium effects of switching tax regimes. A switch from an income tax to the consumption tax increases private savings at the cost of government savings.

2. The wage tax, or the equivalent consumption tax, does not affect the trade-off between consumption at different dates for the individual. It only has a *wealth*

effect—it shifts the budget constraint inward. This has an important corollary, namely, individuals with the same present value of receipts are affected identically, regardless of the timing of their wage income.

3.2. Simple Life-Cycle Model

Consider the simple case of an individual whose life span is divided into two equal periods. He works for a wage w in the first and retires in the second period. He saves from his wage income to provide for his retirement, at a lending rate of interest of k. This is expressed as a budget constraint in the following equation, where C_1 and C_2 represent consumption in each of the two periods,

$$C_1 + \frac{C_2}{1 + k} = w \tag{3.5}$$

The individual is assumed to maximize lifetime utility $U(C_1, C_2)$. The wealth and substitution effects alluded to earlier can now be more explicitly discussed. Note that $p \equiv 1/(1 + k)$ is just the price of consumption in the second period. In addition, note that w represents his lifetime wealth. Then the Slutsky equations can be expressed as follows

$$\frac{\partial C_1}{\partial p} = \frac{\partial C_1}{\partial p}\bigg|_U - \frac{C_2 \partial C_1}{\partial w} \tag{3.5a}$$

and

$$\frac{\partial C_2}{\partial p} = \frac{\partial C_2}{\partial p}\bigg|_U - \frac{C_2 \partial C_2}{\partial w} \tag{3.5b}$$

The first term on the right-hand side represents the substitution effect, while the second term is the income effect. An increase in p as a result of a decrease in the interest rate (k) makes first-period consumption more attractive through the substitution effect. However, a decline of the interest rate makes the individual worse off as a lender and hence the wealth effect on first-period consumption is negative, as $\partial C/\partial w > 0$. The net effect is therefore ambiguous. On the other hand, both income and substitution effects on second-period consumption are negative, and they work to reduce consumption.

In Figure 3.1, the substitution effect with an increase in p is represented by a movement along the indifference curve from Q to P'. This effect depends on the curvature of the indifference curve and it is useful to characterize it in terms of the elasticity of substitution, σ, where

$$\sigma \equiv \frac{d\log(C_2/C_1)}{d\log(1 + k)}\bigg|_U \tag{3.6}$$

Figure 3.1
The Two-Period Consumption Model

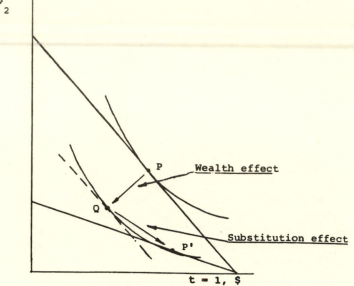

Source: Adapted from A. Atkinson and J. E. Stiglitz, *Lectures on Public Economics* (1980). Used with permission from McGraw-Hill, Inc.

σ represents the percentage change in the relative value of C_2 with respect to C_1 as the slope of the budget constraint $(1 + k)$ changes along the indifference curve. Recalling that $p = 1/(1 + k)$, eq. (3.6) may be expanded as

$$\sigma = \left. \frac{\partial \log C_1}{\partial \log p} \right|_U - \left. \frac{\partial \log C_2}{\partial \log p} \right|_U \qquad (3.6a)$$

A result of the relationship between $\partial C_i/\partial p_j$ (i not equal to j), and the expenditure function is the following[8]

$$\left. \frac{\partial C_1}{\partial \log p} \right|_U + p \left. \frac{\partial C_2}{\partial \log p} \right|_U = 0 \qquad (3.7)$$

Defining s as the savings rate $\equiv pC_2/(C_1 + pC_2)$, and substituting the result from equation (3.7) in (3.6a), yields

$$\left. \frac{\partial \log C_1}{\partial \log p} \right|_U = \frac{pC_2}{C_1 + pC_2} \, \sigma \equiv s\sigma \qquad (3.8)$$

Further, defining λ as the wealth elasticity of first period consumption $(w/C_1)(\partial C_1/\partial w)$, then

$$\frac{\partial \log C_1}{\partial \log p} = s(\sigma - \lambda) \tag{3.9}$$

Thus, savings increase or decrease with the net rate of return depending on the relative magnitudes of elasticity of substitution and wealth elasticity of consumption. For example, if the indifference curves are homothetic, such that $\lambda = 1$, then the effect depends on whether the elasticity of substitution between consumption early in life and later in life is greater or less than unity.

3.2.1. Effects of Taxation. A proportional expenditure tax, or, equivalently, a wage tax, has a pure wealth effect—it shifts the budget constraint inward to a position parallel to the pretax constraint. On the other hand, a proportional income tax that includes the taxation of interest income swivels the budget-constraint so that no wealth is carried forward. If t_w and t_i represent the wage tax and income tax respectively, the after-tax "price" of second-period consumption, $p = 1/[1 + k(1 - t_i)]$. Note that p increases with t_i. Define S as savings in monetary units, where $S = (1 - t_w)w - C_1$. The total change in savings dS with respect to changes in t_w and t_i is

$$dS = \frac{\partial S}{\partial t_w} dt_w + \frac{\partial S}{\partial t_i} dt_i \tag{3.10}$$

or

$$dS = -wdt_w\left(1 - \frac{\partial C_1}{\partial M}\right) - \frac{\partial C_1}{\partial p}\frac{\partial p dt_i}{\partial t_i} \tag{3.10a}$$

where $M = w(1 - t_w)$.

Assume tax rates are positive and the relative tax ratio, $(1 - t_w)/(1 - t_i)$, is constant. Dividing (3.10a) by $dt_i/(1 - t_i) = dt_w/(1 - t_w)$, invoking the relationship in equation (3.9), and recognizing that $\partial p/\partial t_i = rp^2$ yields the condition

$$\frac{\partial S}{\partial t_i} = -\left[w(1 - t_w)\left(1 - \frac{\lambda C_1}{M}\right) + C_1 s(\sigma - \lambda)(1 - p)\right] \tag{3.11}$$

Thus, the condition that the response of savings to an increase in tax will be negative is that the absolute value of the term in the square bracket is positive. Note that in equation (3.11), $s = pC_2/(C_1 + pC_2)$ where $p = 1/[1 + r(1 - t_i)]$. Taking the condition that the term in the square bracket should be positive, dividing by $w(1 - t_w)$ yields

$$so(1 - p) + [1/(1 - s)] > \lambda[1 + s(1 - p)] \tag{3.12}$$

Thus, the response of savings to the income tax depends on the wealth elasticity of first-period consumption (λ), the elasticity of substitution (σ), the savings rate (s), and the price of second-period consumption.

3.2.2. Capital Market Imperfections.

The preceding discussion does not permit borrowing, since the individual is presumed to have only first-period income. Suppose this situation is altered with the assumption that the individual has wage income w_i in period i. Thus, the individual could consume an amount C_1 in excess of his wage w_1 by resorting to borrowing. A change in k, the interest rate, causes the budget constraint to swivel about Q in Figure 3.2. The effect of taxation depends on the deductibility of the interest paid. If there is deductibility, taxation of interest income is analogous to a decline in k, and for individuals to the right of Q there is a positive wealth effect increasing C_1. The Slutsky equation becomes

$$\frac{\partial C_1}{\partial p} = \frac{\partial C_1}{\partial p}\bigg|_U - (C_2 - w_2)\frac{\partial C_1}{\partial M} \tag{3.13}$$

The income effect depends on the difference between consumption and wage income in the second period. If the individual is a borrower in the first period, then $w_2 > C_2$ and the income effect is positive and so is the net effect. If the individual is a first-period lender, then $w_2 < C_2$, and the income effect is negative, so that the net effect is indeterminate. However, if C_2 is approximately equal to w_2, then the

Figure 3.2
Budget Constraint with Interest Income Tax

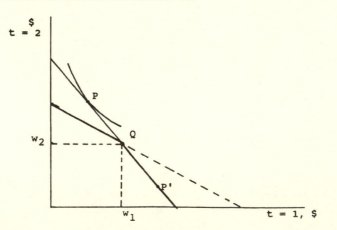

Source: Adapted from A. Atkinson and J. E. Stiglitz, *Lectures on Public Economics* (1980). Used with permission from McGraw-Hill, Inc.

substitution effect tends to dominate and an interest income tax results in an increase in C_1.

If there is no deductibility, the budget line is kinked as in Figure 3.2. Those individuals choosing points to the right of Q, such as P', where $C_1 > w_1$, are unaffected by the tax. The kinked budget constraint is also analogous to a form of capital market imperfection, where borrowing rates exceed lending rates. One possible effect is that individuals may cluster at the kink.

3.3. Tax Design for Developing Countries

Normative tax theory recognizes that the impacts of taxation occur at two different levels. First, taxation affects individual decisions relating to the tradeoffs between current and future consumption as well as between leisure and work. Second, at the institutional level we recognize the tradeoff between raising tax revenue, which has the goal of redistribution of the tax burden among the population, and associated efficiency losses. From purely efficiency considerations, a lump-sum tax is the preferred approach. The difficulty with this approach is that there is inadequate information about the population regarding consumption, incomes, nonmarketed production, etc. If a lump-sum tax is not feasible the second best alternative is income or expenditure tax. In taking this alternative, we recognize implicitly that efficiency losses are inevitable.[9]

4. ISSUES RELATING TO TAXATION IN DEVELOPING COUNTRIES

4.1. Constraints on Taxation in Developing Countries

The preceding discussions indicate that taxes influence individual choice. A tax on earning capacity, such as a head tax, encourages additional work, since money must be earned to discharge the tax liability. Whereas, marginal taxes on increments of income discourage additional effort. Taxes based on consumption affect consumer options in direct relation to the incidence and diversity of the rate structure. If the role of fiscal policy is to eliminate price distortions with a view to maximizing welfare, then it may be concluded that the best policy is the absence of taxes. This conclusion is not warranted, for the price mechanism is not geared to provide essential public goods. These services have to be paid for, which does not present a problem as long as the marginal government expenditure is valued higher than the marginal tax effort. Furthermore, the objective of improving the use of the country's resources are better served if tax measures are used as instruments to countervail distortions. In addition, the tax system may be used as a regulator to align aggregate demand with productive capacity.[10]

Taxation in developing countries is constrained by administrative, sociopolitical and economic factors that tend to magnify the burden. A tax system that limits the excess burden and provides equal treatment for individuals in similar circumstances (horizontal equity) is not easily designed or administered. The problem is complicated by the fact that developing countries are victims of their own underdevelopment. Modern accounting and record-keeping habits are not consistent with an illiterate population. By the same token, tax administrators are generally poorly educated, inadequately paid, and lack a tradition of public service. Furthermore, the absence of a well-established legal system, together with poor transportation, communications, and other infrastructure, contribute to the general difficulty of raising and collecting taxes.

At the sociopolitical level, resistance to taxation, especially in the instance where the goal is the promotion of equity, is always encountered from the privileged classes. With their power and influence they are better positioned to circumvent the tax laws. The government has to counter such negativism by generating confidence in its policies and its stability. An economic objective of tax policy is the promotion of horizontal equity subject to the constraint of minimal excess burden. It is easy to assess and collect taxes through payroll withholdings, but this strategy is vitiated if employment in the economy is such that there are few individuals on properly accountable payrolls. Another economic constraint is the heavily skewed distribution of income in developing countries. There must be adequate political support for progressive taxation to counter this phenomenon. Finally, the attitudes of the wealthy classes towards their portfolio composition contribute to aggregate savings and investment. The more holdings in productive assets are encouraged, the narrower the gap between potential and actual savings and the higher the eventual growth.

4.2. Tax Structure and the Stage of Development

An interesting question relates to the notion of a representative or model system for nations at the same stage of development. Hinrichs (1966) contends that as economic development evolves, the ratio of direct to indirect taxes is high initially. This is followed by a stage in which indirect taxes assume greater importance, and, in the final stage, direct taxes dominate again. At the early stage of development, government revenues are obtained mostly in the form of nontax sources and direct taxation on land, livestock, agricultural output, water rights, and poll taxes. In the transition to modernity, these yield to indirect taxes, such as customs duties consequent to openness to foreign trade and domestic consumption taxes. A higher overall tax ratio is characteristic of this stage. In the advanced stage of development, taxes on foreign trade diminish in importance while modern direct taxes grow. Thus, in the earlier stages, governments are constrained by the size of the alternative tax bases and their administrative capacities. In the highest stages of development, they have greater opportunity to adapt their tax systems to the political preferences of the population. Hinrichs (1966) observes that the structural movement has been from taxation on agriculture, to foreign trade, to consumption, to net earnings, individual and business.[11]

Musgrave (1969) describes tax structures as being determined by economic and socio-political factors. The former determine the size of different tax bases, while the latter influence opinions on tax equity. In the initial stage, tax revenues are obtained from land taxes, import and excise duties, and few excise taxes. Collection of income taxes is limited to individuals within the organized sector, such as civil servants and employees of large enterprises. This stage is described as having limited "tax handles." In the second stage, general income taxes become feasible, and attract support due to egalitarian sentiments, democratic politics, and government decentralization.[12] Musgrave agrees with Hinrichs that in the final stages of development nations have greater flexibility in the design of the tax system than in the earlier stages.

Empirical evidence in a study by Tait, Gratz, and Eichengreen (1979) supports the tax handle explanation. Tax share is found to be positively correlated with the share of mining in GDP and with the share of nonmineral exports to GNP. The tax share is not significantly correlated with the share of per-capita income or with the share of agriculture in GDP. These relationships are significant only for countries with GNP less than $10 billion and per-capita income less than $750. The study draws attention to the importance of mineral taxation and export taxation. Tanzi (1987) also finds that the structure of taxation is related (perhaps weakly) to the level of development. Income taxes are weakly correlated with per-capita GNP, although corporate income taxes are more important. There appears to be some substitution between export tax and corporate tax revenues. Indirect taxes, including domestic sales taxes and taxes on foreign trade, are relatively important. Foreign trade taxes are negatively correlated with per-capita income and the share of domestic sales taxes. This implies that as development proceeds, domestic production of import substitutes become more important and domestic sales tax will account for a larger share of indirect tax revenue. These studies support the viewpoint that corporate taxes and indirect taxes are particularly important for developing countries. Personal income taxes are, however, relatively unimportant.

4.3. Special Characteristics of Developing Countries

Newbery (1987) identifies several characteristics of developing countries for tax analysis.

Importance of the Primary Sector. In most developing countries the agricultural sector provides significant employment opportunities and generates substantial income but has a far lower level of productivity compared to the non-agricultural sector. Thus, there is dualism with the coexistence of two sectors with different levels of labor productivity. However, in most of these countries a significant portion of the workers' time may be spent on nonagricultural activities. If this aspect is taken into account, the disparity in productivity may not be as high as previously indicated.[13]

Dualism. Newbery (1987, p. 168) notes, "A dual economy is one with a significant difference in the economic and social organization of the traditional, rural sector and the modern capitalist sector." The distinctions may be in terms of products produced (food versus nonfood), social organization (semisubsistence or capitalist), or location (rural or urban). From the perspective of tax analysis, two aspects of dualism are noteworthy. The first is the extent to which transactions in the traditional sector can be taxed, and the second is the extent to which dualism is symptomatic of market failure, particularly market segmentation.

Segmentation of the Labor Market. With a segmented labor market, the marginal products of the same kind of labor differ between the two sectors. Squire (1981) identifies two kinds of this dualism, labeled as traditional sector dualism and modern sector dualism. The marginal product of labor in the modern sector exceeds that in the traditional sector. The driving force is the supply price of labor from the traditional to the modern sector.

Dualism, Capital-Market Fragmentation, and the Rate of Savings. The modern sector grows faster than the traditional sector, with higher share of GDP and higher share of profits and savings. The traditional sector is unable to save due to poverty, shortage of investment opportunities, or its institutional nature. On the other hand, due to the lack of financial intermediaries, the traditional sector is unable to transfer its savings to the modern sector. It has been argued that the government should use tax policy to provide incentives to the traditional sector to raise the rate of investment and growth.

Income Distribution. It is well known developing countries exhibit skewed income distributions and these distributions have dynamic characteristics over time. Obviously, these asymmetries have implications for tax policy.

Size Distributions of Firms. In many developing countries, the distribution of firm size is bimodal. There are small firms in the traditional or informal urban sector and larger, organized firms in the modern sector. The latter may be foreign dominated. In other countries, the fear of foreign domination may restrict foreign investment. In some countries, like India, the response to foreign domination has been the development of a monolithic public sector. The activities of the public sector and its size raise questions for tax policy.

Imperfect Competition, Trade Distortions, and Scarcity of Foreign Exchange. The manufacturing sector is usually small in developing countries. With a view to attracting foreign capital, incentives in the form of protection are usually offered. Quotas, licenses and tariff barriers are equally more prevalent in developing countries. All such distortions have implications for tax policy.

Planning, Public Capital Formation, and State-Owned Enterprises. Developing nations attach greater importance to planning and a significant amount of capital is raised through the public sector. This is rationalized on the basis of potential market failure. Infrastructural facilities with substantial economies of scale are lumpy investments that may not be supplied through the market. Facilities, such as, roads, sanitation, irrigation, and urban development, generate benefits that are hard to capture except through the tax system.[14]

4.4. Supply-side Arguments and Taxation in Developing Countries

The relevance of supply-side arguments for economic growth was discussed in Chapter 2. A major focus of the supply-side position relates to taxation. How truly relevant are these considerations for developing nations? Gandhi (1987a), in perhaps the only systematic effort to answer this question, assembles some impressive research. This subsection summarizes some of these important findings.

Supply-side economists emphasize the need to minimize distortions in market-determined prices caused by regulations, subsidies, and high income taxation. They also believe that the reduction of such distortions would permit a free market to offer the necessary incentives to promote savings and production. Two interpretations of supply-side economics have evolved over time.[15] *Basic* supply-side economists, recognizing the importance of efficient resource allocation to aggregate output, advocate the reduction in "distortions in resource allocation that individual taxes and tax structures can cause." How do these distortions arise? These distortions depend on a number of factors, including size of the tax base, tax rules that have differential impacts on producers and factor suppliers and can thus affect the tax base, extent and structure of the tax schedule, and finally, the interrelationship between inflation, tax base, and tax liabilities. On the other hand, the principal emphasis of the *popular* supply-side economists is on the lowering of the marginal tax rate. Their position has been distinguished from that of the *basic* supply-side economists in that their focus is on a narrow aspect of tax policy. They are more concerned with tax policy, and, specifically, with progressivity of income taxation and top marginal income tax rates. They also claim high elasticity of each of the variables—growth rate, increases in tax revenue, rise in savings and reduction in inflation—with a reduction in the marginal income tax rates. Thus, a reduction in the marginal income tax rates is expected to change the economic behavior of households and businesses in favor of work, savings, and productive investments as opposed to leisure, consumption, and unproductive investments. The short-run price elasticity embodied in the behavior of economic agents is presumed to be very large. This "elasticity optimism" is the underpinning of the Laffer curve.[16]

Gandhi (1987a) reviews a number of studies concentrating on the economic effects of direct taxes—income taxes, corporation taxes, and export duties—and examines their optimality in developing countries. Three important questions emerge from this discussion and each is considered in turn.

How responsive are labor supply, savings, and investment to price changes?

Mackenzie (1987) concludes from a theoretical analysis that the price elasticities of labor supply, savings, and investment are the primary determinants of the magnitudes of positive supply-side effects from a reduction of income taxes. Ebrill (1987a) surveys the literature relating to developing countries and determines that labor supply functions are price inelastic, as these supply decisions are based on a number of factors other than the wage rate. The evidence indicates that aggregate savings are affected less by interest rates and more by income and noneconomic factors, such as demographic characteristics, income distribution, life span, occupational patterns, and urban–rural differentiation. However, economic incentives do affect portfolio allocations between financial assets and competing possibilities. Investment in developing countries is affected by a number of factors other than the cost of capital. For example, foreign investment is influenced more by the availability of natural resources, established record of economic performance of the country, threat of expropriation, degree of urbanization, and infrastructural facilities than by fiscal incentives. Domestic investment, on the other hand, is affected by supply of savings, retained earnings of businesses, public investment outlays in support of private productive activity, trade policy, and the degree of protection. Ebrill (1987a) concludes that given the widespread market failure in developing countries, a more promising supply-side approach might be one that corrects for market failure.[17]

How do tax policies affect financial savings? Ebrill (1987b) identifies four characteristics of developing countries that affect optimal tax policy from the perspective of financial savings: artificially low interest rate ceilings, which, given the rates of inflation, result in financial repression; relatively underdeveloped financial markets and institutions, unorganized capital markets; compulsory savings schemes imposed by governments.[18] Ebrill (1987b) develops an optimal tax model in the spirit of Atkinson and Stiglitz (1980), taking into account the existence of financial repression and curb markets. Under standard conditions, the model indicates that the optimal tax on financial savings depends on its own price elasticity. If the degree of financial repression is large, the model indicates that a subsidy in place of a tax is appropriate. If subsidies are not permissible due to, say, fiscal reasons, then the model suggests that consumption, rather than income, is the appropriate tax base. Given the fact that each country represents a unique situation, it needs to be treated individually. The optimal tax treatment of financial savings can run the full range from subsidies to substantial taxation.[19]

Finally, how do tax policies affect investment? The neoclassical approach predicates that the tax rate affects the level of investment through its impacts on the cost of capital. Ebrill (1987c, pp. 115–7) finds that in developing countries with high rates of inflation, tax systems incorporating depreciation and inventory valuations based on historic cost are disincentives for investment. The determinants of investment are seen to be, in addition to the cost of capital, the rate of inflation and growth of exports.[20] This finding has implications for supply-side tax reform proposals.

5. STRATEGIES AND POLICIES FOR TAX REFORM IN DEVELOPING COUNTRIES

Tax reform in developing countries involves broad issues of economic policies as well as specific aspects of tax structure design and administration. However, the gap between desired goals and feasible actions depends on geography, institutions, political environment, and development stage of the country. Like many other aspects of public policy in developing countries, tax reform is not easily generalized or duplicated. Markets tend to be more segregated and imperfect than those available in industrialized countries, mobility is lower, dependence on foreign markets and indigenous markets for specific products is greater, and political and administrative constraints are more pervasive. Given these constraints, taxation is an instrument with multiple objectives.[21] Gandhi (1987c) asserts that, strictly from theoretical considerations, if efficient allocation of resources were the sole concern of policy makers, the tax systems of developing countries would consist of a poll tax, a tax on land area, windfall profits tax, potential income tax, taxes on items with inelastic demand or supply, and taxes on activities that only consume resources or generate externalities.[22] It would exclude popular taxes, such as income tax, corporation tax, capital gains tax, payroll tax, wealth tax, gift tax, and inheritance tax. Export and import duties as well as tax incentives and preferences would be excluded. The tax system would be based on price elasticities and exhibit no progression.[23]

5.1. Tax Incentives, Savings and Investment

The impact of taxation on savings and consumption is important from the perspective of economic development goals. The rate of *household saving* in developing countries is typically low. Most of this saving occurs at the upper end of the income scale and taxation of these income earners jeopardizes the limited saving in this category. But ignoring the taxation of upper-income earners implies bypassing their luxury consumption. Thus the equity–efficiency issue is raised again. Musgrave (1987) suggests that the dilemma may be resolved by a progressive expenditure tax, but points out that there are severe administrative limitations on its feasibility. Rather than provide incentives for household savings, the effort may be better spent in controlling inflation and creating adequate savings institutions, thus promoting more efficient financial intermediation.[24]

The linkage between tax policy and *business saving* is more direct. A survey of the corporate tax structure and incentives in developing countries indicates that while a few have high corporate tax rates (55% and above), most have liberal tax deductions and incentives.[25] These incentives are generous enough to reduce the corporate cost of capital considerably. This observation is supported by Ebrill (1987d) who concludes that governments of many developing countries subsidize productive investments in priority sectors of their economies. Another important element is *public sector* saving. Public investment, financed by taxes drawn from consumption, adds to capital formation; on the other hand, public consumption, financed by taxes drawn from saving, reduces capital formation.

Given the mobility of capital, in the absence of exchange controls, the limit on domestic taxation is set by the level of net returns available abroad. The level of corporate taxation should be modest if domestic capital is to be retained at home. This argument establishes a case for incentives to prevent capital flight. A complementary strategy is the granting of incentives to attract foreign capital. Musgrave (1987) notes that such incentives should not be neutralized by stricter taxation of repatriated earnings in the host country. Furthermore, competition among developing countries to provide tax incentives to attract foreign capital generates tax relief over and above the minimum needed.[26]

What is the role of tax incentives? A tax incentive is defined as: "A reduction in either the tax rate, the tax base or the tax liability, which is granted if a specific action is taken by the selected beneficiary" (Gandhi, 1987b, p. 250). Examples of tax incentives include tax holidays, accelerated depreciation, and investment tax credits. Tax incentives are meant to produce certain desired results—investment, production for exports, employment of labor, and increase in output. Sanchez-Ugarte (1987) observes that tax incentives are not substitutes for an efficient tax system. They cannot neutralize the negative economic effects of high marginal rates of narrowly based taxes, or inappropriate policies with respect to wage rates, interest rates, or exchange rates. Tax incentives are effective only when applied to accomplish specific narrow goals (Sanchez-Ugarte, 1987, p. 261). Sanchez-Ugarte identifies two cases of tax incentives. A "pure" case for tax incentives exists when the goal is to counteract externalities, to promote regional development, research, and development, encourage risk-taking and saving, and to dampen short run output variations. The "impure" case arises when tax incentives are employed solely to compensate for distortionary effects of inappropriate economic policies whose reform may be considered infeasible. Examples are inappropriate trade, tax, and wage policies.[27]

In conclusion, tax incentives are usually rendered ineffective in developing countries. The necessary conditions for them to be effective are: they should be directed at limited economic (not political) objectives; they should be predictable; they should be appropriate for the objectives being pursued; their general equilibrium effects on the economy should be considered, and finally, the administrative mechanism to handle the tax incentives should be available.[28] If an efficient tax system is in place, there is no need for tax incentives.

5.2. Export Duties

The data reveal that a substantial portion of the tax revenue of developing countries is derived from export duties levied on primary products, such as coffee, cocoa, tea, bananas, rubber, tin, groundnuts, bauxite, and phosphates. The average rates of duties on these products are high and affect incentives for production and exports. Sanchez-Ugarte and Modi (1987) conclude, after a review of the characteristics of export duties in developing countries, as follows: export taxation is accentuated by overvalued or multiple exchange rates, producer price ceilings, or quantitative restrictions on exports;[29] second, nondistortionary taxation of "windfall" profits through export taxes is possible only when the tax is temporary and unexpected; finally, producer income stabilization schemes discourage production and exports by reducing the present value of revenue to producers without reducing riskiness.

In the long run, reduction of export taxes will generate beneficial effects to the nation from supply-side perspectives as well as economic efficiency considerations. However, in the short run, market imperfections in commodity markets may preclude developing nations from benefiting from supply-side effects of lowering export taxes. The resulting loss of revenue is the major obstacle to reducing export taxes. If nonrevenue-yielding implicit taxes, such as exchange rate overvaluation, quantitative restrictions on exports, etc., are corrected, the effective level of export taxation can be reduced without losing revenue.[30]

5.3. Elements of Tax Reform in Developing Countries

Tax systems induce distortionary effects in many countries when they are employed as instruments to accomplish multiple objectives. They would be more effective if they were directed at limited goals, such as correcting market failures or providing government with adequate revenues without distorting resource allocation or creating disincentives for factor supplies.

Gandhi (1987b) summarizes tax reform proposals from a supply-side perspective for developing countries.[31] First, the tax system should be broad-based in scope, except for taxes on windfall profits or scarcity rents, or to correct some externality. Second, the high marginal income tax rate in developing countries could be reduced. These proposals should be accompanied by some complementary reforms: expansion of the tax base through the elimination of most allowances, deductions, exclusions, and tax credits; indexation of the tax base for inflation; improvement of income tax laws and their administration. Separate capital-gains taxes, payroll taxes, or social security taxes may be eliminated. Third, income tax on savings needs to be eliminated and replaced by a broad-based consumption tax. Fourth, corporate taxes should not be diluted by tailor-made tax incentives to benefit specific industries or firms. Depreciation allowances and inventory valuation should be indexed for inflation. The former encourages the use of replacement basis for depreciation rather than historical basis. The latter can be accomplished by inventory valuation on LIFO (last in, first out) basis. It has even been suggested that cash flow be the basis for corporate taxation, thus permitting capital outlays to be expensed immediately with elimination of deductibility of interest payments.[32] Similarly, a strong argument can be made for the elimination of double taxation of dividends. Fifth, purely on efficiency considerations, export taxes rates need to be kept at low levels. Only in the instance of temporarily inflated world prices would higher export taxes be justified to soak up demand from "windfall" gains. However, the rate of export taxation should permit an adequate return to exporters. Sixth, taxes should be directed only at those elements of wealth that exhibit inelastic supply, such as land or items limiting personal use (homes, automobiles, etc.). Other elements of wealth tax justifiable on grounds of intergenerational equity are transfers through gifts, bequests, and unproductive assets, such as jewelry, precious metals, or land and real estate bought for speculative purposes.[33] Finally, from theoretical considerations, if income taxes have been designed optimally, there is no justification for commodity taxes. However, there can be a case for differential commodity taxation if income taxes are not optimal. Any commodity taxation scheme should incorporate the following characteristics: final consumption goods, not raw materials or intermediate goods should be taxed; there should be no differential taxation between alternative sources of supply for consumption (domestic goods and imports);[34] to avoid distortions in consumption patterns, both consumer goods and consumer services should be taxed; commodity taxes should be levied as near as possible to the retail stage of the production–distribution process; excise duties are justified on items that have relatively inelastic demand, such as necessities, addictive substances (tobacco, alcohol) or those complementary to leisure, and other "luxury" goods; exports should not attract domestic commodity taxation.

The tax reforms outlined in the preceding discussion are not without their risk of significant revenue loss, at least in the short run. They must be accompanied by expenditure reforms and public enterprise pricing reforms. Such tax systems will have positive impacts on growth only if it is clear that they are permanent. Furthermore, they need to be accompanied by macroeconomic policy reforms relating to exchange rates, interest rates, wage rates, etc.

6. CONCLUSION

This chapter has presented a discussion of the relevance of tax policy for developing nations. Obviously, the role of taxation in the development process is through its linkage with savings. The traditional view of development (for example, Harrod–Domar models) assigns an important role for saving and investment. The structuralist viewpoints consider development from the perspectives of financial structure, social infrastructure, population, agricultural reform, modern technology, and factor-substitution possibilities. Irrespective of whether these perspectives are substitutes or complements, tax policy has an pervasive role in the development of nations in the modern world.

Shome (1987) observes that the goals of development may include increasing rates of savings and investment to increase output, enhancing social investment in health, education, and welfare, ensuring consistency in the rate of population growth and rate of accumulation of capital stock, or safeguarding terms of trade for agriculture. The treatment of taxes is an essential ingredient of any broad strategy to accomplish these goals. Through taxation, the government finances its capital construction projects or offers those resources to the private sector. Tax policy has been an important instrument to reduce the foreign exchange gap through import tariffs, free trade zones, and incentives for export diversification. Again, the special tax treatment of dividends and interest encourages intermediation through financial markets and institutions. On the other hand, tax policy has been used to influence changes in factor proportions through incentive packages such as accelerated depreciation, investment credits, income tax holidays, and deductions for research and development. Other development goals may be accomplished by tax policy. For example, China employs reduced taxation as an incentive to maintain small family sizes. The agricultural sector has attracted attention from a tax perspective. There have been arguments for taxes on the agricultural sector to extract the surplus. On the other hand, there have been counterarguments for tax subsidies, eliminating export duties, and exempting import duties for farm equipment, seeds, and fertilizers. Finally, tax and expenditure policies have been the instruments through which human resource development—social security, social welfare, education, and nutrition—have been attempted.

Clearly, there are necessary conditions for tax policy to succeed in its objectives. First, it must be broad-based in its scope. Otherwise, it may lead to instances where certain sectors, for example, the rural sector, may escape taxes altogether. Second, tax policy must be focused on accomplishing a set of limited objectives, otherwise the effort may get diluted with competing claims. Third, the administrative capacity to implement the schemes should be available. This is particularly important if the goal of tax policy is to accomplish major redistribution of wealth and income. The best-conceived schemes may be easily rendered worthless if the capability to control tax avoidance and evasion is nonexistent. Fourth, the implicit assumption in all tax schemes is that individual behavior is price-responsive. However, if behavior does respond to price, but is also affected by other factors (perhaps less observable) and noneconomic considerations, then tax policy will be vitiated in its attempts to achieve its goals. As Shome (1987) observes, "Sending children—especially female—to school to receive primary education may not depend on whether it is free but on whether it is permitted by society."[35]

Tax policy is an important and necessary ingredient for development finance. Developing countries may be called upon to initiate efficiency-oriented reforms of the entire tax system, including corporate tax incentives and export duties, to reach their full-growth potential.

NOTES

1. See Chelliah, Bass, and Kelly (1975), Tait, Gratz, and Eichengreen (1979), and Tanzi (1983).
2. See Tanzi (1987), p. 225.
3. Ibid., p. 226.

4. Ibid., p. 227.
5. Ibid., p. 232.
6. Ibid., Table 8.9, p. 233.
7. Ibid, Tables 8–10, p. 235.
8. For a formal proof, see Atkinson and Stiglitz (1980), pp. 59–61 ("Note on the Expenditure Function").
9. See Atkinson (1987) for a model illustrating the equity–efficiency tradeoff. This model demonstrates that tax revenue reaches a maximum with increasing tax rates and then declines, providing analytical support for the Laffer curve, which is at the core of the supply-side argument on taxation. The author also demonstrates that there is an upper limit to the lump-sum tax that can be levied, in the sense that it cannot be so high that it drives an individual to destitution. Furthermore, the distribution of the lump-sum tax cannot be such that it penalizes an individual with more assets more than it penalizes one with less assets. These considerations along with information-gathering and -processing costs imply that only simple forms of lumpsum taxes are applicable.
10. See Wolfson (1979), p. 125.
11. See Hinrichs (1966), p. 106.
12. See Goode (1984), p. 90.
13. See Newbery (1987), p. 168.
14. Newbery (1987), p. 175.
15. See Gandhi (1987b), pp. 5–11.
16. Ibid., p. 10.
17. See Ebrill (1987a), p. 82.
18. See Ebrill (1987b), pp. 93–94.
19. See ibid., pp. 105–6 for these results.
20. Ibid., pp. 133.
21. See Gandhi (1987c), pp. 227–28.
22. For example, activities that consume scarce resources without offsetting marketable ouputs or generate outputs that do not have positive values, such as environmental pollution. Ibid., pp. 232–33.
23. Ibid., pp. 234–35.
24. See Musgrave (1987), p. 245.
25. See Tables A13 to A15 in the Statistical Supplement in Gandhi (1987a), pp. 370–6.
26. See Musgrave (1987), p. 246.
27. See Sanchez-Ugarte (1987), p. 251.
28. Ibid., pp. 270–73.
29. See Sanchez-Ugarte and Modi (1987), p. 279.
30. Ibid., (1987), pp. 305–6.
31. Ibid., pp. 33–36.
32. See Ebrill (1987c), p. 134.
33. It is recognized that these forms of wealth taxes are difficult to administer.
34. An argument may be made for some differentiation between indigenous production and imports on grounds of protection of "infant industries." It is essential to ensure that import duties are not excessively high and are phased out gradually so that they do not become entrenched permanently. India is a classic case in point, where "infant industries" have matured under the protective umbrella of a set of hardened import duties.
35. See Shome (1987), p. 330.

4

Conceptual Foundations
of Financial Intermediation

1. INTRODUCTION

Many developing nations have reconsidered their approaches to development consequent to their experiences in the 1980s. Increasingly, these nations have decided to rely on the private sector and market signals to direct the allocation of resources. Efficient financial systems are *sine qua non* if greater reliance is to be placed on voluntary, market-based decision-making systems. An efficient financial system provides services that are essential in a modern economy. Savings will be held in the form of financial assets if their yield, liquidity, and risk characteristics are attractive to savers. Financial intermediaries direct resources to their most efficient uses by evaluating alternate investments and monitoring the activities of borrowers. Economic agents are able to pool, price, and exchange risk by having access to a wide variety of financial instruments.

This chapter provides a conceptual framework for analyzing the functions and activities of financial intermediaries in economic development. The following section discusses the various functions of the financial intermediary, specifically, portfolio diversification, maturity intermediation, reduction in the costs of contracting, management of the payment system, and insurance or risk-shifting. A classical model of financial intermediation with capital markets is presented which concludes that capital markets promote the efficient transfer of funds between borrowers and lenders. Section 3 surveys the literature on financial-structure development and economic growth. The works of Goldsmith (1969, 1983, 1985), McKinnon (1973) and Shaw (1973) provide the impetus to establish this connection. McKinnon (1973) and Shaw (1973) focus on "financial repression" and the urgent need for financial liberalization. On the other hand, the neostructuralists emphasize the role of informal credit markets and argue that the efficiencies of these markets will be adversely affected by financial liberalization. The microfoundations of financial intermediation are explored in Section 4. It casts the financial intermediary as an asset transformer, a portfolio manager, a reducer of transaction costs, and examines its comparative informational advantage. This section also presents a simple model in which the intermediary is seen in the role of monitoring the performance of the borrower, where this function is delegated to the intermediary by other lenders. This chapter provides the conceptual framework for the two following chapters, which examine separately financial intermediation through capital markets and through specialized institutions such as development finance companies.

2. THE CONCEPT OF FINANCIAL INTERMEDIATION

Auction markets are characterized by dealers who buy and sell assets and profit by the "spread,"—the difference between the buying and selling prices. The dealer does not alter the asset in any way or create a new set of assets. Assets are carried purely as inventories and the dealer does not have an interest in holding them over the long term. Financial intermediaries, on the other hand, purchase most assets as investments. Their primary function is *asset transformation*—the creation and distribution of new assets. However, these new assets constitute financial claims on the intermediary rather than on the original issuer, whose assets were purchased by the intermediary. The term intermediation refers to the alteration of the financial claim distributed to the market. Intermediated markets deal in the liabilities of financial intermediaries, where such liabilities are created to fund their assets. Financial intermediaries create new financial claims and promote new markets, simultaneously bridging the gaps between markets. It is therefore relevant to examine the specific services provided by financial intermediaries.

2.1. Specific Services Provided by Financial Intermediaries

The specific services provided by financial intermediaries cover a broad spectrum, ranging from simple management of the payment system to production of sophisticated financial instruments.

Portfolio Divisibility and Diversification. The financial intermediary pools the funds of a large number of investors and invests in a diversified portfolio of assets. Pooling of resources results in two immediate benefits to investors. First, transactions costs are incurred in creating any portfolio. The financial intermediary can exploit the economies of scale inherent in these transactions costs, which are unavailable to individual investors. Second, the financial intermediary provides portfolio divisibility to individual investors. The portfolio is divided into a large number of smaller units and, thus, investors can obtain a stake in a highly diversified portfolio with limited capital.

Maturity Intermediation. Financial intermediaries are uniquely positioned to intermediate across maturities. They accept funds from investors who desire to lend for the short term and in turn lend to borrowers who desire long-term maturities. Thus, borrowers and lenders with different preferred maturities are not compelled to agree on a common maturity. The intermediary bears the risk associated with borrowing at volatile, short-term interest rates and lending at stable, long-term interest rates. While the intermediary cannot reduce the risk involved in bridging the gaps in preferred maturity habitats, it can perform this function more efficiently than other forms of market organizations. The intermediary is in a unique position to achieve certain economies. First, it can estimate the risks involved in lending long term more easily than the individual provider of short-term funds. Second, the intermediary is able to package short-term liabilities and long-term loans in economical units.

Financial Intermediaries and Costs of Contracting. Costs of contracting include the cost of writing and understanding the contract. A second element is the cost of monitoring the activities of the parties to the contract to ensure the contract terms are observed and enforcing the terms if they are not. Specialized contracts to meet the particular needs of borrowers and lenders are more easily produced by financial intermediaries. Furthermore, in the event they are required to be re-negotiated by borrowers, it is more convenient to do so with a financial intermediary than with a collection of lenders. The costs of monitoring and enforcement are reduced by centralizing them in the financial intermediary, which can provide the degree of required specialization with the appropriate expertise.

Information Production. Financial intermediaries expend considerable resources collecting, processing, analyzing, and interpreting information relating to the assets in which they invest. The intermediary produces this information for its own consumption and not for general distribution to the market. Some of this information may have strategic importance to borrowers. They may be more willing to divulge the information to a financial intermediary than to the general market, relying on the former's reputation for preserving confidentiality. A related issue is whether the intermediary produces and employs information in a scrupulous manner consistent with the interests of the lenders. The extent of funds provided by the owners to the intermediary is a measure of their commitment. The larger the contribution by the owners to the capital base of the intermediary, the smaller is the probability of improper investment decisions.

Management of the Payment System. Commercial banks and other thrift institutions provide the bookkeeping function of keeping track of receipts and disbursements for their customers as well as handling the exchange of funds. It is not necessary that the management of payments be handled by a financial intermediary which also manages funds. In some European countries payments are made through the giro system, which is not linked to commercial banks. In the United States, the Federal Reserve System provides the check-clearing services for the banking industry. With innovations in computer technology and communications, electronic funds transfer has made the payments system more efficient.

Insurance. Finally, there are some financial intermediaries providing insurance. This is a service, similar to the management of the payments system, which is closely related to the management of investments. Insurance spreads the risk of a large potential loss sustained by a small group of insurers among the large number of other insurers who do not sustain the loss. Such risk-shifting becomes economical when the risk is diversifiable. Risk-shifting is beneficial to the economy, as it induces individuals to undertake productive activities that they would otherwise perceive as excessively risky.

2.2. A Conceptual Model of Financial Intermediation with Capital Markets

Financial intermediation is performed by institutions providing the varied services described in the preceding paragraphs. The intermediation function is facilitated by capital markets, which serve to modify individual consumption and investment decisions. Consider Figure 4.1, in which the horizontal axis represents monetary values in dollars in the current period ($t = 0$), while the vertical axis

Figure 4.1
The Capital Market Line

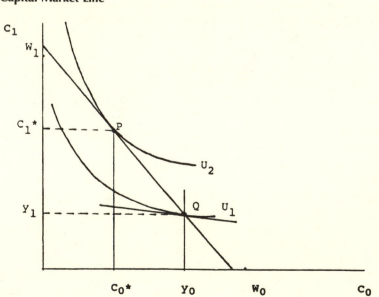

relates to the next period ($t = 1$). An individual has an endowment (y_0, y_1) consisting of current and future incomes and is located on utility indifference curve U_1 at Q. Given a market interest rate i, the individual's current wealth, W_0, is defined as the present value of the income stream,

$$W_0 = y_0 + y_1/(1 + i) \qquad (4.1)$$

By lending or borrowing at the market interest rate, the individual can reach any point on the capital market line W_1PQW_0. Thus, the decision-maker maximizes utility by moving along the market line to point P, where the subjective time preference equals the market interest rate. At Q, the subjective time preference, represented by the slope of the line tangential to indifference curve U_1, is less than the market rate of return. Therefore, the individual prefers to lend. Ultimately, the decision maker reaches point P, where the consumption decision (C_0^*, C_1^*) maximizes utility. The equation for the capital-market line is

$$C_1^* = W_0(1 + i) - (1 + i)C_0^* \qquad (4.2)$$

Since $W_0(1 + i) = W_1$, it follows

$$C_1^* = W_1 - (1 + i)C_0^* \qquad (4.3)$$

Now consider a world with capital markets in which the consumption–investment decision is facilitated by the exchange of funds at the market rate of interest. Figure 4.2 combines production possibilities and such market exchange possibilities. From point Q, with the goal of maximizing utility, the individual can move either along the production-possibility set or along the capital-market line. Both alternatives offer higher return than the rate of subjective time preference; but as production offers a higher return than the capital-market rate, the decision maker invests and moves along the production-possibility frontier. If there are no opportunities to borrow or lend along the market line, the individual would invest at S, where the marginal return on investment is equal to the rate of subjective time preference. The individual has moved now from indifference curve U_1 to U_2. With the opportunity to borrow, the decision maker's position is improved. The borrowing rate represented by the slope of the capital-market line is less than the return on the marginal investment at S represented by the slope of the investment-opportunity set. Further investment returns more than the cost of borrowed funds and the individual invests at P, where the marginal return on investment is equal to the borrowing rate. At P, the individual receives the output from production (P_0, P_1) and wealth has increased to W_0^* . Since time preference at P is greater than the market rate of return, the decision maker consumes more than P_0, the current payoff from production. By borrowing, the individual locates the point R on the market line. Optimal consumption is found where the decision maker's subjective preference is equal to the market rate of return. Utility has increased from U_1 at

Figure 4.2
Consumption and Investment with Capital Markets

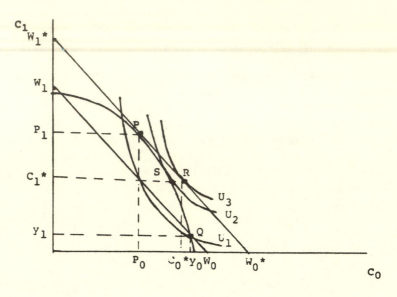

Q to U_2 at S to U_3 at R. Clearly the individual is better off with the existence of capital markets.

The individual makes the decision with production opportunities and capital market exchange opportunities in two distinct steps: the first choice is optimal production by undertaking projects until the marginal return on investment equals the market rate; the second choice is optimal consumption by borrowing or lending along the market line to equate subjective time preference to the market rate. This separation of the consumption and the investment decisions is known as Fisher's separation theorem.

Thus, capital markets promote the efficient transfer of funds between borrowers and lenders. Individuals are not constrained by insufficient wealth, for they can still take advantage of investment opportunities that yield returns higher than the market rate by borrowing funds through the capital markets. Funds are efficiently reallocated from individuals with limited productive opportunities but more wealth to individuals with many opportunities but insufficient wealth. Thus, everyone is better off with capital markets.

3. FINANCIAL STRUCTURE AND ECONOMIC GROWTH

The importance of financial structure development and its implications for economic growth has been recognized in the literature only in the last twenty years. The works of Goldsmith, McKinnon, and Shaw provided much of the needed impetus in this direction. Whereas, McKinnon and Shaw focused on financial repression and urgent need for financial liberalization, the neostructuralists emphasized the role of informal credit markets.

3.1. A Historical Background

The strategic role of money, credit, and finance in the promotion of economic growth has long been known to economists. While it was implicit in the earlier literature, Schumpeter (1911/1935) explicitly acknowledges the crucial role of bank credit in economic growth. He views economic development as a process of innovations, some of which may be discrete and even disruptive. Entrepreneurial function, which involves development of new sets of factor combinations, is dependent on bank credit for acquiring real resources. Schumpeter distinguishes between real credit, which finances entrepreneurial innovations, and routine credit, which provides working capital. He concludes that the interest rate is the product of economic development. In addition, innovations can occur in both the real and financial sectors. In the financial sector, such innovations extend from the early joint-stock banks to the modern Eurocredit markets, institutions such as mutual funds, and instruments such as currency and interest rate swaps. The interaction of innovations in both sectors provides the impetus for economic development and growth. Furthermore, Schumpeter assigns a primary role to the banking sector, which promotes growth by its willingness to finance the entrepreneur at the appropriate time.

Many case studies document the role of banks in the industrialization of European nations and Japan.[1] The "Gerschenkron hypothesis" assigns an important role to the banking sector in promoting capital and entrepreneurship in nations lagging in their development. The growth-oriented version of this model favors the proactive German system of "universal banking" against the passive British form of commercial banking.[2]

The seminal works of Goldsmith (1969, 1983, 1985) relate to the role of financial institutions, both banks and nonbanks, in economic growth and development. His major finding is that the financial interrelations ratio (FIR), defined as the ratio of the value of all financial instruments outstanding at a given date to that of national wealth, tends to increase with the growth of the real economy.[3] However, he is cautious in equating this finding with causality. He observes that there is no possibility of determining whether financial factors are responsible for the growth of the economy or vice versa. But it is clear that "the financial superstructure, in the form of both primary and secondary securities, accelerates economic growth and improves economic performance to the extent that it facilitates the migration of funds to the best user, i.e., to the place in the economic system where the funds yield the highest social return."[4]

Gurley and Shaw (1955, 1956, 1960, 1967) are concerned with the role of financial intermediation, by both banks and nonbanks, in the saving and investment process. They note that, given the complex differentiation of financial intermediaries and instruments in a developed economy, money is not easily defined. They argue that financial structures are functions of the real economies—as nations grow in income and wealth, their financial structures tend to become richer and more sophisticated in terms of financial assets, institutions, and markets. However, differences in financial systems cannot be explained by differences in income and wealth alone. The major reason for this is that there are alternative techniques for generating and allocating savings. The permutations and combinations of these techniques are so numerous that no two countries are likely to follow the same financial growth trajectory or reach the same ratio of financial assets to national wealth.

Most of these theories take for granted the institutional setting of a developed economy, and do not address the specific realities of developing nations. This deficiency is rectified in the McKinnon and Shaw approaches.

3.2. McKinnon and Shaw Models

3.2.1. Financial Restrictions and Repression.

Shaw (1973) notes that developing economies are "financially repressed." This description covers indiscriminate "distortion of all financial prices, including interest rates and exchange rates" (p. 3). Further, he observes that "shallow" finance or financial repression "has reduced the real rate of growth and the real size of the financial system relative to nonfinancial magnitudes."[5] Fry asserts that "the original policy" in many developing countries was targeted "not at indiscriminate financial repression but at financial restriction." Hence, these nations seem to have "slipped into financial repression inadvertently."[6]

Who benefits from financial restrictions? The government is the principal beneficiary. By promoting money and banking systems, the government can channelize resources for its own needs and for the growth of the public sector. For example, this goal may be accomplished by imposing reserve requirements and by requiring banks to hold government bonds. Governments do not favor bond or equity markets because it is not easy to impose and implement such restrictions on these institutions. Nevertheless, governments may impede the smooth functioning of these institutions with transaction costs, such as taxes and stamp duties. Interest ceilings are imposed to curb competition with the public sector and "crowd out" the private sector. Flows of domestic resources to the public sector without higher tax, inflation, or appropriate interest rates are ensured by the imposition of foreign exchange controls, interest rate ceilings, high reserve requirements, and the suppression of private capital markets.

Governments may also employ directed credit or selective credit controls to accomplish their goals of promoting the public sector. Such policies result in interest rates on loans for approved public investments being subsidized. Financial restriction is a necessary condition for selective credit policies, as otherwise resources would be channelled to uses with the highest private returns. Financial markets must be kept segmented and restricted for such selective credit policies to work.

3.2.2. McKinnon Model.

3.2.2. McKinnon Model. Both McKinnon (1973) and Shaw (1973) argue that the implicit assumptions of the neoclassical models are irrelevant for developing nations.[7] These assumptions suggest that the economy is fully monetized and capital markets are perfect; that physical plant is homogeneous and of uniform productivity; and that input indivisibilities are unimportant.

It follows from these assumptions that real money balances and physical capital are competing assets. The neoclassical model is an asset-substitution model. McKinnon (1973) contrasts real-world conditions in developing nations with the foregoing assumptions. He argues that the typical developing economy is highly fragmented, capital markets being rudimentary or nonexistent, with wide varia-tions in the quality of physical capital, and indivisibilities that are disadvantageous to small economic units. In such economies, he points out that real money balances are complements rather than substitutes for physical capital. He assumes that in developing economies all economic units are self-financed; that investments are characterized by indivisibilities, that is, small enterprises are unable to undertake discrete investments based on best-practice technology; and that the government does not participate directly in capital formation through fiscal or monetary policies (p. 56). The indivisibilities assumption implies that the priority facing productive units is to accumulate real money balances before physical capital.

Define M = money balances, including interest-bearing deposits
P = general price level
Y = real current income
I = investment
d = nominal deposit rate
P^* = expected rate of inflation

The demand-for-money function is expressed as

$$(M/P)_d = D(Y,\ I/Y,\ d - P^*) \tag{4.4}$$

The last argument, $d - P^*$, represents the real return on holding money. If D_i is defined as the partial derivative of D with respect to its ith argument, then eq. (4.4) is further specified as $D_i > 0$, for all i. The condition, $D_2 > 0$, represents the basic complementarity between money and physical capital in "fragmented economies."

The demand-for-money function can also be expressed with the real rate of return in place of the investment–income ratio. McKinnon notes that actual rates of return vary widely in developing nations. This is represented by a distribution of rates of return, indicating the variable productivity of capital, around a mean value, r^*. Equation (4.4) is now

$$(M/P)_d = D(Y, r^*, d - P^*), D_i > 0, \quad \text{for all } i \tag{4.5}$$

In contrast, the conventional demand-for-money function is expressed as

$$(M/P)_d = F(Y, r, d - P^*), F_1 > 0, F_2 < 0, F_3 > 0, \tag{4.6}$$

where r is the real return on all assets other than money. The condition, $D_2 > 0$, in the McKinnon model representing the complementarity relationship in developing nations, is in sharp contrast with the traditional substitution effect, $F_2 < 0$. Money is viewed by McKinnon as a *conduit* through which capital is accumulated. If the real rate of return on holding money balances increases, so will self-financed investment over a significant range of investment opportunities. However, McKinnon concedes that the conduit effect will not dominate the investment function indefinitely; at some point the conventional substitution effect will come into play.

The complementarity and substitution effects are displayed in Figures 4.3 and 4.4. Under the assumptions of self-finance, the relationship between I/Y and the real return on money balances is shown in Figure 4.3. The curve reaches a maximum at B and then falls off. In the segment AB, the conduit effect is dominant. The process of self-financed investment is constricted by the small size of the monetary system. The higher real return on holding money relaxes the saving–investment restriction by enlarging M/P. As $(d - P^*)$ increases toward the best marginal return on self-financed investments, the substitution effect takes over to the right of B, and reduces the flow of investment. If the increase in real return on money leads to improvements in the quality of physical investment, as

Figure 4.3
Effect of Real Return on Holding Money on Self-Financed Investment

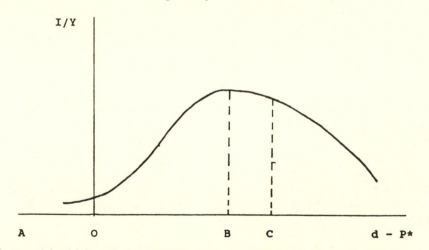

Source: Adapted from R. I. McKinnon, *Money and Capital in Economic Development* (1973). Used with permission from The Brookings Institution.

Figure 4.4
Effect of Holding Money on Self- and Externally Financed Investment

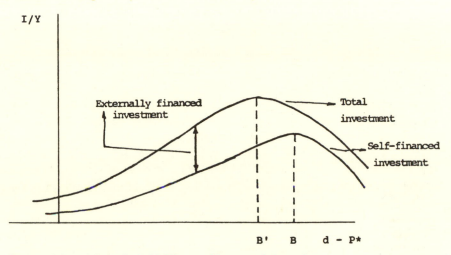

Source: Adapted from R. I. McKinnon, *Money and Capital in Economic Development* (1973). Used with permission from The Brookings Institution.

individuals shift from nonproductive inflation hedges to cash balances, the conduit effect is extended and the social optimum shifts from *B* to *C*.

The assumption of self-finance is relaxed in Figure 4.4. Direct external finance provided by lenders supplement the flow of self-financed investment. These lenders perceive a reduction in their risk with the greater liquidity of the borrower and his self-financed equity component invested in the enterprise. Total investment increases initially through its self-financed and externally financed components, as $d - P^*$ is increased. The widening of the shaded area represents increases in the flow of external lending. However, the increase in the return in holding money reinforces the substitution effect and makes money a more competitive asset. Thus the total investment the authorities can encourage in this manner remains restricted.

3.2.3. Shaw Model. Shaw (1973) focuses on the expanded role of financial intermediaries resulting from financial liberalization (higher real institutional interest rates). A characteristic of financially repressed economies is fragmented markets. The law of one price is not operative in such segmented markets. Each segment carries its own price, which may differ from those in other segments. Participants in such economies function myopically in the sense that their horizons are very short. High variability in returns due to imperfect and expensive information causes such returns to be high.

The functions and advantages of financial intermediaries have been discussed in preceding paragraphs. Financial intermediation is inefficient and is impeded when interest rates are administratively fixed below their equilibrium levels, whereas when interest rates are free to find their own levels, then the intermediation of a large volume of investible funds can be performed efficiently. Whereas in liberalized markets a homogeneous product would be acceptable as a medium of exchange, in repressed markets, only money would be acceptable. Shaw's demand-for-money function is

$$(M/P)_d = D(Y, r, r_c, r_m, d - P^*) \tag{4.7}$$

where r is a vector of opportunity costs in real terms of holding money, since there are differential returns to assets in segmented markets; r_c is the rate of individual time preference; and r_m is the return on money.[8]

Both McKinnon and Shaw emphasize the importance of real money balances in a developing nation characterized by a limited array of financial assets. A steady growth in real balances is obtained by either keeping the price level relatively stable with growth in nominal money supply, or keeping the latter constant accompanied by decline in the price level. To induce individuals to hold the enlarged real balances, the real return on money, $d - P^*$, should be attractive. This implies maintaining d, the nominal deposit rate, stable while inflationary expectations are declining, or increasing d during relatively stable inflationary expectations. The common thrust of the McKinnon–Shaw approaches of financial deepening is the elimination of artificial repression and restrictions on financial variables, particularly interest rates, and permitting steady growth in nominal money supply.

3.3. Extensions of the McKinnon–Shaw Framework

A number of researchers have extended the basic McKinnon–Shaw models, notably, Kapur (1975, 1976a, 1976b), Mathieson (1979, 1980), Galbis (1977), and Fry (1980).[9]

Kapur (1975) develops a monetary growth model based on two assumptions descriptive of developing nations: unlimited supply of labor and differential saving propensities of profit-earners and wage-earners. An important finding is that while an increase in the rate of monetary growth definitely increases the steady-state capital intensity (capital–labor ratio), this will not in itself generate higher growth. On the contrary, it may even reduce the steady-state growth of the economy. This conclusion is explained as follows. First, real balance is assumed to be an argument of the aggregate production function; but if inflationary expectations reduce the level of real balances, it will result in the reduction of productive efficiency and thereby the economy's real growth. Second, the typical developing nation has a labor surplus and an expansionary monetary policy that stimulates capital intensity may adversely affect employment and output. The trade-off between higher level of employment generated by labor-intensive techniques and higher rate of growth generated by more capital-intensive techniques is nonexistent beyond a certain level of monetary growth.

Kapur (1976a, 1976b) considers alternative financial reform and stabilization policies for countries experiencing financial repression and high inflation. He examines the optimal mix of two policy variables—the rate of monetary growth (μ) and the nominal deposit rate on money holdings (d)—in a model in which entrepreneurs are dependent on the banking system for working capital. He concludes that in the initial phase of reform and stabilization, if the goal is to minimize loss of employment and output and to dampen inflation, then an increase in d to its equilibrium level is more effective than a drastic reduction in μ. The reason being that an increase in d, *ceteris paribus*, raises the real return to money, creates a demand for money relative to its supply, and generates an instantaneous deflationary effect. On the other hand, a reduction in μ can only increase the expected real return after it has worked through the entire system to reduce inflationary expectations. Furthermore, an increase in d stimulates the flow of savings to the banking system and maintains the flow of real bank credit, thus sustaining or even raising the level of output or employment. Whereas a drastic reduction in μ, if not accompanied by wage–price flexibility, will cause an unacceptable level of unemployment and loss of output, even if limited to the short run. Thus, μ should be reduced gradually only when inflationary expectations have subsided.

Jao (1985) observes that the difficulty with Kapur's models is d cannot be indiscriminately increased without adversely affecting the profitability of banks. The management of the maturity structures of their assets and liabilities is increasingly important in this scenario. Furthermore, an increase in the deposit rates may be accompanied by an increase in lending rates, which in turn affects the profitability of entrepreneurial activities and thus investment in real assets. Kapur acknowledges this difficulty by noting there is probably an upper bound for d.[10]

Mathieson (1980) addresses the issue of bank profits by specifying the constraint that the nonbank private sector will have confidence in the banking system, only if an interest rate decontrol policy is adopted that keeps the cumulative flow of profits to total deposits above some critical value. He concludes that financial liberalization should be integrated with stabilization in two stages. In the initial phase there should be fairly large increases in deposit and lending rates and reductions in monetary growth. Deposits are expected to expand with increases in deposit rates to meet the demand for loans despite the reduction in monetary growth and increases in lending rates. Thus, the increase in the supply of real bank credit for working capital will expand output. In the second phase monetary growth is increased and interest rates are decreased consistent with the decline in inflationary expectations—the policy variables are adjusted to their long-run values.

Galbis (1977) develops a two-sector model to examine the effect of financial repression on the average efficiency of investment. His scenario describes an economy consisting of two kinds of productive units operating with different technological processes and subject to different financial constraints. Thus, his model captures the essential elements of a fragmented developing economy. He demonstrates that improvements in the process of financial intermediation may result in increases in the rate of economic growth. This result is brought about by higher equilibrium interest rates that shift resources from traditional low-yielding investments to investments in the modern, high-technology sector.

Empirical investigations by Fry (1978, 1980, 1981) generally lend support to the McKinnon–Shaw framework.

3.4. The Neostructuralist Viewpoint

Taylor stresses that macro models describing developed economies are not applicable to the developing economies.[11] Developed and developing economies are distinct from each other, particularly with regard to their sectoral differences. Whereas developed nation economies are represented as one homogeneous sector, developing nation economies have distinct, heterogeneous sectors. For example, the agriculture and manufacturing sectors differ with respect to technology employed. Agricultural technology tends to be more labor-intensive than capital-intensive. Consumer demand in developing nations is price- and income-inelastic; furthermore, the markets for consumer products exhibit large price variations. The structure of the manufacturing industry in developing nations is mostly markup oligopolistic. Capital-goods-producing sectors are differentiated from consumer-goods-producing sectors in terms of size and technology employed.

A second distinction between developed and developing economies relates to the role of money and other assets. Money has no substitute financial products in developing economies and, hence, there are no financial markets offering such substitute products. Finally, income distribution effects are more pronounced in developing economies. Price changes may affect particular income groups (wage earners, for example) more severely than they affect other income groups (such as savers).

The implications of these structural distinctions between developing and developed economies are captured in van Wijnbergen (1983a, 1983b, 1982) and Buffie (1984). In particular, curb markets or "unorganized money markets," which supply working capital to firms, are common in developing economies. McKinnon's (1973) arguments for financial liberalization are based on the assumption that increases in time deposits will lead to more funds being intermediated through banks and will thus lead to higher investment and higher economic growth. The implicit assumption is that resources are held in the form of "unproductive assets," such as cash, precious metals, physical commodities, etc. In fact, savers find it more beneficial to invest in the curb markets than hold resources in unproductive assets. Curb markets intermediate more efficiently than commercial banks for two reasons. There is less asymmetric information between lenders and borrowers in informal credit market, which is not the case in the formal credit markets. Furthermore, lending institutions in the formal credit markets are required to maintain relatively high reserve ratios, which is not required of lenders in the curb markets.

In this scenario, if the time-deposit rates are increased, there will be outflows from the curb markets with consequent decrease in the supply of working capital for firms. Thus, the firms' outputs will be reduced. Furthermore, increases in the time-deposit rates, which in turn increase the cost of capital for firms, lead to inflationary conditions in the economy. The combined effects of reduced output and increased inflation result in stagflationary conditions. An additional effect of the increased inflation is the loss of competitiveness of firms, which results in reduced profitability, reduced investment, and, thus, reduced medium term growth. Of course, it is possible that increased time deposit rates increase the supply of savings, which compensate for the decreased supply of working capital and decreased investment. The outcome is probabilistic, depending on which effect is dominant.[12]

Diaz-Alejandro (1985) presents a comprehensive discussion of financial liberalization programs in Latin America and why they had adverse effects, such as bankruptcies, government interventions, or nationalizations, and low domestic savings levels. Two aspects deserve special mention. First, deposit insurance is a feature that protects depositors by guaranteeing repayment of deposits up to some limit, even if the financial institution were to experience bankruptcy. It provides a safety net for depositors and thus encourages deposits. But this very safety net causes depositors to view all commercial banks as identical and depositors are thus unable to discriminate among them. A type of moral hazard problem is created by the deception of averages. Second, large banks deal with large numbers of depositors. The risks to which these banks are exposed increase disproportionately with the number of depositors. Furthermore, large banks have a number of cross-institutional relationships. The number of interdependencies increase dramatically with the size of the bank.

The financial instabilities created in Latin American nations in the 1980s are traced partly to liberalization programs and partly to other endemic problems. Diaz-Alejandro (1985) identifies several factors that contributed to adverse impacts of the liberalization programs. First, there existed a general belief that governments would not permit sick financial institutions to fail. Statements to the contrary by the authorities were treated with scepticism. Second, a similar lack of credibility existed among the international lenders as well. Third, these problems were compounded by inadequate bank regulation. Fourth, financial liberalization gave rise to a number of risk-taking private financial institutions. Fifth, most of the transactions were not at arms length and frequently involved concessionary loans to friends and relatives of bank officials. Sixth, and perhaps most important, financial liberalization does not necessarily imply an increase in long-term financial instruments. Seventh, while it is true in some instances that financial liberalization was accompanied by apparent increases in savings, the principal reasons were foreign inflows and not intrinsic improvements in the savings rate. Eighth, there was no perceptible improvement in the volume or efficiency of investments. Finally, the combination of fixed nominal exhange rates, free capital movements, moral hazard, and other imperfections led to "microeconomic misallocation and macroeconomic instability."[13] Private markets alone do not have the capability to raise long-term capital for long-term investments. The author notes, "private uncertainties and scepticism of all sorts, which will not disappear by freeing interest rates, reduce the scope for private long-term finance and for stock markets."[14]

In conclusion, there is a kernel of truth in both the financial liberalization and the neostructuralist arguments. One can certainly accept the notion that administratively suppressed interest rates do not promote increased savings and thus inhibit resources for financial intermediation. On the other hand, one cannot ignore the presence of curb markets, which are institutional descriptors of developing nations. The assumptions one makes in this regard partly determine the conclusions. As Fry (1988, p. 106) observes, if one believes that commercial banks are the most efficient mechanism for financial intermediation, liberalization of interest rates will lead to increased savings and rapid economic growth. However, if one believes that curb markets are more efficient than any other financial intermediary, then it follows that liberalization of interest rates will not attain the desired objectives.

Two additional factors enter into this discussion. If the size of the curb market is large in relation to the size of the financial sector, there is greater support for the neostructuralist position that financial liberalization will choke an efficient mechanism for intermediation with adverse consequences for economic growth. Of course, if the relative size of the curb market is small, then there is greater support for the financial liberalization position. A second aspect relates to the maximum size of transaction that the curb market can process. The smaller this upper bound, the greater the probability that the curb market will limit its service to the small-scale sector consisting of family (or one-person) businesses with limited scope of activities. Financial liberalization could have widespread adverse consequences in this instance, choking resources to a sector perhaps not reached by the organized banking sector. On the other hand, if this upper bound is high, bank intermediation may be a reasonable substitute for the curb market.

4. MICROFOUNDATIONS OF FINANCIAL INTERMEDIATION

In macroeconomics, financial intermediaries are viewed typically as conduits for effecting monetary policy objectives. Macroeconomic issues are examined by focusing on the money multiplier process by which an increase in the money base gets multiplied by a fractional-reserve banking system. The traditional monetarist position has been that financial intermediaries are unimportant unless they issue liabilities that have the characteristics of money.[15] The intermediation process, by itself, is considered irrelevant for aggregate activity; more relevant is how disturbances to the system affect monetary assets.

Some microapproaches have viewed financial intermediaries as firms with specific input–output relationships. A technology is specified by which inputs are converted into outputs. For example, Pesek (1970) and Towey (1974) describe the firms employing loans as inputs and money as outputs. On the other hand, Hyman (1972) and Melitz and Pardue (1973) view the firms using deposits as inputs and credit as the output of the production process. None of these models really differentiate the financial intermediary from any other real output-producing firm. Other approaches of this genre have cast the financial intermediary in an optimizing framework, maximizing, alternately, profits, growth or, anthropomorphically, utility, as in Klein (1971).

4.1. A Taxonomy of Microtheories of Financial Intermediation

Several independent approaches have been taken in the development of microtheories of financial intermediation. These viewpoints have described the financial intermediary as an *asset-transformer* in its function as a portfolio manager, its ability to reduce transaction costs, and in terms of its comparative informational advantage. These classifications are not mutually exclusive and some degree of overlap among them is inevitable. Each of these is now considered in turn.

4.1.1. The Asset-Transformation Function of the Financial Intermediary.
Some intermediaries, such as banking firms and mutual funds, are able to transform large denomination assets (bank loans and investments) into smaller units with greater liquidity. Asset transformations by financial intermediaries increase the liquidity of the rest of the economy if the aggregate claims of the nonbank sector against the banks are more liquid than the reverse claims of banks on the nonbank sector. Financial intermediaries perform a qualitative transformation on the funds they handle. Thus, investors and depositors are provided with divisibility of their assets. The banking firm, in particular, has a mismatched balance sheet, consisting of short-term, liquid depository liabilities and longer-term assets. Thus, the bank, rather than its depositors, deals with the risk of interest rate changes. This risk is mitigated by interest rate forecasting and hedging techniques. This description is the essence of the approach taken by Klein (1971).[16] Another intermediary, the insurance firm, also deals with the reduction of policy holders' risks by pooling their collective risks.

4.1.2. The Portfolio Management Function of the Financial Intermediary.
The approaches taken by Parkin (1970), Pyle (1971), and Hart and Jaffee (1974) apply the general theory of portfolio behavior to the theory of the financial firm. The financial firm is treated as a collection of financial assets with exogenously determined stochastic rates of return, and liabilities treated as negative assets. Pyle (1971) examines conditions conducive for intermediation, when a firm sells deposit liabilities (a negative asset) in order to acquire positive amounts of other financial assets. Parkin (1970) assumes that the collection of assets and liabilities held by the firm are institutionally dictated, and discusses the properties and comparative statics of portfolio choice. Whereas, Hart and Jaffee (1974) consider features unique to depository institutions, such as reserve and liquidity requirements and constraints on selection of assets and liabilities.

Pyle (1971) considers an intermediary with choices among three securities, namely, a risk-free asset, risky "loans," and risky "deposits." All securities can be held in positive and negative amounts. Let α_0, α_1, and α_2 denote the proportions invested in the risk-free asset, "loans," and "deposits," respectively, where $\alpha_0 + \alpha_1 + \alpha_2 = 0$. Let their respective returns be represented as r_0, r_1, and r_2. Then the firm's profit is $\pi = \alpha_0 r_0 + \alpha_1 r_1 + \alpha_2 r_2 = \alpha_1(r_1 - r_0) + \alpha_2(r_2 - r_0)$. The firm maximizes expected utility of π, where the utility function, $U(\pi)$, is concave (exhibits risk aversion). Pyle develops the conditions for financial intermediation in two scenarios. First, in the event the returns of assets and liabilities are stochastically independent, intermediation ($\alpha_1 > 0$, $\alpha_2 < 0$) will occur only if $E(r_1) > r_0$, i.e., there is a positive risk premium on loans, and $E(r_2) < r_0$, i.e., there is negative risk premium on deposits. Thus, there should be a positive yield spread in the returns of assets and liabilities. Second, if the returns have positive dependence, these conditions are still sufficient. Positive dependence is more favorable than independence, since the probability of a negative yield differential is reduced. Intermediation can occur even if there is a nonnegative risk premium for deposits, $E(r_2) \geq r_0$, so long as there is a strong dependency in returns. Profitability from intermediation activities increases with the expected yield spread $E(r_2) - E(r_1)$, and with the degree of positive correlation.

But why would depositors be willing to accept a return less than that obtained by the firm on its lending? Or why would borrowers be willing to accept borrowing rates greater than that obtainable on their deposits? Revealing though Pyle's analysis is, it does not provide any answers. The common answer is embedded in the additional services provided by intermediaries, which are described in the following subsections.

4.1.3. The Transactions-Cost-Reduction Function of the Financial Intermediary.

Benston and Smith (1976) view the role of the financial intermediary as creating specialized financial commodities. Individuals derive utility from consumption and financial commodities facilitate the intertemporal and intratemporal transfers of consumption. The authors assert that financial intermediaries have been created to reduce transactions costs. Components of these costs broadly include those associated with the purchase and sale of securities, costs to the individual of transportation and inconvenience, and costs to the intermediary of collecting information, documentation, and monitoring. At the most basic level, market makers, such as stock exchanges, bring potential buyers and sellers together and thus reduce information costs. At the intermediate level is a dealer who takes a position in the asset being transacted—a specialist. A more sophisticated form of intermediation is the set of financial commodities produced by mutual funds and consumer finance companies. These intermediaries permit individuals to purchase shares in diversified portfolios of securities, in odd amounts, for indefinite lengths of time, at much lower transaction cost than could be achieved by direct purchase of securities. The intermediary has a comparative advantage in servicing the needs of this particular group. It exploits the returns to scale implicit in the transaction costs of a security exchange by purchasing large blocks of securities, packaging them in the form demanded by investors, and selling the package at a suitable price. Thus, the essential feature of financial intermediation is the reduction of transaction costs related to inter- and intratemporal consumption. In fact, Benston and Smith (1976) observe "the *raison d'etre* for this industry is the existence of transactions costs."[17]

Impacts of Transactions Costs. Transactions costs affect the individual's consumption possibilities. First, they reduce the amounts of present and future consumption, should the individual wish to defer current consumption. Transfers of consumption among periods is inhibited by transactions costs and there is encouragement for consumption patterns to align themselves with the income stream.[18] Second, in a perfect market it is optimal to hold a portfolio with risky assets. However, the presence of transactions costs may inhibit the inclusion of risky assets in the portfolio. Third, even if the inclusion of risky assets is utility-increasing, transactions costs affect the choice of portfolio. With proportional transactions costs, the market portfolio is still one of the components of the individual's investment, but the amount invested is reduced by transactions costs. However, with other forms of transactions costs, the separation property of the Sharpe–Lintner Capital Asset Pricing Model may be destroyed.

Reduction of Transactions Costs by Financial Intermediaries. The creation of financial instruments involves documentation, information, and monitoring activities. However, financial intermediaries have a comparative advantage in performing such activities. First, they achieve economies of scale through specialization. Specific institutions specialize in serving the needs of specific customers with specific instruments and specific technology. Examples include consumer finance companies, wholesale and full-service commercial banks, and thrift institutions. Second, some important information, such as details regarding a borrower's financial condition, may be obtained by specific financial institutions at lower cost than by others. Such institutions acquire reputations for handling sensitive information with discretion. Hence, the information may be more easily forthcoming, thus reducing the related costs of collection. Finally, financial institutions can reduce the transaction costs of identification, to a lender in search of a borrower or vice versa.

4.1.4. The Comparative Informational Advantage of the Financial Intermediary. *Information Signalling in Imperfect Markets.* Leland and Pyle (1977) emphasize that financial markets are characterized by informational asymmetries. While entrepreneurs know the true value of their collateral and the industriousness and quality of their projects, investors are not aware of these facts. Moral hazard prevents the direct transfer of information. There may be rewards to exaggerating facts and verification may not be possible. Firms can profit from the gathering, packaging, and sale of certain types of information. Such firms can create portfolios based on their information. The firms' information is embodied in a private good, namely, portfolio returns. Returns to the firm's information-gathering efforts is captured through increased portfolio value. The best guarantee of the quality of the firm's information is its willingness to take an equity position in its portfolio. Leland and Pyle (1977) claim that informational asymmetries provide a stronger explanation for financial intermediation than transactions costs.

Campbell and Kracaw (1980) describe a rational-expectations equilibrium in which both the values of firms are correctly identified and this is accomplished in the most efficient manner. Their model requires equilibrium in both the capital market and the market for information. Similar to Leland and Pyle (1977), the authors assert that the moral-hazard problem relating to the reliability of information is resolved by the information producer taking a large enough equity position. The authors argue that financial intermediaries emerge because they can *jointly* produce information as well as other products and services valued by investors. Thus, their reasoning straddles both the transaction costs as well as the asymmetric information approaches.

Chan (1983) casts the asymmetric information problem in the scenario of an entrepreneur developing a project of given quality. The returns from the project provide him with the opportunity to consume perquisites. The entrepreneur's actions are generally unobservable by investors, but by incurring search costs they can learn more about the entrepreneur's activities. However, the presence of highly informed investors who do not have to incur search costs forces the entrepreneur to select high-return projects and, at the same time, curtails the consumption of perquisites. In the absence of such well-informed, zero-cost investors, the entrepreneur prefers low-return (LQ) projects, and extracts high-perquisite (HP) consumption. Table 4.1 describes this scenario.

Financial intermediaries substitute for well-informed, zero-cost investors. Furthermore, since information about the firm is reusable, i.e., it can be recycled, there are attendant benefits of economies of scale to the intermediary. Chan (1983)

Table 4.1
Project Quality–Perquisite Combinations with Asymmetric Information

Perquisites	Absence of well-informed investors	Presence of well-informed investors
	LQ HP	HQ HP
	LQ LP	HQ LP

Project Quality

concludes that financial intermediaries provide two benefits. First, they conserve societal search costs; second, they increase investors' welfare by inducing a Pareto-preferred allocation of resources.

Delegated Monitoring. Diamond (1984) describes a financial intermediary as being entrusted with the task of monitoring loan contracts written with entrepreneurs who borrow from investors. There are two alternatives to monitoring by the financial intermediary. The first is direct monitoring by every lender, which entails high societal costs. The other, less-desirable, option involves a free-rider problem, in that no lender monitors because his related benefit is perceived to be too small. The author suggests the delegation of the monitoring function to the specialized agent, namely, the financial intermediary. An associated benefit of this arrangement is that the financial intermediary has a cost advantage in monitoring.

What are the methods used in delegated monitoring by the financial intermediary? A typical example is the bond covenant. In the event of a default, the financial intermediary renegotiates the contract with new interest rates and contingent promises. The intermediary must choose an incentive contract, such that it has the incentives to monitor the information and make adequate payments to depositors to attract deposits. Diamond (1984) notes that diversification by the intermediary on both sides of its balance sheet is a necessary condition for a successful monitoring arrangement. The author concludes that no other monitoring structure will have lower costs.

4.2. A Simple Model of Financial Intermediation

Consider a situation in which an entrepreneur has access to a project that entails an investment I_0, where I_0 is far greater than e, the endowment of individual lenders. The collective endowments of n lenders are required to finance an entrepreneur, i.e., $I_0 = \sum_{j=1}^{n} e_j$. For simplicity, consider a two-period horizon for all participants. If a project is funded at $t = 0$, it is either successful yielding a cash return C_2 in period two with probability π, or unsuccessful, i.e., $C_2 = 0$, with probability $1 - \pi$. Only the entrepreneur can observe the outcome of a funded project without incurring a cost. Furthermore at $t = 1$ the project information is adequate for the entrepreneur to assess the project outcome with probability one, i.e., at this stage, the project is no longer probabilistic. Other agents incur a monitoring cost M at $t = 1$ to observe the project outcome. Thus, it is costly for others to learn about the outcome of a particular project but costless for the entrepreneur. All participants are equally informed, before the project is funded, about its potential payoffs and probability of success.

A potential moral hazard arises in the absence of monitoring, for an entrepreneur can label an successful project as unsuccessful and consume its entire returns. Hence lenders would not fund projects without the provision for monitoring. Contracts need to be written so that entrepreneurs have the incentive to report project results truthfully and lenders can economize on monitoring costs.

Let x_j be the liquidating payment to lender j at the end of the second period if the project is successful. Then these payments cannot exceed project cashflows at $t = 2$, i.e.,

$$\sum_{j=1}^{n} x_j \leq C_2.$$

If the entrepreneur declares success at $t = 1$, there is no need for monitoring. The payoff to the lenders is zero only when the project has failed. On the other hand, the lender has an incentive to monitor when the entrepreneur declares failure. Being aware of this monitoring strategy, the entrepreneur always reveals the true project outcome at $t = 1$. The payoff matrix is illustrated in Table 4.2. If G_j is the present value of the expected net gain of the jth lender, then the collective expected gain of the group if every member monitors is

$$\sum_{j=1}^{n} G_j = \pi \sum_{j=1}^{n} x_j (1 + k)^{-2} - Mn(1 + k)^{-1} \tag{4.7}$$

and the present value of the expected net gain of the entrepreneur is G_e, where

$$G_e = \pi(C_2 - \sum_{j=1}^{n} x_j)(1 + k)^{-2} \tag{4.8}$$

where k is the appropriate discount rate.

The Case for Delegated Monitoring. An alternative to independent monitoring by each lender, with the group collectively incurring a cost of Mn, is to delegate the monitoring function to one of its members. There are economies of scale in delegation with fixed costs of collecting information and monitoring (M_f) and variable costs of diseminating the information to the members of the group

Table 4.2
Payoff Matrix of Entrepreneurial Announcements and Project Possibilities

		Project is a	
		success (π)	failure ($1-\pi$)
Entrepreneur announces at t=1	success	$x_j > 0$ <--No monitoring-->	$x_j = 0$
	failure	$x_j = ?$ <---Monitoring--->	$x_j = 0$

(M_v). Thus $M = M_1 + M_v n$. If the present value of the expected net gain of each lender with delegated monitoring is G_j^d, then the collective gain of the group is

$$\sum_{j=1}^{n} G_j^d = \pi \sum_{j=1}^{n} x_j (1 + k)^{-2} - (M_f + M_v n)(1 + k)^{-1} \qquad (4.9)$$

Obviously, delegated monitoring is advantageous if there is a critical mass (n^*) of lenders in the group, where $n^* = M_f/(M - M_v)$. If $n > n^*$, delegated monitoring is preferred, otherwise the group is better off with individual monitoring.

Moral Hazard and Reputational Capital. A potential problem in the arrangement described is moral hazard explicit in collusion between the entrepreneur and the delegated monitor (DM). Both parties could agree to announce failure of the project when it was a success and share the gains of the project. The DM incurs some nominal cost M' in reporting the failure of the project, where clearly $M' < M$, and M being the monitoring cost with full-fledged monitoring and reporting. The present value of the expected gain from collusion that accrues to the DM is $G_c = [\pi C_2(1 + k)^{-2} - M'(1 + k)^{-1}]p$, where p is the proportionate share of the DM. The present value of the expected gain of the entrepreneur is $[\pi C_2(1 + k)^{-2} - M'(1 + k)^{-1}](1 - p)$. However, other lenders will suspect collusion and obtain confirmation later by observing performances of similar projects. The DM is barred thereafter from monitoring or syndicated lending activities by the group. Thus the DM's gain from collusion is just one-time.

If there is no collusion, the DM is selected more frequently to perform this function, gradually acquires expertise in monitoring and reporting and is eventually appointed as a permanent monitor. The DM is now eligible to an infinite stream of payments, whose expected present value is

$$G_{dm} = [\pi X_d - (M_f + M_v n)(1 + k)n^{-1}]k^{-1}(k + 2)^{-1}$$

where X_d is the cashflow that accrues to the DM. The DM will not collude if $G_{dm} > G_c$, i.e.,

$$\frac{\pi X_d - (M_f + M_v n)(1 + k)n^{-1}}{k(k + 2)} > \left[\frac{\pi C_2}{(1 + k)^2} - \frac{M'}{(1 + k)} \right]p \qquad (4.10)$$

For $k < k^*$, where, $G^*_{dm} = G^*_c$, i.e.,

$$\frac{\pi X_d - (M_f + M_v n)(1 + k^*)n^{-1}}{k^*(k^* + 2)} = \left[\frac{\pi C_2}{(1 + k^*)^2} - \frac{M'}{(1 + k^*)} \right]p, \qquad (4.10a)$$

the opportunity cost of funds is low and there is no incentive to collude. For $k > k^*$, the opportunity cost of funds is high enough to make collusion attractive, i.e., $G_{dm} < G_c$, as shown in Figure 4.5. Other lenders cannot observe if condition (4.10) really holds, and, hence, the selection of the DM is crucial. A particular lender will

Figure 4.5
Gains to Reputational Capital and Collusion

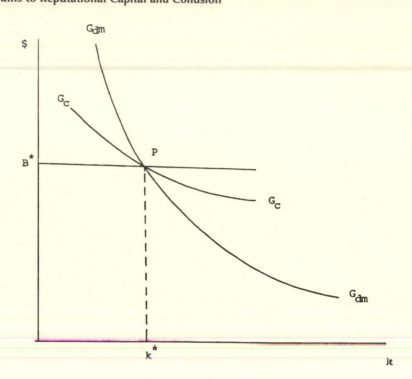

be selected as DM if the lender has established a reputation for scrupulous honesty and fair play.

In other words, this lender is deemed to have accumulated reputational capital. The reputational capital, B, is in the nature of a bond or guarantee of performance and is allocated by the DM among the n lenders, so that the allocation per lender is B/n. This is an additional cost charged to the other lenders, who now find delegation to be attractive if the present value of expected cashflows net of monitoring and reporting costs exceed the allocated reputational capital of the DM, i.e.,

$$\pi[x_j(1 + k)^{-2}] - (M_f + M_v n)n^{-1}(1 + k)^{-1} > B/n \tag{4.11}$$

The DM will accept the monitoring function if $G_{dm} > B$. Otherwise, the infinite stream of gains from monitoring do not provide returns to the DM's reputational capital. Typically, large consulting or law firms do not find it worthwhile to accept small assignments. The optimal bond to be provided is B^*, where $G^*_{dm} = G^*_c$. If

$B < B^*$, then the reputational capital is not adequate to prevent collusion. If $B > B^*$, while collusion is prevented, the return to reputational capital is diluted.

The Role of Financial Intermediaries. Given the preceding scenario, the role of the financial intermediary is easily perceived. The DM can function as a financial intermediary, which collects funds from a number of lenders and lends to a number of entrepreneurs. If there is a diversified portfolio of entrepreneurs, the intermediary can commit to make a fixed payment to lenders (depositors) without linking these payments to project returns. If r_d is the certain return to the lender–depositor and the payment received from the ith entrepreneur is X_i, then

$$\sum_{i=1}^{m} \pi_i x_i = mM^* + \sum_{j=1}^{m} r_d D_j \tag{4.12}$$

All the monitoring is delegated to the financial intermediary and the depositor–lenders do not incur the cost of monitoring.

Reputation and Financial Intermediation in Developing Nations. Asymmetric information is a distinguishing characteristic of the developing world. Borrowers know the true worth of the collateral they offer or have better estimates of the costs and benefits of their projects. Lenders have no or little access to such information. The financial intermediary, through its delegated monitoring activities, mitigates the risks faced by lenders. However, the lenders also face the risk of collusion between the intermediary and the borrower. Risks associated with such asymmetric information are mitigated by the reputations of the intermediary and the borrower. An intermediary that has acquired the reputation for protecting the interests of its lenders gains their confidence. Similarly, a borrower who has acquired the reputation for timely discharge of his responsibilities gains the confidence of the financial market. Reputation is an important element in reducing the risks associated with imperfect information in developing nations.

5. CONCLUSION

A financial intermediary represents an institutional arrangement to reduce transaction costs. North (1987) argues that "the costs of transacting are the key to the performance of economies." Furthermore, industrialized nations developed the elaborate institutional structures needed for complex, interpersonal exchanges to be consummated with minimum cost. Thus, it appears that economic growth can be adversely affected without such institutional development. Financial intermediaries produce a wide variety of services, ranging from simple management of the payment system to portfolio diversification and maturity intermediation.

McKinnon (1973) and Shaw (1973) argue for elimination of financial repression in favor of financial liberalization. On the other hand, the neostructuralists assert that the curb or noninstitutional credit-market-determined nominal interest rate adjusts to equate demand for and supply of money and credit. In their models, the curb or informal markets have important roles to play and their intermediation efficiencies may be adversely affected by financial liberalization. Microtheories of financial intermediation focus on some specific function of intermediaries and provide a wealth of representations. Thus, the financial intermediary is seen as an asset transformer, a portfolio manager, and a reducer of transaction costs. The most interesting representations capitalize on the comparative informational ad vantage of the intermediary.

The following two chapters focus on specific financial intermediaries, namely, security markets and specialized institutions, such as development banks. The former permit free pricing mechanisms adjusting according to the risks and fundamental characteristics of the issuers, while the latter develop the skills and expertise needed for the delegated monitoring function.

NOTES

1. See Gerschenkron (1962, 1968), Cameron (1972), Cameron et al. (1967), Patrick (1967), and Patrick et al. (1966).
2. See Khatkhate and Richel (1980).
3. The financial interrelations ratio as defined is a *stock* measure. The *flow* analogue is the ratio of issues of financial instruments in a given period to the period's gross national period.
4. See Goldsmith (1969), p. 400.
5. See Shaw (1973), p. 3.
6. See Fry (1988), p. 14.
7. For an excellent survey of this literature, see Iao (1985)
8. See Shaw (1973), chapters 2 and 3.
9. See Fry (1988) for an extensive review of this literature.
10. See Kapur (1976a), pp. 792–93.
11. See Taylor (1979, 1983).
12. Kapur (1992) argues that even though the formal financial intermediaries carry the burden of higher reserve ratios, their benefits outweigh this cost. These benefits are "liquidity enhancement" and "seignorage creation." Kapur demonstrates that when these effects are taken into account, financial liberalization is welfare-increasing.
13. See Diaz-Alejandro (1985), p. 15.
14. Ibid., p. 20.
15. See, for example, Friedman and Schwartz (1963).
16. See Baltenspreger (1980) for an exhaustive discussion of the theory of the banking firm.
17. See Benston and Smith (1976), p. 215.
18. This conclusion runs counter to the Fisherian model in Section 2.2.

5

Financial Intermediation through Capital Markets

1.0. INTRODUCTION

Developing nations have reconsidered their approaches to financing as a result of their experiences in the 1980s. The global trend towards financial liberalization has been unmistakably set on its course. The political metamorphoses in Eastern Europe in the early nineties has provided additional impetus to structural economic transitions. Increasingly, developing nations have chosen to rely on the private sector and market signals to direct the allocation of resources. Efficient financial systems are *sine qua non* if greater reliance is to be placed on voluntary, market-based decision making.

This chapter examines the role of securities markets in financing development. The following section delineates the nature and functions of capital markets and discusses the applicable definitions of efficiency. Section 3 provides an outline of pricing mechanisms in competitive securities markets. Section 4 details some issues relating to the role of securities markets in financing development. Specifically, it provides answers to questions such as: How relevant are securities markets to developing nations? At which stage of their development should securities markets be considered? This section also considers in some detail microanalytical issues relating to financial intermediation through banks and equity markets. Problems of adverse selection and moral hazard in the presence of asymmetric information confound the efficiency of capital investment. Credit rationing can be an outcome in such conditions with bank financing. However, principal–agent relationships, imperfect information, legal forms of corporate organization, and market performance are factors that can affect the efficiency of investments through equity markets. Section 5 considers strategies for securities markets development leading to efficient financial intermediation. It emphasizes the stage of development at which securities markets should be considered, the regulatory framework, promotion of institutional investors, and considers portfolio investments from abroad. The concluding section draws attention to the "infrastructure" necessary for the efficient functioning of securities markets, such as the legal structure, accounting standards, and communications technology.

2.0. NATURE AND FUNCTIONS OF CAPITAL MARKETS

The capital market is the network of facilities that provides for the purchase and sale, or exchange, of long-term claims or securities. The money market, in which near-money financial assets and claims are traded, is quite distinct from the capital market. The capital market provides a channel for *augmenting* the flow of investible funds—by adding to the stock of financial assets and liabilities—as well as a means for *readjusting* a given stock of financial assets and liabilities. By performing these functions efficiently, the capital market contributes to the growth of the real economy.

2.1. Functions of Capital Markets

Capital markets perform three important functions. First, they permit gains to be made through *economic specialization*. Clearly, if all economic units were homogeneous and self-sufficient, all assets would be financed from internal sources and there would be no necessity for capital or other financial markets. However, differences in preferences, talents, and opportunities demand specialization for efficiency. Specialization, of course, promotes exchange. Households, for example, tend to specialize in saving and in demanding financial assets, whereas businesses specialize in borrowing and in supplying financial assets. Second, capital markets accommodate *interpersonal differences in consumption time preferences*. Even if current saving and investment were to balance in all sectors individually and in the aggregate, tastes of economic units change in the course of their life cycle. The altered demand patterns of economic units promote secondary markets for financial assets distinct from the primary markets in which they are first issued. Finally, capital markets allow for *interpersonal differences in attitudes towards risk*. Each economic unit makes its choice of financial assets based on individual risk–return preferences. However, these preferences need not be identical across economic units.

Thus the saving–investment imbalances in the various sectors lead to new issues of securities—the development of the primary capital market. However, variations in risk and time preferences across economic units lead to adjustments in outstanding financial assets, which promote secondary capital markets. The secondary market reinforces the primary market, inasmuch as it provides essential liquidity to the new issues of financial assets. In fact, an active secondary market provides a guarantee of redemption to issues made in the primary markets and thus ensures their survival.

2.2. Capital Market Efficiency

When scarce current savings are exchanged for financial assets, the economy as a whole benefits. There are two ways of promoting economic welfare through efficient use of scarce resources. *Allocational efficiency* calls for ordering of all possible uses in decreasing desirability and allocating resources in that order until they have been exhausted. Not all uses may be satisfied, but the procedure assures that resources are put to their best use. Ends chosen for priority should be met with least expenditure of resources. *Operational efficiency* assures that, given the list of priorities, as many uses down the list as possible are satisified, given the scarce resources.

Tobin (1984) identifies four separate concepts of efficiency. *Information arbitrage efficiency* measures the extent to which it is possible to gain on average from trading on generally available information. *Complete information arbitrage efficiency* implies it is not possible to gain from such trading.[1] *Fundamental valuation efficiency* measures the extent to which market values of financial assets reflect accurately the present value of the stream of future payments expected from holding that asset. *Full insurance efficiency* refers to the extent to which the financial system offers possible hedging (insuring) opportunities against future contingencies.

A competitive capital market promotes both allocational and operational efficiency. It encourages allocational efficiency when it directs savings flows to investments with the best risk-adjusted return. A competitive capital market promotes operational efficiency when the allocation of funds is performed with least cost of transfer. Thus, operational efficiency is measured in terms of floatation costs, brokerage charges, and economies of scale in the capital market. Economies of scale are obtained by both diversification and specialization. Both kinds of efficiency are likely to exist if funds are allocated to the highest bidder (risk-adjusted return) by least-cost intermediaries. It is clear that Tobin's fundamental valuation efficiency is impounded in the notion of allocational efficiency. A broadly diversified capital market should provide opportunities for full insurance efficiency.

Fry (1988) describes *functional efficiency* as relating to the main economic functions of the financial sector—administering the payment mechanism and intermediating between savers and investors. Functional efficiency is determined by market structure and the regulatory framework in which the financial sector operates. Market structure encompasses the degree of competition, concentration, and mutual relationships between financial intermediaries and business enterprises, and the extent of specialization within the financial sector. Internal organization and management of financial intermediaries influence market structure. These factors are in turn affected by the degree of government ownership and control.

The regulatory framework is directed towards monetary policy and ensuring prudent management. It includes the legal environment, adequacy of commercial law, and efficacy of the judiciary system. Market structure and the extent of government intervention are clearly interrelated.[2]

In conclusion, a dynamic capital market, in addition to optimal allocation of resources, stimulates the supply of savings. By widening savers' choices, both risk averters and risk seekers are encouraged to save more, for such capital pooling operations increase the risk-adjusted rate of return. Thus, a competitive capital market not only promotes optimal use of existing funds, but also augments the level of available funds by reducing the required rates of return on investment and raising the rates of return for given risk classes.[3]

3.0. CONCEPTUAL PRICING MECHANISMS IN COMPETITIVE CAPITAL MARKETS

The principal product of competitive markets is a system of prices that functions both as a signalling device and as a provider of incentives. In this context, Meier (1983) observes, "The more developed a country's price system, the more effectively it will exercise the functions of providing information, rationing, allocation and mobilization of resources, and distribution of income."[4]

Dorfman (1967) refers to prices as the "coefficients of social choice."[5] A relevant question is, "How do conceptual competitive capital markets price their products?" The following discussions provide some answers.

3.1. Capital Asset Pricing Model

The principal contributors to a theory for pricing financial assets in a competitive market are Sharpe (1964), Lintner (1965), and Mossin (1966). Their Capital Asset Pricing Model (CAPM) develops a partial equilibrium framework for relating the expected return of a financial asset to a measure of its risk. They assume an environment in which risk-averse investors are single-period expected-utility maximizers with homogeneous expectations of future returns of financial assets. The environment provides a perfect market in which all participants are price-takers. Furthermore, the participants have full and costless access to information, and are subject to zero taxes or transaction costs.

Risk-averse investors who seek to diversify their portfolios confront two types of risk. Systematic risk is ever-present in the broad economic environment within which all financial assets are traded. It reflects the sensitivity of returns of a particular financial asset to changes in the economic environment. Systematic risk includes elements such as purchasing power risk, interest rate risk, market risk, political risk, etc. Unsystematic risk is the component that is issuer-specific. It reflects the financial characteristics of the entity issuing the financial assets. Unsystematic risk includes operating risk, which measures variability of the operating earnings of the issuer, and financial risk, which is determined by the composition of the issuer's capital structure. In a diversified portfolio, unsystematic risk can be eliminated or minimized, as the financial characteristics of an issuer may be neutralized by those of another issuer. However, systematic risk can never be eliminated, as it is determined in the economic environment in which all financial assets are individual components. Thus, in this competitive market, financial assets are priced according to the level of their systematic risk—the expected returns of financial assets are directly related to their systematic risk.

Define R_{jt} and R_{mt} as the random return to asset j and the aggregate market m, respectively, in period t. The returns are assumed to have a simple linear relationship,

$$R_{jt} = \alpha_j + \beta_j R_{mt} + e_{jt} \tag{5.1}$$

where α_j and β_j are the intercept and slope, respectively. Equation 5.1 posits that the random return to asset j consists of a market-dependent component, $\beta_j R_{mt}$, a market-independent component, α_j, and a random component, e_{jt}. β_j measures the sensitivity of the asset's return to the return of the aggregate market. The last component (e_{jt}) is assumed to be distributed with mean zero and standard deviation σ_{ej}. Furthermore, all the variables abide by the assumptions of the ordinary least squares regression model, so that

$$E(R_j) = \alpha_j + \beta_j E(R_m) \tag{5.2}$$

and

$$\sigma_j^2 = \beta_j^2 \sigma_m^2 + \sigma_{ej}^2 \tag{5.3}$$

If X_j is the proportionate allocation to asset j in a n-security portfolio p, then

$$E(R_p) = \sum_{j=1}^{n} X_j \alpha_j + \sum_{j=1}^{n} X_j \beta_j E(R_m) \tag{5.4}$$

and

$$\sigma_p^2 = \left(\sum_{j=1}^{n} X_j \beta_j \right)^2 \sigma_m^2 + \sum_{j=1}^{n} X_j^2 \sigma_{ej}^2 \tag{5.5}$$

The term $\Sigma X_j \beta_j$, replaced by β_p, measures the sensitivity of the portfolio returns to those of the aggregate market. The first term on the right-hand side of equation 5.5 measures the systematic risk of the portfolio, while the second term represents its unsystematic risk. In a broadly diversified portfolio, the unsystematic risk can be made insignificantly small; with large n, average proportionate allocation, X_j, tends to approach zero and the second term on the right hand side of the equation can be ignored. Then

$$\sigma_p^2 = \beta_p^2 \sigma_m^2 \tag{5.6}$$

Equation 5.6 implies that a well-diversified portfolio exhibits only systematic risk. Since σ_m^2, the variance of the returns of the aggregate market, is a parameter constant for all assets, the portfolio's systematic risk is determined only by its β_p. Thus the β-parameter of an individual asset or a portfolio is taken to be a measure of its systematic risk.

Sharpe (1964), Lintner (1965) and Mossin (1966) develop a partial equilibrium framework for pricing assets in a perfectly competitive capital market. Given the assumptions described earlier, they demonstrate that an asset will be priced such that its expected return is determined only by the measure of its systematic risk, β_j. As unsystematic risk can be diversified away, the market does not offer rewards for carrying this risk in the portfolio. Specifically,

$$E(R_j) = R_f + [E(R_m) - R_f] \, \beta_j \tag{5.7}$$

where R_f is the risk-free rate of interest. Note that R_f and R_m are market-wide parameters. Equation 5.7 states that the expected return of the jth asset consists of a base rate, R_f, and a risk premium. The risk premium is proportional to the assets's measure of systematic risk, β_j, where the constant of proportionality is the market risk premium, $[E(R_m) - R_f]$.

The CAPM is perhaps the most important development in the theory of capital markets. It posits that in perfect capital markets, all the needs of risk-averse investors are met by allocations between just two assets, namely, the market portfolio and the risk-free asset. This principle is known as portfolio separation in perfect capital markets. The empirical evidence generally supports the theory, although low-β assets have been found to have higher expected returns and high-β assets have been associated with lower expected returns than predicted.[6]

3.2. Arbitrage Pricing Model

Equation 5.1 specifies a particular form of the return-generating process. Other forms of the return-generating process, called factor or index models, posit that the return on a security is sensitive to the movements of various factors or indices. This characterization is plausible, as more factors than the movements of the market portfolio appear to affect asset returns. Thus, within the economy more than one pervasive factor affects asset returns. It is therefore important to identify these factors in the economy and the sensitivities of asset returns to movements in these factors. This relationship is termed a factor model of asset returns. Such models contain both common factors that affect all securities to a greater or lesser extent, for example, growth rate of GNP, and sector factors that affect only one particular subgroup of securities, for example, industries.

The arbitrage pricing model (APM), like the CAPM, represents a system of asset pricing in equilibrium. The APM differs from the CAPM in that it assumes that returns are generated by a n-factor model. The model does not specify the

number or the identity of the factors. Furthermore, it requires only the innocuous assumption that investors prefer higher levels of wealth to lower levels of wealth.[7]
An n-factor model is specified as

$$R_j = a_j + b_{j1}F_1 + b_{j2}F_2 + \ldots + b_{jn}F_n + e_j \qquad (5.8)$$

Given adequate securities with different characteristics, it is possible, theoretically, to construct a "pure factor" portfolio that has unit sensitivity to a particular factor, no sensitivity to other factors, and zero nonfactor risk. Thus

$$R_{pk} = \alpha_{pk} + F_k \qquad (5.9)$$

where R_{pk} is the return of the portfolio sensitive to the kth factor. In practice, not all the conditions are met completely; it may be only possible to create "impure factor" portfolios that are largely sensitive (not exclusively) to one factor with little nonfactor risk.

The relationship in equation 5.9 can be restated as the expected return of the kth pure factor portfolio consists of the riskfree rate of interest and a residual Φ_k, defined as the expected return premium per unit of sensitivity to the factor. Thus

$$R_{pk} = R_f + \Phi_k \qquad (5.10)$$

It is possible that many alternative combinations of securities produce a pure factor k portfolio. In theory, each such portfolio should have the same expected return. In the event that two factor k portfolios had different expected returns, this could be due only to differences in their α values. By selling short the portfolio with the lower expected return and purchasing the portfolio with the higher expected return, an investor makes an abnormal return, irrespective of the level of factor k. In equilibrium, therefore, the two identical assets will be priced to provide the same expected return. Otherwise, the actions of arbitrageurs will ensure that this result follows.

It is possible to demonstrate that the n-factor return-generating process of an individual asset j in equation (5.8) is equivalent to the return of a portfolio, pj, such that,

$$R_{pj} = R_f + b_{j1}\Phi_1 + b_{j2}\Phi_2 + \ldots + b_{jn}\Phi_n \qquad (5.11)$$

In eqs. 5.8 and 5.11, the sensitivities of the jth asset and pjth portfolio to the various factors are identical. In equilibrium, the expected return of the jth asset is equal to the expected return of the pjth portfolio. Thus the expected return of asset j is

$$R_j = R_f + b_{j1}\Phi_1 + b_{j2}\Phi_2 + \ldots + b_{jn}\Phi_n \qquad (5.11a)$$

Equation 5.11 is a representation of the arbitrage pricing model. It states that the expected return of a security is linearly related to the sensitivity of each pervasive factor. Furthermore, the common intercept term is the risk-free rate.

3.3. Concluding Observations on Asset Pricing Models

Both the CAPM and APM linearly relate the expected return of assets to their various attributes. The CAPM posits that the relevant asset attribute is β_j, i.e., its sensitivity to the market portfolio, whereas the APM specifies the attributes as the sensitivities to major factors, b_{jk}, $k = 1,2, \ldots, n$. It is not clear from the APM the number of relevant factors for a particular asset or what they represent. Nevertheless, it can be argued that conditions necessary for both the CAPM and APM to hold are available. Due to their complex statistical nature, actual usuage of these models is limited to professional money managers who have the necessary resources. As investors gain more experience with these models, more variations will be generated. Such efforts contribute to better understanding of markets and in promoting their informational, and thus operating, efficiency.

4.0. SOME ISSUES RELATING TO THE ROLE OF CAPITAL MARKETS IN DEVELOPING NATIONS

This section considers some issues relating to the role of capital market development in the overall scheme of economic development. It discusses the relevance of capital markets in the context of developing nations, the stages of financial structure development and the place of capital markets therein. This section also highlights some conceptual microanalytical issues relating to debt intermediation through commercial banks as against intermediation through equity markets.

4.1. Relevance of Capital Market Development to Economic Development

Capital market (in particular, equity market) development is an intrinsic component of the overall strategy for economic development for three reasons. First, equity capital is an effective cushion against adverse circumstances. Second, equity capital markets are considered to be more efficient than bank-based debt markets (this issue is discussed in more detail later in this section). In this context, McKinnon (1986) asserts that the absence of open security markets in developing countries places too much risk on bank-based capital markets. The lack of direct financial markets may lead to higher intermediation costs. In fact, Watson et al. (1986) observe that, as a result of recent capital market liberalization and innovation in OECD countries, intermediation costs have been reduced by lower commissions and increased competition consequent to substitution of bank credits by direct transactions in securities. Third, inadequate provision of term finance and the lack of direct financial markets have resulted in high inflation in developing nations. In Turkey, for example, between 1978 and 1981, inflation accelerated as the debt–equity ratios of large business corporations increased from 3.2 to 5.7 with the shrinking of equity markets.[8] Finally, efficient securities markets provide liquidity and marketability, divisibility of assets, diversification possibilities, and promote widespread ownership. The last factor is important for the promotion of equitable distribution of investment opportunities.

A formal analysis of the contributions of equity markets to economic growth is made by Levine (1990, 1990a). The model extends and links two strands of literature. In the *endogenous growth* literature, agents make decisions that fully determine the economy's steady state growth rate [Romer (1986, 1990) and Lucas (1988)]; financial contracts emerge in the *financial structures* literature as optimal responses to an economy's informational and risk characteristics [Townsend (1979), Diamond (1984), Diamond & Dybvig (1983)]. Levine constructs an endogenous growth model in which the stock market emerges to allocate risk and it alters investment incentives to impact steady state growth rates.

Each individual is assumed to live for three periods. There is an infinite sequence of such generations of individuals and infinite individuals are born each period. The arguments of their utility function are consumption in periods 2 and 3—thus all income in period 1 is saved.

$$U(c_1, c_2, c_3) = \frac{(c_2 + \phi c_3)^{-\gamma}}{\gamma} \tag{5.12}$$

where $\gamma > 0$ and c_i is age i consumption. ϕ is a $(0,1)$ random variable with probabilities $1 - \pi$ and π, respectively. If $\phi = 0$, agents want to consume their wealth at age two. The fact that some agents may experience $\phi = 0$ and others may not induces "liquidity risk." The two types of individuals are not publicly observable and hence there are no insurance contracts to eliminate private liquidity risk. Agents born in period t work, receive wage w_t, and make investment allocation decisions.

There are two production opportunities available. The first is a liquid "storage" technology—investment of one good at t yields $n > 0$ at $t + 1$ or $t + 2$. The second is the risky and illiquid activity of forming and investing in firms that have a higher expected return than the liquid technology. Consumption goods are produced using capital, labor, and human capital. Human capital is nontradable and represents knowledge and skills embodied in individuals. In the first stage, individuals accumulate human capital. This accumulation is over period $t + 1$ and some of $t + 2$, so that only age three agents have human capital. Human capital is accumulated by the agent's interactions with others, as well as the amount of resources invested by the agent, and the average amount of capital invested and maintained in the firm for two periods. A public-good element is intrinsic to the creation of human capital. First, there is a public-good externality associated with firm resources; second, a member who benefits by his own investment will influence the human capital of others through interactions; and finally, resources invested by a member allows him to interact more with others, so that the human capital of other members increases independently of their own investments.

Age 3 members with human capital ("entrepreneurs") hire age 1 workers and produce goods according to a production function, the arguments of which are labor and human capital. There is a firm-specific productivity shock, a random variable with expected value of unity, which appears as an argument of the production function. Human capital positively influences production, wage rate, and return to entrepreneurs.

In this scenario, the presence of liquidity and productivity risks promote the creation of stock markets. Productivity risk lowers welfare and discourages agents from investing in firms. Stock markets allow investors to invest in a large number of firms and diversify away idiosyncratic productivity shocks. Thus, welfare, resources invested in firms, and the economy's steady state growth rate are increased. Liquidity risk lowers welfare and firm investment. Public stock markets provide mechanisms for satisfying liquidity requirements and allow individuals to hold diversified portfolios, thus protecting against productivity and liquidity risks.

The stock market influences aggregate growth in two ways. First, the stock market increases firm efficiency by eliminating the premature withdrawal of capital from firms, which accelerates the growth rate of human capital and per-capita output. Second, the stock market increases the resources devoted to firms. By increasing liquidity of firm investment, reducing productivity risk, and improving firm efficiency, stock markets encourage firm investment, which in turn stimulates human capital production and growth. Thus, in this scenario, stock markets prevent premature liquidation of firm capital and increase the fraction of resources allocated to firms; by providing the opportunity to risk-averse investors to diversify, they are encouraged to invest more. In conclusion, Levine (1990, 1990a) develops an interesting model capturing the essence of the contribution by stock markets to economic growth. However, the model does not reflect the possible feedback effects between economic growth and stock markets that can compound growth over several periods.

4.2. Stages of Financial Structure Development

Kumar and Tsetsekos (1992) develop a general theory of security market development with a sequential process of economic development. They link Rostow's celebrated "stages of growth" concept with parallel phases of financial sector development. To summarize, the economy is characterized initially as a traditional society with low productivity and consumption at subsistence levels. In the second stage, assets expand with productivity improvements to promote the emergence of a dominant sector, such as agriculture. Further increases in the proportion of savings and investment to national income promote the development of other leading sectors in manufacturing and agriculture together with the proliferation of social and political institutions. Thus, in the third phase the growth of the economy is poised to increase dramatically (Rostow's "takeoff stage"). Higher growth with the development of new leading sectors in manufacturing industry and services together with further increases in investment drive the economy towards maturity. Technology and export development have major roles in the fourth stage. The final stage is characterized by additional leading sectors in consumer goods and services, all of which are heavily technology-intensive. These five stages are depicted in Figure 5.1.

Factors such as investment, manufacturing activity, export development, absorption of technology, human capital, and institutional development, are undoubtedly necessary; however, the financial sector is the vital catalyst that activates the interrelationships among them. Specifically, the authors posit that the development of a subset of the financial sector, namely the securities markets, is necessary for the economy to progress to the final stages of economic growth.

The traditional society is characterized by the total absence of the financial sector. In this barter economy, all savings are held in the form of real output and participants bear the consequent risks of nonexchangeability, obsolescence, etc. With the emergence of the dominant sector in the second phase, the economy gets monetized. Outside money, commodity money, or money backed by government debt appears. However, with no financial asset other than money, there are restraints on saving, on capital accumulation, and on the allocation of savings to investment. Such restraints tend to depress the rate of growth and income. In the third phase, as savings and investment increase, and social and political institutions proliferate, the banking sector is organized, with some accompanying activity in the curb markets. With the development of new leading sectors and demand for even higher levels of investment in the fourth stage, the banking subsector and curb markets continue to grow. However, efficiency of financial intermediation through the banking sector leaves scope for improvement and securities markets providing for the trading of claims by other economic entities are developed. As formal securities markets develop, the importance of informal curb markets diminishes. In the final stage, the banking subsector matures, with reduced growth, and activities in the securities markets increase dramatically. Financial innovations in the form of derivative financial instruments based on contingent claims lend dynamism to the securities markets. The curb markets virtually disappear at this stage.

Securities markets develop and grow in the final stages. This development is closely paralleled by growth in the economy. As the securities markets intermediate efficiently, the allocation of investment in the economy improves and output increases further. In turn this creates new demand for intermediation services from the securities markets with the concomitant increased growth in the economy. There are mutually reinforcing feedback effects between real output growth and increased securities market activities, as displayed in Figure 5.1.

4.3. Conceptual Microanalytical Issues Relating to Financial Intermediation through Banks and Equities Markets

The literature advocating financial liberalization has overlooked the aspects of imperfect information and equity capital market structure. Feedback effects be-

Figure 5.1
Security Market Development and Economic Growth

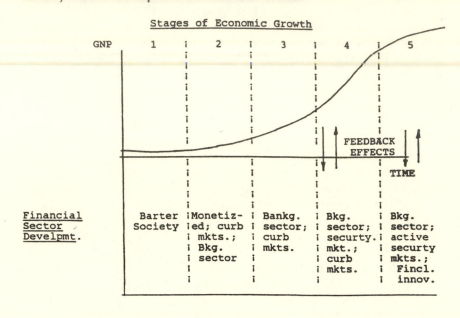

tween inadequately developed equity markets and high dependence on bank loan financing have made financial liberalization difficult. Cho (1986) considers the question whether full-scale liberalization of the banking sector would be efficient given the current state of capital markets in developing nations. He concludes that in the absence of well-functioning equity markets, full-scale liberalization of the banking sector would not result in efficient capital allocation. Substantial development of an equity market is a *necessary* condition for complete financial liberalization. This argument unfortunately focuses on one side of the issue, namely, the adverse selection and incentive effects that result in high-risk bank loans. However, the aspect of financial signalling effects in equity markets has been ignored. The following discussion develops both these conceptual aspects in detail.

4.3.1. Financial Intermediation through Bank Loans. The analysis is based on work by Stiglitz and Weiss (1981). These authors demonstrate that in equilibrium a market for bank loans, in which interest rates are set by borrrower characteristics, may be characterized by *credit rationing*. This constraint may be due to *exogenous* factors—interest rate ceilings due to legal and/or institutional considerations. *Endogenous* factors in the form of informational imperfections may also affect this constraint. Banks may find it costly to distinguish among the risk characteristics of their borrowers. As a consequence, even if interest rates were liberalized and free competition existed among banks, information constraints can inhibit the efficient allocation of capital.

Stiglitz and Weiss (1981) suggest that a bank's return from lending to a specific group of borrowers is not a monotonically increasing function of the interest rate it charges for two reasons. First, borrowers who are deterred from borrowing by the higher cost of capital may be precisely the safe borrowers to whom the bank can profitably lend. This reason is termed the *adverse selection* effect. Second, borrowers who have a choice tend to favor projects that have higher probabilities of default when interest rates are increased. This reason is described as the *incentive* effect. These two effects are mutually reinforcing and as a consequence banks are deterred from raising interest rates in response to increasing demand for loans. Thus, as interest rates are increased, the expected bank profit from lending to a specific group has an interior maximum and is not a monotonically increasing function.

The assumptions of the Stiglitz and Weiss (1981) model are 1) the borrower provides a fixed amount of equity in financing the project; 2) borrowers and lenders are risk-neutral; 3) supply of loanable funds is independent of the interest rate; 4) cost of the project is fixed; and 5) projects are indivisible.

Define R as the cash flow to the borrower from operations, and C as the collateral offered against a borrowing of B at interest rate i. Then the profit to the borrower, $\pi(R,i)$, and to the bank, $\beta(R,i)$, are:

$$\pi(R, i) = \text{Max}[R - (1 + i)B, -C] \qquad (5.13)$$

$$\beta(R,i) = \text{Min}[R + C, (1 + i)B] \qquad (5.14)$$

Consider the case in which the "Walrasian" equilibrium interest rate—the level at which demand for funds equals the supply of funds—such that there exists a lower interest rate at which level bank profit, β, is higher. The demand for funds depends on the interest rate charged by banks, whereas the supply of funds depends on β. In Figure 5.2, L_d is the demand for loans, a decreasing function of the interest rate in the first quadrant. The relationship between the profit earned on loans (β) and the interest rate charged is displayed as a nonmonotonic function in the fourth quadrant. There is a direct relationship between β and the supply of loanable funds, L_s, as shown in the third quadrant. In the first quadrant, L_s is shown as a function of the interest rate through the impact of the interest rate on the return of each loan, and hence on the interest rate banks can offer to attract loanable funds.

A credit rationing equilibrium exists in Figure 5.1, as L_d at i^*, the bank profit-maximizing interest rate, is greater than L_s. Any bank increasing its interest rate on loans greater than i^* reduces its profitability, β. Excess demand is represented by z. The "Walrasian" interest rate is obtained at i_w, where $L_d = L_s$. But i_w is not an equilibrium interest rate, as the bank can increase its profits by charging interest

Figure 5.2
Stiglitz–Weiss Equilibrium for Bank Loans

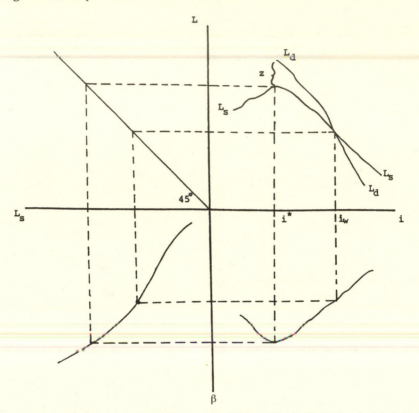

Source: Adapted from J. E. Stiglitz and A. Weiss, "Credit Rationing in Markets with
    Imperfect Information," *American Economic Review, 71* (1981), p. 397. Used with
    permission from the American Economic Association.

rate i^* rather than i_w. Thus, at the lower interest rate, the bank can attract all the
borrowers it had at i_w and still make larger profits on each loan.

Cho (1986) extends the Stiglitz and Weiss analysis specifically to developing
nations. He considers the issue whether full-scale liberalization of the banking
sector would promote efficient allocation of capital, given the existing structure of
capital markets in developing nations. Let there be n groups of potential borrowers
in the economy. Banks can distinguish among these groups according to their
innate characteristics—size, industry to which they belong, etc. Banks can approximately estimate the productivity of each group, measured by R, the cash
flow. However, within each group there is diversity, in that the riskiness of each
member varies due to unsystematic factors, such as managerial abilities. Information imperfection affects the banks in that they can distinguish among groups of
borrowers, although not among members of any particular group. The Stiglitz and

Weiss conclusion holds in the sense that the expected profit of a bank from lending to a group of borrowers is not monotonically increasing and there exists an interior optimal interest rate for each group. Consider two groups, k and j. The maximum expected profit to a bank $E(\beta)$ from lending to a group of a borrowers is a function of the variability of riskiness in the group.[9] The bank's expected profit from lending to group k can be higher than that from lending to group j even though the expected productivity of j is higher, i.e., $R_j > R_k$.

Figure 5.3 displays the expected profit of the bank $E(\beta)$ against its lending rate (i). Borrowers are ordered according to their productivities, i.e., $R_1 < R_2 < R_3 < \ldots < R_n$. Suppose there is an administratively imposed lending rate ceiling at i_a. The bank's preferred order of borrowers is group 1, group 2, group 3, etc., since $E\beta_1(i_a) > E\beta_2(i_a) > E\beta_3(i_a), \ldots$ This selection runs counter to the efficiency of allocation criterion, i.e., according to their productivities. Now consider the situation when the interest rate ceiling is eliminated. The preferred order of borrowers is group 3, group 2, group 1, group 4, group 5, etc., since $E(\beta^*_3) > E(\beta^*_2) > E(\beta^*_1) > E(\beta^*_4) > E(\beta^*_5)$. The efficiency of allocation is improved, but only partially. If the competitive bank deposit rate is i_d (indicated on the vertical axis, since at the

Figure 5.3
Expected Return of the Stiglitz–Weiss Bank

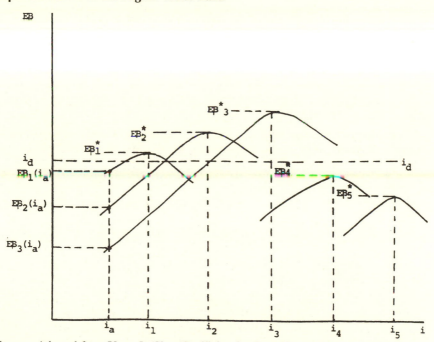

Source: Adapted from Yoon Je Cho, "Inefficiencies from Financial Liberalization in the Absence of Well-Functioning Equity Markets," *Journal of Money, Credit, and Banking,* 18, no. 2 (May 1986). Copyright 1986 by the Ohio State University Press. Used with permission.

competitive rate bank profit is zero), only groups 1, 2, and 3 will be eligible for loans, to the exclusion of the most productive groups, 4 and 5. The important conclusion is that in a situation of imperfect information, a free interest regime is not a sufficient condition for full allocative efficiency of capital.

Cho (1986) argues that with the existence of equity markets, the risky groups will obtain financing. Thus, full allocative efficiency is assured with the presence of equity markets. This would happen because equity finance is free from adverse selection and moral hazard effects whereas these effects hamper bank loan finance in the presence of asymmetric information. However, this argument does not consider distortions in the allocative efficiency of equity markets caused by principal–agent relationships, informational imperfections, and legal forms of corporate organization. These topics are explored in the following paragraphs.

4.3.2. Financial Intermediation through Equity Markets. Are equity markets free from distortions in allocative efficiency as claimed by Cho (1986)? The answer is an unequivocal negative. Indeed, there are distortions in allocative efficiency caused by principal–agent relationships, informational imperfections, legal form of corporate organization, and market performance. It is not clear if such distortions are less than those caused by bank financing. The following discussions focus on these features in detail.

Principal–Agent Relationships. Myers and Majluf (1984) argue that, with asymmetric information, managers who favor the interests of old, passive stockholders may decide to forego issuing new shares and thereby increasing equity capital, even at the cost of passing up good investment opportunities. Managers may prefer to rely on internal sources of finance and prefer debt to equity if new capital is needed. Thus, real capital investment is misallocated and firm value is reduced. Firms whose operating cash flows are less than the level of investment opportunities available may forego these good investments rather than issue risky securities to finance them. Stockholders are made better off when the firm carries sufficient financial slack, defined as the sum of cash, marketable securities, and low-risk borrowing capacity, to undertake good investment opportunities. The ex ante loss in value increases with the size of the required equity issue. Thus, increasing the required investment or reducing slack equivalently increases the ex ante loss.

Informational Imperfections. The principal Stiglitz and Weiss (1981) (SW) assertion is that when the bank increases the interest rate, good borrowers are crowded out and only inferior quality borrowers remain to accept loans. Thus the adverse-selection problem arises. Further, there is greater propensity for such borrowers to present high-risk, low-quality projects for financing, resulting in the incentive effect. If the demand for such loans is sufficiently high, it results in a credit-rationing equilibrium in which banks select their profit-maximizing interest rate. DeMeza and Webb (1987) (DW) argue that with an increase in the interest rate, only superior projects clear the hurdle rate of acceptance and the probability of success of the marginal project accepted increases. Thus, inferior projects are rejected. If there is ample supply of high-quality projects, the SW credit-rationing equilibrium cannot exist. Banks recognize that the supply of such high-quality projects is not indefinitely large and reducing the interest rate at the cost of the profit per contract results in a larger volume of loans and increasing total profit. The interest rate falls to the level of the zero-profit, market-clearing equilibrium value. As long as the rate of return on the marginal project is not less than the return on the safe asset, social efficiency of investment is assured. DeMeza and Webb thus conclude that the total investment at this competitive equilibrium exceeds the socially efficient level. They also demonstrate that in these conditions leading to *overinvestment*, the equilibrium method of finance is a *debt* contract. Further, in the SW model, which yields the *underinvestment* result, the equilibrium method of finance is shown to be *equity*.

The critical difference between the two models is that the DW model assumes that the marginal project has the worst quality in the opportunity set and thus the lowest probability of success. Conversely, the SW model assumes that the marginal project has the best quality associated with the highest probability of success. The important DW conclusion germane to the question raised earlier is that the presence of equity markets alone is not sufficient to prevent underinvestment. Thus, full allocative efficiency is not accomplished with equity markets.[10]

Greenwald, Stiglitz, and Weiss (1984) argue that informational imperfections limit the ability of a firm to raise equity capital for two reasons. First, incentive problems may intensify when a firm is equity financed. Managers in the firm are less restricted in the diversion of profits for their private uses with equity than with debt capital. In the case of debt finance, large bankruptcy costs may cause managers to act responsibly. Lenders can discipline managers by threatening to withdraw funds. This sanction is more effective than majority shareholder voting. Second, signalling effects may restrict a firm's access to equity markets. Bankruptcy risk and the marginal increase in bankruptcy risk with expanded debt levels is less severe for "superior" firms than "inferior" firms. Greater reliance on debt capital by "superior" firms implies that only "inferior" firms issue equity capital. The issuance of equity capital carries negative connotations and affects firm value. Greenwald, Stiglitz, and Weiss demonstrate that the firm issues equity capital only if its operating earnings are not adequate to prevent bankruptcy. If the operating earnings are large enough to sustain debt-related payments, debt is the preferred form of financing. The important conclusion that the availability of capital and not its cost determines the level of investment has implications for developing nations.

Legal Form of Corporate Organization. Does the legal organization of the corporation affect the relations among the various principals? If so, what are its implications? Limited liability is a common characteristic of the modern corporation. It restricts the aggregate claims of the various claimants on the corporation to the market value of the firm. When the claims of suppliers, customers, and workers exceed the total value of the corporation's assets, its owners are not obliged to use their personal wealth to meet these claims. The minimum value of the equity stock is zero. The limited liability condition offers the unlevered firm's stockholders a call option to buy the firm at zero exercise price. John and Senbet (1988) argue that corporate limited liability induces conflict of interest between equity stockholders and nonfinancial claim holders, i.e., other stakeholders. Corporate insiders make investment decisions that are suboptimal from the welfare of all stakeholders. Thus, corporate limited liability induces investment decisions that deviate from the social optimal level.

Cash flows from investments and all claims against the firm are settled according to prespecified sharing rules, which accompany the securities in question, as well as the tax and legal structure in place. Private investment is controlled by corporate insiders, such that writing and enforcing contracts on the level of productive investments to be undertaken by the firm is prohibitively expensive. This condition implies that the firm cannot be forced to invest any amount. Incomplete contracting ability gives rise to conflict of interest among various claimants. Therefore, once the outside claims are sold, corporate insiders will make investment decisions that maximize the value of current equity claims. Such decisions deviate from the maximization of firm value principle. Given these conditions, it is plausible that corporate insiders *overinvest* in risky technologies relative to socially optimal levels.

Can risky debt financing align public and private interests? John and Senbet demonstrate that outstanding risky debt induces *underinvestment* relative to the all-equity-financed optimal level. This effect may offset the *overinvestment* effect under the limited liability conditions. In a private economy, the social planner cannot mandate a particular financing strategy and the firm may choose to have no debt. However, the social planner can provide incentives for debt financing relying upon subsidies and tax deductions. John and Senbet demonstrate that the incentive effects of corporate taxation alone undo some of the distortions caused by corporate limited liability. Furthermore, tax deductibility of debt payments can provide endogenous incentives for debt financing of firms, where the optimal capital structure chosen induces ex post investment choices close to the social optimum.

Market Performance. What is the degree of efficiency with which the market diversifies and prices project risk? This concern is fundamental and specific to stock markets. A relevant issue is whether the pattern of prices in capital markets reflects changes in the underlying fundamental factors. For example, questions have been raised as to whether the observed volatility in world capital markets in the 1980s were intrinsically justified. Undoubtedly, unjustified volatility has adverse implications for capital formation and social welfare.[11] A related issue is whether inordinate concern of corporate managers with stock price performance induces myopic focus on near-term profits. Does this divert corporations from long-term investments on which their secular performance depends?

Implications for Developing Nations. The features of equity markets detailed in the preceding paragraphs, namely, principal–agent relationships, imperfect information, legal form of corporate organization, and market performance, are clearly prevalent in developing nations. They compound the problem of mis-allocation of investments.

Distortions in investments in developing countries may be exacerbated by specific principal–agent problems. Many small and medium firms are family owned and managed. With management and equity stock holdings embodied in the same entity, decisions may be made that are not in the interests of other equity stockholders or debt holders. The consumption of perquisites is a case in point. Resources may be diverted from the firm in the form of perquisites, which promote the welfare of the insider manager-owners. The need to retain managerial control within the insider group may limit the size of investment, even though many projects may be available. Barriers to supply of external equity capital may exist in the form of exclusionary criteria, such as, membership in a caste or sect, common geographical ties, etc.

Problems of imperfect information are compounded in developing nations. Asymmetric information, with the attendant problems of adverse selection and moral hazard, is severe, with inadequate disclosure. The impact may be felt not only by other equity shareholders and debt holders, but also other stakeholders in the firm, such as consumers and society at large. Obviously, the strategies to promote capital-market development need to recognize these specific features.

5.0. STRATEGIES FOR CAPITAL-MARKET DEVELOPMENT

The promotion of capital markets is vital to developing nations. Obviously, specific strategies are necessary to ensure that such efforts meet with success. This discussion covers prerequistes for security market development, regulatory basis, institutional development, and finally, opening emerging securities markets to foreign investors.

5.1. Security Markets and the Stage of Development

Studies of international comparisions of methods of financing conclude that the share of securities markets has been relatively small.[12] Even in developed nations banks are the primary source of external funding of corporations. Developing nations are characterized by limited managerial resources. The role of financial institutions is then to provide effective substitutes/proxies for or to supplement available management skills. It follows that in the early stages of development bank involvement has, by necessity, to be pervasive. This consequence is not so much the result of market failure per se but a reflection of the limited availability of managerial resources. With further progress of economic development the corporate sector breeds its own indigenous managerial skills and the dependency on banks is minimized. At this stage, the role of securities markets becomes clarified.[13]

5.2. Regulatory Environment

The promotion of securities markets in developing countries can be enhanced by creating the necessary regulatory environment. Markets can win the confidence of the investing public by steps taken by the authorities to ensure open, free, and fair price formation. Such steps should include, for example, rigorous listing requirements, establishing adequate standards of investor protection, and requiring full and reliable disclosure by promoting full dissemination of information. Policies that guarantee such steps should lead to active and liquid securities markets in developing nations.

5.3. Institutional Development

The participation of institutions in securities markets has increased dramatically in developed nations. Activities of units trusts, contractual savings companies, mutual funds, pension funds, etc., have contributed to liquidity and efficient pricing in these markets. Indeed, in United States securities markets, institutional activities, measured in terms of block transactions (i.e., 10,000 shares or more), have increased from 2,171 in 1965 to 920,697 in 1987.[14] Two issues relating to the activities of such institutions are worth noting.

First, institutional investors tend to focus on large capitalization companies. This specialization has created tiered equity markets in the United States, which occur when investors are willing to pay different prices for stocks with essentially the same growth and risk characteristics. Hence, secondary markets for large institutional stocks have improved substantially, while those for small firms have deteriorated, adversely affecting their primary markets.[15] Second, conventional wisdom has supported the existence of a strong positive relationship between institutional trading activity and stock market volatility. Empirical studies have proved such concerns to be misplaced.[16]

In general, a capital market dominated by institutional investors in which all are actively involved provides the best environment for securities, since they provide liquidity for each other and other noninstitutional investors. Developing nations could examine the possibility of sponsoring the creation and growth of such institutions to promote liquidity and efficient pricing.

5.4. Foreign Portfolio Investments in Developing Nation Securities Markets

Asset managers in developed nations for institutions, such as pension funds, insurance companies, mutual funds, and for wealthy individuals are investors in developing nation securities markets. It is estimated about $7.5 trillion have been invested in the principal markets of the United States, Europe, and Japan. Furthermore, it is estimated this pool of assets is growing at the rate of 15% annually.[17]

The goal of diversification has been the principal motivation for portfolio flows to developing nation securities markets. The returns in these markets have been attractive. However, there are several specific risks facing investors in these markets. For example, accounting standards are frequently inferior and do not conform to commonly accepted international standards. Furthermore, the quality and timeliness of company and market information are inadequate. Second, the underlying value of securities is difficult to estimate, partly due to unreliable company information, and partly due to a variety of factors, such as, distortions of floatation pricing, the speculative nature of some markets and thinness (lack of or limited trading) in others. Third, there is widespread insider trading, and corruption and political interference compound risks in these markets. Finally, while transactional efficiency is regarded as improving in developing nation securities markets, supervisory standards are uneven and lack of price transparency (immediate publication of prices at which significant trades are conducted) magnify the risks.[18]

Authorities in developing nations have taken a cautious attitude towards opening their securities markets towards foreign investors for several reasons. First, portfolio investments in developing nation securities markets are easily reversible if economic conditions deteriorate and can exacerbate the balance of payments situation. Further, portfolio inflows may become relatively costly when future dividend, interest, and withdrawal or repayment of accumulated capital is taken into account. Second, equity investments provide foreign investors potential control over domestic corporations. Third, as a consequence, foreign investors may dominate the market, key sectors of industry, and the financial services sector.[19]

Developing nations have responded by erecting a variety of barriers to foreign portfolio investments. First, as an alternative to opening securities markets, domestic authorities may limit investments to approved-country funds. This strategy facilitates the control of the flow of funds in and out of the country. However, the disadvantage is that the country's funds accrue the premium over net asset value, which price benefit does not readily translate to the individual corporations that constitute the fund portfolio. Second, authorities implement restrictions on foreign exchange transactions by requiring registrations of purchases and authorizations of remittances. Delays associated with these administrative procedures create a separate currency risk for the investor. Third, barriers may be created to retain domestic ownership and control of the corporate sector. These barriers may be in the form of limits on foreign ownership, the use of nonvoting stock for foreign investors, or different classes of stock with limited or nonexercisable voting rights. A final barrier relates to tax policies on dividends and capital gains on foreign investments. Tax disincentives should be carefully evaluated in developing nations seeking to attract foreign capital.[20]

5.5. Conclusion

Given the issues discussed in the preceding paragraphs, it is clear developing nations need to design specific strategies to promote the creation and growth of securities markets. First, tax and monetary policies that favor borrowing rather than financing through the issue of securities need to be reformed. In some countries, dividends are subject to double taxation when investors pay withholding taxes and corporations pay taxes on profits, whereas the real cost of borrowing may even be negative. Second, institutional investors, such as pension and mutual funds and unit trusts, are prohibited in some developing nations from investing in securities markets. Such institutions impart liquidity and contribute to active securities markets; hence, appropriate regulations need to be introduced.

6.0. SOME CONCLUDING REMARKS

The role of securities markets in developing nations has been delineated. The global trend towards financial liberalization has been unmistakably set on its course. The political metamorphoses in Eastern Europe in the early nineties has provided additional impetus to the structural economic transition.

Previous discussions in this chapter have emphasized the benefits provided by securities markets. Foremost among these is the fact that they promote direct investment by savers, irrespective of the level of investment, and thus provide effective portfolio diversification. Conversely, corporate users of these funds are able to pool investments from a large body of individuals. An active secondary market for securities provides liquidity to these investments, which is further enhanced by the presence of institutional investors. Finally, securities markets instill managerial discipline by imposing the overhanging threat of corporate takeovers.

Given the sophisticated nature of securities markets and the instruments traded in them, developing nations are required to provide an essential "infrastructure." A legal framework within which contracts can be designed and implemented is the basic prerequisite. Accounting information needs to be standardized and brought in conformance with accepted international standards. Communications and computing technologies are essential to the functioning of a modern securities market. Finally, an efficient banking system promotes the smooth flow of transactions. A substantial portion of this "infrastructure" is based on the development of human capital. Thus securities markets have an important downstream role along the path of development.

Problems of adverse selection and moral hazard in the presence of asymmetric information abound in developing ecomomies. Neither bank-loan financing nor equity-market financing is immune to such problems. Future research will indicate whether the net efficiency of investment improves with either alternative or with some optimal combination of the two.

NOTES

1. The efficient market hypotheses (EMH) literature posits three levels of capital-market efficiency. *Weak form efficiency* implies that current prices impound the past history

of prices. *Semistrong-form efficiency* posits that current prices reflect not only the past history of prices, but also all current publicly available information, which includes company reports and announcements, macroeconomic, and regulatory information. *Strong-form efficiency* postulates that current prices impound the past history of prices, publicly available information, as well as privately available information. Tobin's *complete information arbitrage efficiency* refers to semistrong-form efficiency. If the market were to be semistrong-form efficient, it would not be possible to gain on average from trading on the basis of generally available information.

2. See Fry (1988), pp. 237–40.
3. See Sametz (1981).
4. Meier (1983), p. 231.
5. See Dorfman (1967), p. 113.
6. See Black, Jensen, and Scholes (1972). However, for an argument that the CAPM cannot be tested, see the critique by Roll (1977).
7. The initial development of the APM was in Ross (1976).
8. See Fry (1988), p. 289.
9. This conclusion follows from Theorems 3 and 4 in Stiglitz and Weiss (1981).
10. From a practical standpoint, it is questionable whether the DeMeza and Webb assumption of an ample supply of high-quality projects is descriptive of developing countries.
11. See Shiller (1982), Leroy and Porter (1981), Cutler, Poterba, and Summers (1988), and DeLong, Shleifer, and Summers (1989).
12. See Mayer (1989).
13. This argument reinforces the stages of financial development posited by Kumar and Tsetsekos (1992). An extension of this idea is as follows. If management-skills creation is a consequence of investment in human capital, then an underdeveloped nation is characterized by a corporate sector with an accumulated stock of human capital less than that accumulated in the banking sector, whereas in a developed nation the accumulated stock of human capital in the corporate sector is larger than that in the banking sector.
14. See Reilly (1989), Table 3.7, p. 104.
15. Reilly and Drzycimski (1981), in their study of common stocks in three market tiers, report that lower-tier firms experienced a decline in relative market liquidity and dividend payout and a increase in stock price volatility and financial leverage.
16. See Reilly and Wachowicz (1979) and Reilly and Wright (1984).
17. See World Institute for Development Economics Research (1990). It is estimated that the net investment in developing nation securities markets has been of the order of $1 billion a year for the past five years.
18. Ibid., p. 18.
19. Ibid., p. 20.
20. Ibid., pp. 21–22.

6

Financial Intermediation
through Development Banks

1. INTRODUCTION

With the advent of the industrial revolution in the early nineteenth century, long-term financing of investment to promote economic growth was provided by some commercial banks. These financial institutions performed the entrepreneurial function of providing risky, long-term funds for enterprises engaged in new economic activities. Such institutions, which primarily concentrated on promoting industrial activities, were known as industrial banks. They provided "risk" or "equity" capital and long-term loans for promising projects promoting new products or technology. These institutions were particularly active in the period 1890–1930, selling stocks and bonds all over the world to finance industrial activities.

Modern-day development banks perform functions similar to those of the erstwhile industrial banks. They underwrite securities and offer financial advice in the creation of new enterprises. In the 1930s, the first public financial institutions were established in Mexico, Chile, Japan, and Venezuela to channelize public credit into long-term funds to finance investments. After World War II, these institutions assumed even greater importance as the need for the reconstruction of war-ravaged countries gained top priority. Table 6.1 presents a recent survey, which estimates the world-wide distribution of DBks.[1]

The contributions of development banks to project identification, selection, financing, and performance monitoring are "catalytic" in nature. They assist entrepreneurs in selecting technology and disseminating technical knowledge. Hence, they are described as creating and promoting human capital. This concept is developed further in this chapter, which is arranged as follows. Section 2 describes the five-fold functions of a development bank. Section 3 develops a linear programming model of a development bank that maximizes the human capital created through the projects it finances. Four broad issues relating to the

Table 6.1
World-wide Distribution of Development Banks

Region	Number	Percentage of Total
Latin America	150	35
Asia and Pacific	90	21
Africa	100	24
Europe and Middle East	85	20
TOTAL	425	100

Source: Bruck (1991), p. 21

operations of development banks are described in Section 4. Section 5 describes financial strategy and the role of development banks in the 1990s.

2. THE NATURE OF DEVELOPMENT BANKS

A development bank (DBk) is a financial institution explicitly charged with financing development in specified economic sectors. Activities of DBks are project-oriented; these projects are long-term and risky.

2.1. Functions of a Development Bank

Functional activities of DBks can be categorized into five broad areas. First, DBks supply credit on the *appraisal of specific projects*. In this respect, they are unlike commercial banks, which extend credit to enterprises on the strength of their finances. Through careful appraisal of the financial, economic, technical, managerial, and legal aspects of the project, DBks reduce the risks of a specific loan. Further, by creating a portfolio of such carefully appraised projects, overall lending risk to the institution is reduced. A second important function of DBks is *project promotion*. Promotional activities include identification of unexplored economic opportunities and motivation of entrepreneurship. Third, DBks can be important vehicles for *capital-market development*. Institutions, such as capital markets, for raising long-term capital are absent in the early stages of development of a nation. DBks serve as effective substitutes or proxies for capital markets. By initiating the flow of long-term capital, DBks contribute to capital-market development. Fourth, DBks also function as *syndicate managers*, when the funds needed to finance a project exceed its capabilities, by combining private, official, external, and domestic sources. By arranging *co-financing* packages, DBks integrate different loans, such as, multilateral loans, supplier's credits, bilateral loans and private bank credits. In this activity, DBks assume a "catalytic role" when they assist potential borrowers in locating new sources of financing. Through its endorsement of a project, the DBk facilitates co-financing arrangements.[2] In addition, DBks play a key role in the selection and transfer of appropriate technology. Finally, specialized technical services for the design and operations of modern production facilities are lacking in many developing nations. DBks perform a *technical assistance function* by either importing or assisting in building indigenous strengths in technical fields. This function may take the form of creation of domestic research institutions, consulting firms, and institutional capacities for technical training. The provision of technical assistance is an activity that distinguishes development banks from commercial banks.[3] Thus, DBks need to acquire expertise in diverse fields, such as financial engineering, risk management, corporate restructuring, and investment banking.

Performances of DBks in financing industrial investment have been mixed. Even though DBks have provided a small fraction of total loans in most countries, their share of term finance and foreign exchange loans has been higher.[4] DBks lending to small-scale enterprises have provided their clients with technical assistance, including production, marketing, and financial planning. DBks have introduced greater discipline in investment appraisal and these techniques have been adopted by other financial institutions. DBks have also contributed to the national accumulation of human capital by creating a pool of trained operations officers, accountants, engineers, and economists, whose expertise has been available to other financial institutions, industry, and government. The following section describes a linear programming model, which focuses on the human capital creation characteristic of the DBk.

3. A CONCEPTUAL MODEL OF THE DEVELOPMENT BANKING FIRM

3.1. Development Banks as Creators of Human Capital

The contributions of DBks in project identification, selection, financing and monitoring have been largely "catalytic" in nature. DBks assist entrepreneurs in selecting technology and disseminate technical knowledge for development. Thus, DBks create and promote human capital.

The recent literature on aggregate growth identifies human capital as a significant variable in the process of economic development. Lucas (1988) uses human capital to explain the differences in growth rates of nations. He defines human capital as an individual's general skill level, so that "a worker with human capital $h(t)$ is the productive equivalent of two workers with $h(t)/2$ each, or a half time worker with $2h(t)$" (p. 17). Furthermore, the way an individual allocates his time over various activities in the current period affects his productivity, or his $h(t)$ level, in future periods. Romer's (1990) model implies that an economy with a larger total stock of human capital will experience faster growth. Levine (1990) describes growth as occuring only if agents invest a sufficient amount in projects that augment human capital and stimulate technological innovation. He assumes productivity growth to occur in firms in which groups of people invent, innovate, and produce together.

The primary function of a development bank is creating, augmenting, and promoting human capital. By undertaking long-term investments, the DBk ensures that the average quantity of resources maintained in firms increases the human capital of each agent, which in turn contributes to increased economic growth.

Let us assume that entrepreneurs provide seed capital in the form of their equity, S_j, in the jth firm. This equity component is a small component of the total financing needs of the firm, which is completed by borrowing D_j at interest rate k_j from the DBk. The DBk therefore maximizes its portfolio of loans to firms, which in turn increases human capital and thereby aggregate growth, subject to a set of constraints.

3.2. Constraint Set of the DBk

Assume that the DBk has a capital structure consisting of debt B and equity S. It allocates this capital in the form of loans to individual firms. If FRR_j is the financial rate of return of the jth firm's project (each firm has only one project), then the return on the DBk's portfolio should equal at least its opportunity cost of capital (OCC). This constraint is represented as

$$\sum_{j=1}^{n} FRR_j D_j / (B + S) \geq OCC \tag{6.1}$$

The DBk's portfolio of projects should not only be financially viable but should have satisfactory economic rates of return. The economic rate of return (ERR) of a project is the discount rate at which its discounted economic benefits equal its discounted economic costs. Economic costs and benefits exclude "transfer payments," such as duties and taxes, and rely on international or border prices for traded goods and "shadow prices" for nontraded goods.[5] The average ERR of the projects in the DBk's portfolio should equal at least its opportunity cost of capital (OCC).

$$\sum_{j=1}^{n} ERR_j D_j / (B + S) \geq OCC \tag{6.2}$$

Financial and economic rates of return relate to the cash flows over the entire life of the project. However, it is important that each project have adequate liquidity to meet its interest payments in every period. If R_j represents the revenue generated by the project, M_j is the material consumed at a cost C, L_j is the labor input in the jth project at wage w, this constraint requires that the interest coverage ratio be not less than the desired level (IC_j)

$$(R_j - M_j C - L_j w) / k_j D_j \geq IC_j, \quad j = 1, 2, \ldots, n \tag{6.3}$$

or

$$OI_j/k_jD_j \geq IC_j, \quad j = 1, 2, \ldots, n \tag{6.3a}$$

where $(R_j - M_jC - L_jw) = OI_j$ is the operating income of the jth firm.

The DBk sets an internal constraint to ensure adequate diversification among the projects it finances. This constraint states that the amount lent to each project does not exceed a specified fraction θ (<1) of its total resources

$$D_j \leq \theta(B + S), \quad j = 1, 2, \ldots, n \tag{6.4}$$

The DBk needs to earn an adequate spread on its loan portfolio over its cost of funds to ensure its financial viability. This constraint states that the weighted average interest rate on its loan portfolio is not less than some multiple ϕ (>1) of its weighted average cost of capital $WACC$

$$\sum_{j=1}^{n} k_jD_j/(B + S) \geq \phi WACC \tag{6.5}$$

The DBk is subject to a budget constraint that ensures that the allocations to various projects do not exceed its available financial resources

$$\sum_{j=1}^{n} D_j \leq (B + S) \tag{6.6}$$

Material resources in the economy are limited to some aggregate level M. Material consumption in a project is determined by the technology adopted. If the material consumed in each project is proportionate to the level of investment, and is thereby a multiple (μ_j) of each DBk loan, then

$$\sum_{j=1}^{n} \mu_j D_j \leq M \tag{6.7}$$

Similarly, the supply of labor is limited to some aggregate level L. Labor absorption in the project is determined by the technology adopted. If labor input in each project is proportionate to the level of investment and is therefore a multiple (λ_j) of each DBk loan, then

$$\sum_{j=1}^{n} \lambda_j D_j \leq L \tag{6.8}$$

The DBk allocates its resources to maximize the human capital created. Human capital depends on the capital invested in each project and, hence, on lending by the DBk. However, projects are not homogenous in the creation of human capital. Inputs to human capital may be measured by the success of the projects, that is, financial and economic rates of return and their liquidity—all of which are desirable financial qualities—cost of financing, labor employed, and material consumed. The multiplier h_j, which is determined by the technology selected, differentiates among projects. The objective function of the DBk is therefore

$$\max_{D_j} \sum_{j=1}^{n} h_j D_j \tag{6.9}$$

The nonnegativity constraints are $D_j \geq 0, j = 1, 2, \ldots, n$.

Equations (6.1–6.9) represent the primal version of the linear programming model of the DBk. We now consider the primal along with its complement, the dual model, to gain useful insights. Both models are expressed in their expanded, canonical form.

3.3. The Primal Model

The complete primal model with the objective function and the constraint set is presented below.

$$\max_{h_j} \quad h_1 D_1 \quad + \quad h_2 D_2 \quad + \quad \ldots \quad + h_n D_n \tag{6.10}$$

$$\text{ST} \quad - FRR_1 D_1/(B + S) - FRR_2 D_2/(B + S) - \ldots - FRR_n D_n/(B + S) + u_1 = -OCC \tag{6.11}$$

$$- ERR_1 D_1/(B + S) - ERR_2 D_2/(B + S) - \ldots - ERR_n D_n/(B + S) + u_2 = -OCC \tag{6.12}$$

$$IC_1 k_1 D_1 \qquad\qquad\qquad\qquad\qquad\qquad + u_{3.1} = OI_1 \tag{6.13.1}$$

$$IC_2 k_2 D_2 \qquad\qquad\qquad\qquad + u_{3.2} = OI_2 \tag{6.13.2}$$

$$\cdots \qquad\qquad \cdots \qquad\qquad \cdots$$

$$IC_n k_n D_n \qquad\qquad\qquad + u_{3.n} = OI_n \tag{6.13.n}$$

$$D_1 \qquad\qquad\qquad\qquad\qquad + u_{4.1} = \theta(B + S) \tag{6.14.1}$$

$$D_2 \qquad\qquad\qquad + u_{4.2} = \theta(B + S) \tag{6.14.2}$$

$$\cdots \qquad\qquad \cdots \qquad\qquad \cdots$$

$$D_n \qquad + u_{4.n} = \theta(B + S) \tag{6.14.n}$$

$$-k_1 D_1/(B + S) \quad - k_2 D_2/(B + S) - \ldots \quad - k_n D_n/(B + S) + u_5 = -\phi WACC \tag{6.15}$$

$$D_1 \quad + \quad D_2 \quad + \ldots + \quad D_n \quad + u_6 = (B + S) \tag{6.16}$$

$$\mu_1 D_1 \quad + \quad \mu_2 D_2 \quad + \ldots + \quad \mu_n D_n \quad + u_7 = M \tag{6.17}$$

$$\lambda_1 D_1 \quad + \quad \lambda_2 D_2 \quad + \ldots + \quad \lambda_n D_n \quad + u_8 = L \tag{6.18}$$

$$D_j \geq 0, j = 1, 2, \ldots, n. \tag{6.19}$$

$$u_i \geq 0, i = 1, 2, 3.1, \ldots, 3.n, 4.1, \ldots, 4.n, 5, \ldots, 8. \tag{6.19'}$$

3.4. The Dual Model

Let y_i be the dual variable associated with the ith constraint. Then the dual model with its objective function and the constraint set appears as below.

$$\min_{y_j} - (OCC)(y_1 + y_2) + OI_1 y_{3.1} + \ldots + OI_n y_{3.n} + \theta(B + S)(y_{4.1} + \ldots + y_{4.n})$$

$$- \phi(WACC)y_5 + (B + S)y_6 + My_7 + Ly_8 \tag{6.20}$$

$$ST - (FRR_1)y_1/(B + S) - (ERR_1)y_2/(B + S) + IC_1 k_1 y_{3.1} + y_{4.1} - k_1 y_5/(B + S)$$

$$+ y_6 + \mu_1 y_7 + \lambda_1 y_8 - v_1 = h_1 \tag{6.21}$$

$$- (FRR_2)y_1/(B + S) - (ERR_2)y_2/(B + S) + IC_2 k_2 y_{3.2} + y_{4.2} - k_2 y_5/(B + S)$$

$$+ y_6 + \mu_2 y_7 + \lambda_2 y_8 - v_2 = h_2 \tag{6.22}$$

$$\ldots \qquad\qquad \ldots \qquad\qquad \ldots \qquad\qquad \ldots$$

$$- (FRR_n)y_n/(B + S) - (ERR_n)y_n/(B + S) + IC_n k_n y_{3.n} + y_{4.n} - k_n y_5/(B + S)$$

$$+ y_n + \mu_n y_7 + \lambda_n y_8 - v_8 = h_n \tag{6.23}$$

$$y_i \ge 0, \; i = 1, 2, 3.1, \ldots, 3.n, 4.1, \ldots, 4.n, 5, \ldots, 8. \tag{6.24}$$

$$v_j \ge 0, \; j = 1, 2, \ldots, n. \tag{6.24'}$$

3.5. Interrelations between the Primal and Dual Models

The optimal values of the objective functions of the primal and dual are equal. Hence

$$h_1 D_1^* + h_2 D_2^* + \ldots + h_n D_n^* = (OCC)(y_1^* + y_2^*) + OI_1 y_{3.1}^* + \ldots + OI_n y_{3.n}^*$$

$$+ \theta(B + S)(y_{4.1}^* + \ldots + y_{4.n}^*) - \phi(WACC)y_5^* + (B + S)y_6^* + My_7^* + Ly_8^* \tag{6.25}$$

Decision variables marked with asterisks are at their optimal levels, i.e., the variables are optimal solutions to the primal and dual problems.

Dual variables ("shadow prices") have positive, nonzero values only if the corresponding constraint in the primal is binding, i.e., the related primal slack variable is zero. Hence

$$u_1^* y_1^* = u_2^* y_2^* = u_{3.1}^* y_{3.1}^* = \ldots = u_{3.n}^* y_{3.n}^* = \ldots = u_{4.1}^* y_{4.1}^* = \ldots = u_{4.n}^* y_{4.n}^*$$

$$= u_5^* y_5^* = u_6^* y_6^* = u_7^* y_7^* = u_8^* y_8^* = \ldots = 0 \tag{6.26}$$

Decision variables in the primal have positive, nonzero values only if the corresponding constraint in the dual is binding, i.e., the surplus variable is zero. Hence

$$D_1^* v_1^* = D_2^* v_2^* = D_3^* v_3^* = \ldots = D_n^* v_n^* = 0 \tag{6.27}$$

Equations (6.26) and (6.27) provide useful intuition into the decision framework of the DBk. The dual variable is a "value" attached to each primal constraint that indicates the marginal increase (decrease) in the primal objective function (eq. 6.25) with the increase (decrease) of the constraint limit (right side of the constraint equation). Equation (6.26) assigns a nonzero "value" ($y_k > 0$) to constraint k only if the constraint is binding, i.e., the constraint is met with equality or $u_k = 0$. If the constraint is met with inequality, i.e., $u_k > 0$, an increase in the constraint limit does not improve the objective function value beyond its current level in eq. (6.25). In this case the constraint has no value, or $y_k = 0$. For example, if the average financial rate of return on the DBk's portfolio is 15% when the opportunity cost of capital is 12% in equation 6.11, any decrease in the opportunity cost of capital will not improve the objective function value. Or if the funds available for investment in the DBk were $10 million (eq. 6.16) and it could disburse only $8.5 million, an increase in its resources would not improve the objective function.

When will the DBk choose to finance the kth project? The constraints in the dual model state that the contribution to human capital development by the kth project is a linear function of its appropriately valued attributes. The argument set ("inputs") of this function includes, *inter alia,* the kth project's contribution to the DBk portfolio financial rate of return, contribution to the portfolio economic rate of return, consumption of material inputs, employment of labor, and interest rate earned on the loan. The appropriately valued "inputs" are required to be in equilibrium with the human capital generated by the kth project. For example, the larger the kth project's financial and economic rates of return and interest earned on its loan, and the smaller its material consumption or labor absorption, the more likely its loan by the DBk.

3.6. Policy Interventions and DBk Performance

Policy interventions in the operations of the DBk may take the form of directed investments and interest rate controls. Requiring the DBk to lend to certain sectors or to certain kinds of projects can affect the optimal level of human capital generated. For example, if the new project had less than average financial and economic rates of return, these slack variables may be nonzero and the corresponding dual variable equal to zero, which would affect the equilibrium between the kth project's "inputs" and its contribution (human capital) to the objective function. The kth project thus may not be ordinarily selected for investment.

If the DBk were forced to subsidize certain projects with low-interest financing, it reduces the probability of default as well as the spread earned over the DBk's cost of capital. It is also possible that the subsidized projects contribute very little to the portfolio financial and economic rates of return. Obviously, which effect dominates depends on the relative magnitudes of the parameters. If the cost of capital to the DBk were increased administratively, e.g., the authorities increased the interest rate the DBk pays on its borrowings, its optimal allocations and thus the human capital generated by its portfolios are affected.

4. ISSUES RELATING TO THE OPERATIONS OF DEVELOPMENT BANKS

Perhaps the most pervasive concern is that few DBks have transformed themselves into financially viable, autonomous institutions with the capacity to raise resources both at home and abroad. While pursuing developmental objectives, DBks need to maintain portfolio quality and earnings. Arrearages on their loan portfolios have eroded the quality of DBk assets. The average return on assets would have been negative had there been adequate provisions for loan losses. The immediate cause for this problem has been the impact of global recession in the 1980s, currency devaluations, and higher real interest rates at home and abroad. Four broad reasons identified in the following paragraphs have contributed to the perceived problems of DBks.

4.1. Corporate Reliance on Debt Financing

Few developing nations in the 1960s and '70s had devoted resources to the creation and promotion of capital markets. Consequently, DBks provided debt capital to finance corporate investments. Such borrowing firms had inadequate equity financing to withstand the shocks of the early 1980s. The inability of these firms to service their debts is reflected in the arrearages of DBk portfolios. Risky ventures financed with debt capital distribute asymmetric benefits. The benefits of the high returns of successful, risky projects accrue to their private sponsors, while lenders share in the losses of the unsuccessful projects. On average, a portfolio of such loans will reflect arrears and operating losses.

4.2. Directed Credit

In the 1970s, DBks were viewed as tools of development policy, channeling their resources to priority sectors that commercial lenders found unattractive. Many governments directed credits from DBks for low interest rate lending to public and quasipublic enterprises. The spreads in such loans did not reflect operating costs or incorporate adequate risk premia. When economic problems arose in the 1980s, the priority sectors financed by the DBks were unable to service their debts, thus contributing to the financing institution's arrearages. In cases of such directed credit, financial discipline was poor, and political considerations prevented DBks from foreclosing delinquent loans. The beneficiaries of subsidized credit, therefore, had strong incentives to delay servicing of debt.

In some instances, government intervention in credit markets has been directed at correcting financial market imperfections. Financial markets are fragmented and distorted and do not allocate resources efficiently. Financial markets may be distributed among geographic regions, between urban and rural sectors and, in some cases, among classes of borrowers. Lack of communication between suppliers and users of funds prevents the flow of funds. Equity funds outside the immediate family for risky new ventures may be nonexistent. In some cases, oligopolistic banks affiliated with certain industrial groups may restrict the free flow of funds and contribute to credit rationing.

The experience of the World Bank indicates that directed credit programs have not been successful.[6] Subsidized credit does not compensate for intrinsic distortions in the real sector.

4.3. Resource Mobilization

A few DBks, such as ICICI (India), BNDES (Brazil), KDB (South Korea), and BNDE (Morocco), have successfully raised resources from foreign commercial sources. Others, such as the Colombian *financieras*, have raised a substantial portion of their resources in domestic markets. In practice, few DBks met the mobilization objectives to become self-sufficient institutions. They had little or no impact on overall resource mobilization activities in the country. Easy availability of funds from governments and foreign official lenders vitiated DBk efforts at resource mobilization.

4.4. Structure of Interest Rates

A related issue is the overall structure of deposit and lending interest rates. This issue has implications both for the operational efficiency of DBks and for resource mobilization. DBks were required to make loans at interest rates that precluded mobilization of resources at commercial terms. These interest rates did not incorporate loan loss premia and the cost of promotional services they were asked to provide. DBks were also facing competition from other financial institutions, such as commercial banks, and, hence, were unwilling to increase interest rates. Furthermore, larger and more creditworthy enterprises were able to raise funds in international capital markets, either directly or indirectly, with the assistance of commercial banks. Thus the impact of DBk operations on reform of interest rate structure has been minimal.

5. FINANCIAL STRATEGIES AND THE ROLE OF DBks

DBks were not the engines of finance for promoting economic growth in 1970s and 1980s as was expected. For the most part, the reasons for their performances falling short of expectations may be attributed to some, if not all, factors falling outside their control. Unfavorable interest rate regimes and directed credit affected their profitability and eventual solvency. With the global movement towards market-oriented decision systems in the 1990s, the prospective role of DBks has undergone a major change. These institutions can assume a catalytic role in the transition. The primary role for DBks lies in influencing and assisting the authorities to build free and healthy financial systems. Such policy actions will improve the liquidity and solvency of both firms and financial institutions. In the long run, these actions will contribute to increasing the growth in the supply of finance.

The extent of the catalytic role possible for the DBk will depend on the size, state of development, and degree of distortions in the country. For example, in small, least developed countries, the DBk should promote simple financial systems with limited number of institutions and instruments. Some distortions in financial markets are inevitable but perhaps these are at acceptable levels. In more complex economies, however, the challenges facing the DBk are greater. Financial institutions, instruments, policies, and infrastructure need to match the development of the productive sectors. Depending on the state of the national economy, three sets of strategic activities are identified for the DBk.

5.1. Diversification of Activities

Given the challenges placed on the DBks, they should improve their profitability and flexibility over the business cycle through diversification. Examples of such activities include the provision of working capital and trade finance to the firms they support. Leasing, a form of term financing with better provisions for asset recovery in the case of default, is a less risky form of diversification. Provision of consultancy services for product identification, selection of appropriate technology, and marketing is another possibility. The guiding principle to selection of such activities is that they should be complementary to the existing term-finance business of the DBk. Activities that focus on the accumulated experiences of their staff and established client relationships are potential low-cost candidates.

5.2. Development of Capital Markets

In most developing nations, financial markets for nondepository instruments, such as money market instruments, debentures, long-term bonds, and equity shares are underdeveloped. Development of these markets is essential for two reasons. First to encourage financial savings, and second, to provide competition for conservative, oligopolistic banking systems. In particular, the provision of equity capital calls for a variety of financial institutions. These include *equity financing institutions*, such as venture capital companies and mutual funds, which provide direct capital for new companies as well as capital for restructuring of established companies; *security market institutions*, such as brokerage firms, merchant and investment banks, securities-finance companies, asset-management companies, credit-rating agencies, and mutual fund management companies; *specialized term-finance institutions*, such as leasing and hire–purchase companies, housing- and export-financing companies; *contractual savings institutions*, such as pension fund management companies and insurance companies; and *foreign-investment trusts,* which facilitate foreign-portfolio investment in domestic securities markets, such as the proliferating company funds. While the DBk cannot legitimately claim participation in all these activities, it is particularly suited for investment and merchant banking. As a result of their long-term association with firms, they are in a postion to "certify" issue prices as reflecting future prospects of these firms.

5.3. Promotion of the Financial Infrastructure

DBks can assist in creating the financial infrastructure that facilitates transactions. This includes the creation of accounting and auditing standards to ensure uniformity and transparency of transactions. Communications technology that permits quick transfer and uniform accessibility of information is essential for modern financial transactions. Finally, there needs to be in place the legal framework to enforce contracts and a regulatory environment that encourages financial prudence, discipline, and arms'-length relations among financial institutions, savers, and borrowers.

6. CONCLUSION

Given the political changes of the 1990s, DBks face major challenges and opportunities. Three goals can be identified to ensure their continued participation in the development process. First, they should be self-supporting—they must develop strengths to raise funds in domestic and foreign markets at reasonable costs and in amounts adequate to maintain an acceptable scale of operations. Second, quality of operations should ensure profitability with diversified financial services. Third, the DBk needs to accumulate human capital with organizational and management strengths to ensure its capacity to develop independently.

Performances of DBks have been mixed. The problems they have encountered have been partly of their own making and partly due to policy interventions. Inadequate supervision and monitoring of projects and client firms have led to arrearages and defaults. These problems have been further exacerbated by pressure on the DBks in the form of directed credit and controlled interest rates. Will DBks have a role in providing development finance in the 1990s? In nations that are in the early stages of their development, DBks will have a major role. With a dearth of other financial institutions, DBks may be the only channel for development finance. As the nation evolves in its development process towards more market-oriented decision systems, DBks need to evolve as well. They need to provide additional services, such as working capital and leasing facilities. DBks may be required to participate in the process of creating and sustaining capital markets. Their accumulated experience in project selection and monitoring may stand them in good stead in providing valuable investment banking services.

NOTES

1. For a detailed description of the history of these financial institutions, see Bruck (1991).
2. The endorsement of the project may be seen as offering the DBk's reputational capital

as a performance guarantee or bond. Further, DBk's financing of a project is analogous to a firm-commitment contract offered by an investment banker. See Chapter 4 for a discussion of this point.

3. See Bruck (1991), pp. 27–30.
4. Recent data on the performances of DBks are not available. Gordon (1983), for example, discusses data drawn from the 1977–79 period.
5. Developing nations exhibit wide disparities between financial and economic rates of return on projects, due to subsidies and other policy elements that create mispricing. In perfect markets, of course, financial and economic rates of return are equal.
6. See *World Development Report, 1989*, pp. 55–57.

7

The Trend towards Privatization

1. INTRODUCTION

The 1980s have witnessed a revolutionary innovation in the economic policies of developed, developing, and the erstwhile socialist nations. In Great Britain, Prime Minister Margaret Thatcher had made privatization the cornerstone of her economic policy. The French government had embarked on a program to sell off a large number of state-owned companies and banks. In the African nations of Angola, Benin, Congo, and Tanzania, governments had begun turning to private-sector management of inefficient state-owned firms. Czechoslovakia, Hungary, and Poland collectively had placed close to 10,000 state-owned firms up for private ownership. *The Economist* reports that in the four years preceding 1993, approximately $200 billion of government assets were privatized throughout the world, of which about 25% were in the developing nations. Privatization in Mexico alone amounted to about $22 billion.[1] All over the world, privatization has become an intrinsic component in the strategies for raising development financing and for allocating resources according to market priorities based on a redefinition of the role of government.

Different descriptions have been applied to the privatization concept. These include "transformation," "denationalization," "rationalization," "commercialization," and "democratization of capital." Barletta (in Hanke, 1987, p. ix) defines privatization as contracting with or selling to private parties the functions or firms previously controlled or owned by governments. Broadly speaking, privatization includes the transfer of functions from government agencies or enterprises to the private sector under conditions where market forces can govern economic choices. Specifically, privatization in one instance may imply the sale of shares (or assets) to private investors including employees. In other cases it may include restructuring certain public-sector activities into smaller businesses, which are then transferred to the private sector. In a third instance it may involve contracting with a private-sector firm to manage an enterprise, sharing in the profits when the enterprise becomes profitable. In other instances privatization may be accompanied by elimination of government pricing regulations, licensing requirements, foreign-exchange controls, subsidies, tariffs, and other restrictions or special treatments to create a level playing field so that private firms can profitably enter the market to offer competitive services.[2]

Many nations had nationalized private firms on the grounds that the existence of large, private firms concentrated power and wealth in the hands of a few individuals. Such concentrations were perceived as diluting the commitment to an egalitarian society. According to this viewpoint, denationalization is a retrograde step towards the reconcentration of wealth. In contrast, privatization calls for the conscious implementation of the sale of firms to *large numbers of individual shareholders*. In this sense, privatization embodies and promotes "peoples' capitalism." Hence, any research into sources of development finance needs to include privatization as an element of policy.

The rest of this chapter has the following organization. The next section describes problems associated with state-owned enterprises and motivations for privatization in developing nations. The conceptual foundations of privatization are discussed in Section 3. Various issues related to privatization, such as legal, tax, political, financing, valuation or pricing, and costs of privatization are covered in Section 4. An overview of the common techniques adopted in privatization is provided in Section 5. Strategic considerations in privatization are described in Section 6. Some of the broader impacts and implications of privatization on wealth distribution and wider share ownership are discussed in Section 7. Section 8 concludes the chapter with the precaution that competitive structures are vital to ensure the success of any privatization program.

2. SOME PRELIMINARY DETAILS

This section identifies the principal motivations for privatization. It is useful to start at the source, namely, state-owned enterprises (SOEs), their characteristics and the potential problems they may create.

2.1. State-Owned Enterprises: Characteristics and Problems

The special characteristics of SOEs can be categorized into those relating to their management or administration and aspects stemming from political considerations.

Management in SOEs tend to be bureaucratic in nature, with emphasis on processes rather than on results. Frequent changes in top personnel may result in discontinuity in management. There may be a reluctance to delegate authority, which fosters a general lack of accountability at all levels. Given its political nature, management in SOEs finds itself unable to negotiate freely. Lack of accurate or up-to-date financial records may compound the management problems of SOEs. Inadequate planning may result in underutilized assets and disregarding market values may lead to overvalued assets. Management may lack marketing knowhow and consequently may be insensitive to consumer tastes and desires. A particular weakness exists in personnel management, which results in the inability to penalize unsatisfactory performance due to strong labor union pressures.

Political considerations encourage overstaffing, nepotism, and wasteful practices, such as excessive overtime. Employment of civil service and/or militiary personnel at senior executive levels may be mandated. There may be permanent confusion over conflicting social, political, and economic objectives. These factors result in excessive political interference in routine decisions and operations. Several forms of economic subsidies contribute to such financial losses, such as tariff protection and import restrictions, sole-source supplier status awarded to government agencies, tax exemptions, low-interest borrowing with government guaranties, and legal restrictions to limit market entry by competitors. Politicization of management results in ready acceptance of financial losses for social reasons.

Potential problems arise from government ownership or control of enterprises. First, there are implications for generation and utilization of resources. Scarce resources are diverted for political purposes or personal gain. Capital flight is exacerbated by the lack of private-sector opportunities. These resources are augmented by foreign borrowings, which add to the country's foreign-exchange problems. Operating losses by SOEs have negative impacts on the government's budget deficit and outstanding debt. Activities and transactions in the informal sector expand, with negative impacts on tax revenues and, hence, on the budget deficit. In addition, new investments are either not undertaken or are postponed, contributing to deterioration of facilities and infrstructure. Further, politicians are preoccupied more with SOE operations and less with aspects of policy.

2.2. Motivations for Privatization

The basic reason for privatization is the belief that government-owned and -managed enterprises are not as efficient as privately owned and managed enterprises. The reasons, in most cases, are clear. Citizens in most developing nations depend on their governments to satisfy their basic human needs. Governments find it expedient to absorb the unemployed in the state-owned enterprises. SOEs face two kinds of costs. The explicit cost is the compensation to bureaucrats and the implicit cost is graft and misuse of funds on a large scale. The results are inefficiency, excessive costs, and major losses for the SOEs. The limited resources of developing nations have been diverted to supporting these activities. Slow economic growth and fiscal deficits have led to the realization that these nations cannot afford to support and sustain resource-consuming SOEs. In these circumstances, privatization is a logical alternative. The following motivations for privatization include these and other objectives.

1. *Reduce the financial drain on government.* As mentioned in the preceding

paragraph, operating losses by SOEs cannot be sustained indefinitely. In most cases, it is not possible to privatize the large "loss-generators" in the first round. A sequence of successful privatization transactions demonstrates government's commitment to develop a strong private sector.

2. *Unlock frozen capital in nonproductive government investments.* A second motivation in developing nations is the lack of capital. In some instances, it may be possible to raise cash by the sale of the assets of SOEs. In many cases, the cash raised may be lower than expectations, due to the divergence between market values and book values.

3. *Broaden the base of domestic equity ownership.* In enterprises large enough to support a public stock offering or employee ownership, "democratization of equity capital" is an important objective. A politically acceptable set of buyers is a critical factor determining the eventual acceptance of the privatization scheme.

4. *Attract new capital.* Privatization programs can be means to attract equity capital, both at the domestic and foreign levels. These schemes can attract foreign capital as well as domestic-flight capital from abroad. Funds to finance debt–equity swaps in privatization transactions do not create inflationary pressures, as the nation's debt is not monetized. Thus, privatization is an effective tool to convert foreign debt into equity investment when integrated into the country's debt–equity swap program.

5. *Growth of domestic capital markets.* The rudimentary capital markets available in most developing nations are enlarged by the significant source of new equity offered by the privatized state enterprises.

6. *Create growth-oriented jobs.* The ultimate objective of privatization is the creation of unsubsidized jobs, which have a future.

7. *Enable government to focus on policy.* Privatization enables government to redirect its attention from operations to policy formulation.

3. CONCEPTUAL FOUNDATIONS OF PRIVATIZATION

Two conceptual questions are central to privatization. First, does the ownership structure of the firm affect allocative efficiencies in the marketplace and internal efficiencies? Second, what role do competitive forces have in determining managerial incentives, behavior, and performance? The nature of ownership, public or private, affects the objectives of owners as well as the systems they adopt in monitoring managerial performance. Thus, changes in property rights affect the incentive structures and behavior of management.

3.1. Nature of Ownership and Managerial Incentives

The transfer of an enterprise from the public to the private sector (or vice versa) implies changes in the entitlements of residual profits from its operations. This transfer is accompanied by shifts in the relationships between those individuals responsible for the operations of the enterprise (managers) and the beneficiaries of its profit flows (owners). Such shifts are accompanied by different structures of incentives for management and hence affect managerial behavior and firm performance. These conceptual issues are considered in the following subsections.

3.1.1. Private Ownership. Consider the classic agency problem. A principal seeks to motivate an agent(s), who is contracted to take actions in the interests of the principal, through a suitable incentive structure. The inherent difficulty with this arrangement is that the objectives of the two parties are divergent. Furthermore, there is asymmetry of information—the information set available to each participant is different. The issue then revolves around the optimal incentive schemes that the principals can design to ensure that managerial behavior is not detrimental to their interests. On the other hand, such an incentive scheme needs to be attractive to the agent, who is primarily motivated by considerations of self-interest.

In a private enterprise, the actions of managers (agents) are constrained by internal mechanisms—monitoring by stockholders (principals). In addition, there are external factors constraining management—potential takeover threats by other investors or agents, or by the firm's creditors in the event of bankruptcy.[3] It is usually assumed that shareholders seek to maximize their financial returns from investments in the firm.[4] External auditors and outside directors ensure proper monitoring of management's activities. In addition, the existence of an active market for managerial talent mitigates monitoring activities. On the other hand, public-sector managers are beset by an indentification problem—they cannot associate themselves with a set of clearly unidentifiable owners. Natural consequences are managerial inefficiencies and waste of resources.

Would privatization provide incentives for internal efficiency? The property rights literature responds affirmatively.[5] Two specializations emerge from the availability of private ownership. First, individuals with comparative advantages in certain fields of specialized knowledge capitalize on their knowledge by specialization of ownership.[6] Thus, the potential availability of property rights promotes and facilitates entrepreneurial activity. On the other hand, the absence of property rights deters the search process intrinsic to private entrepreneurial activity. A second specialization made possible with property rights is the separation of ownership and control. Entrepreneurs with the comparative advantage of specialized knowledge have active roles in controlling and managing the activities of the firm, whereas other suppliers of capital—stockholders and debtholders—have passive roles. Such specialization is made possible by divisibility of property rights into smaller transaction-facilitating units, ownership of which may be transferred in secondary markets. Such distinct separation of ownership and control and the accompanying advantages are not available with public ownership structures.

How do property rights arise? Demsetz (1967) offers an interesting explanation. Opportunities to invest are continuously being created in markets. Such opportunities arise from changing tastes, new technologies, more efficient methods of meeting demand, etc. Entrepreneurs evaluate such opportunities and capitalize on them when the accompanying benefits exceed the related costs. Demsetz (1967, p. 350) observes, ". . . property rights develop to internalize externalities when the gains of internalization become larger than the cost of internalization." On the other hand, public ownership is characterized by asymmetry of information between political decision makers and entrepreneurs; thus the former do not have the comparative advantage in identifying worthwhile projects that the latter have.

3.1.2. Public Ownership. In publicly owned firms, the function of monitoring managerial performance is entrusted to government departments. A comparision with privately owned firms reveals the following differences. First, the principals of publicly owned firms do not seek to maximize their market value because there are no marketable shares. Hence, there is no market for corporate control. Second, there is no equivalent to the bankruptcy constraint on financial performance.

Public-interest theories generally assume that government departments maximize economic welfare—they act in the interests of their citizens. The welfare function is represented as a linear combination of consumers' and producers' surpluses. Public ownership may have potential advantages over the private alternative *if and only if* monitoring is equally effective under both types of ownership. What are the stated benefits of public ownership? First, public ownership can deal more effectively with failures in product and factor markets; for example, public ownership may be the preferred alternative to a profit-maximizing monopolist whose practices may run counter to public interest.[7] Second, monitoring by a government department is more focused and hence more effective than monitoring by disparate shareholders. Third, public ownership avoids the transactions costs associated with share purchases by corporate raiders seeking to gain control of a firm. Fourth, government departments can directly intervene in the managerial decision-making process or can set appropriate incentive structures for managers of publicly owned firms.

Successful performance monitoring depends on the supply of relevant information. Competition in the process of information search leads to greater efficiency. In public ownership, there is just one body monitoring performance; with private ownership, specialists and institutions participate in a competitive market for information, thus leading to more effective monitoring of private ownership.

Would privatization provide incentives for internal efficiency? When an enterprise is transferred from the public sector, private ownership of shares creates a market for corporate control. This transfer provides incentives for promoting internal efficiency. When management does not maximize market value by deploying existing and potential resources of the enterprise effectively, it is susceptible to takeover bids from other participants, with consequent loss of control. However, takeovers are also motivated by managerial preferences for control of large asset bases ("empire building"), possibilities of increasing market share, or reduction in corporate tax liabilities. Vickers and Yarrow (1989, pp. 19–21) develop a simple model of corporate takeover linking managerial effort and the probability of takeover. Lower internal efficiency results in a more active market for corporate control. Since there are other motivations for takeovers than the potential capital gains from correction of poor managerial performance, the creation of freely transferable property rights associated with privatization does not imply an automatic improvement in internal efficiency. Whether the general threat of takeover results in improvements in internal efficiency depends on country-specific factors, such as the extent of shareholder protection provided by law, extent of permissible competition, and the relevant fiscal system.

3.1.3. Ownership and Economic Efficiency. Consider the case when public monitoring arrangements are no less efficient than private mechanisms. Public managers are assumed to set price equal to marginal cost, whereas profit-maximizing private managers set marginal price equal to marginal cost. In this situation, public managers produce more and set a lower price than private managers. Furthermore, public managers have greater incentives to reduce unit costs, since the resultant savings are spread across their larger volume of output. Hence, it can be concluded that public managers produce more and make greater cost-reduction efforts, leading to higher levels of social welfare. Private ownership will be superior to public ownership only if it provides significantly better managerial incentives than the control system for public enterprise. Nevertheless, there are several reasons for suboptimal control in publicly owned enterprises in actual practice. First, it is easy for social objectives to be superseded by political objectives. Second, there is a preference for direct political intervention in managerial decisions than an "arms'-length" relationship would dictate. Third, internal inefficiencies prevent adequate control in public enterprises.

The empirical evidence generally supports the view that privately owned firms tend on average to be more internally efficient when competition in product markets is effective.[8]

3.2. Privatization and Competitive Forces

While the concepts of privatization and liberalization are interrelated, it is helpful to distinguish between them. Privatization refers to the transfer of ownership, whereas liberalization is the unshackling of market forces. The presence of public enterprises does not necessarily preclude the existence of a competitive environment. However, as a practical matter, public enterprises and the lack of competition have been coexistent for two reasons. First, in industries where competition is impossible or undesirable or where major externalities exist, public ownership has been the traditional solution to problems of market failure. These concerns have led to natural monopolies in industries, such as gas, electricity, railways, water, and telecommunications. Second, public-sector managers and related bureaucrats have vested interests in promoting and perpetuating the linkages between these enterprises and competition-free environments. Two issues merit consideration. The first is the tradeoff between allocative efficiency and scale economies and the second refers to the role of public-sector enterprises in markets where they compete with private firms.

3.2.1. Allocative Efficiency and Scale Economies.

In industries with economies of scale, it has been argued that entry should be restricted to avoid duplication of fixed costs. This argument leads to the natural conclusion that one large firm (a less preferred alternative is a small number of medium-sized firms) is preferable to a large number of small firms. However, the problem with this situation is that market power is enhanced with fewer firms and monopolies usually are associated with allocative inefficiencies. A relevant question is what is the optimum number of firms when there exists a tradeoff between allocative efficiency and scale economies?

An ideal solution would be a single firm operating where price equals marginal cost. The cost of producing every additional unit is precisely the price consumers would be willing to pay for it. Such an outcome would combine allocative and productive efficiencies. The difficulty with this solution is that the firm would end up with losses and hence would not want to operate at such levels of output.

The tradeoff between allocative efficiency and scale economies has important policy implications.[9] First, policies that affect the number of firms in the industry should be considered together with policies which have direct impacts on firm behavior. Second, the threat of entry by itself can affect significantly the behavior of firms in the industry. This fact has important implications for privatization programs. Finally, there are informational advantages from having more competitors in the industry. Furthermore, incentives for internal efficiency can be enhanced.

3.2.2. Competition and the Public Enterprise.

Can competition improve the performance of an industry that includes public enterprise? The answer is affirmative and it relies on the traditional arguments in favor of competition. Briefly stated, threats of competition discourage managers from developing complacent attitudes. Furthermore, competitive forces disseminate information about the industry, effectively breaking the "monopoly of information." Second, competition stimulates innovation in products, processes, and management, which the isolated public firm has no incentive to attempt.

Critics have argued that privatization can lead to restricted output by private monopolies, price gouging, and concentrated market power.[10] The counterargument has been that public ownership impedes entrepreneurial discovery and the market coordination process. In this context, a monopoly need not be a real problem unless it involves exclusive ownership of an essential input.

3.3. Conclusion

This section has considered a number of questions. The first question relates to ownership and its impacts on allocative and internal efficiencies of firms. The nature of ownership affects the objectives of owners as well as the systems they adopt to monitor managerial performance. Thus, changes in property rights affect incentive structures and behavior of manangement. Private ownership promotes internal efficiency through the potential realignment of corporate control. A priori, it would appear that public ownership promotes greater allocative efficiency. But experience dictates that there is suboptimal control in publicly owned firms. The second question relates to competition and its impacts on the performances of public firms. The overwhelming conclusion is that competitive forces improve the performances of industries, including those dominated by public firms.

4. BROAD ISSUES RELATING TO PRIVATIZATION

Given its complex nature, it is not surprising that there are several issues surrounding privatization. There are political and legal issues as well as issues relating to methods of financing, valuation, and pricing, and costs of privatization. Each of these is now considered in turn.

4.1. Political Issues

Elicker (1987) observes that privatization is a political process that operates in the field of economics and not vice versa. Political obstacles to privatization are placed by distinct interest groups, such as the bureaucracy, militiary, labor, and the private sector, particularly in an oligarchic setup. Poole (1987) identifies several obstacles to privatization arising from political misconceptions. First, an argument for the status quo of state provision of a good or service is based on the belief that an adequate number of suppliers will not enter the market to make it competitive. This contention assumes that a permanent public monopoly is preferable to a temporary private monopoly. It ignores the possibility that consumer welfare is likely to be enhanced with competitive product markets. A second justification is that many public services are natural monopolies and hence should be provided by the public sector. This argument raises the issues whether the services are really monopolies and further whether public ownership is optimal. A competitive private sector is an insurance against the guaranteed monopoly of a public sector bureacracy and offers protection for consumers. A third argument in favor of public provision of goods and services is that it ensures that lower-income groups will have access to the supply. Such services are provided at subsidized prices and these subsidizations have other unwanted consequences in the form of implicit costs. Examples of such costs are lack of cost consciousness by management and employees, continued supply of products or services despite poor demand, salary scales in excess of market levels, and inefficient work policies. These subsidizations benefit free-riders, since individuals who can afford to pay market prices also consume at subsidized prices. Thus low-income groups are not the exclusive beneficiaries. Finally, it is argued rather idealistically that public services should not be organized for profit. It is worth noting there are costs associated with the provision of any good or service. These costs are best met by those who benefit by the consumption of the service. If it is desired to protect some segment of the population, for example, low-income groups, it can be effected by issuing vouchers to its members. All other consumers should pay the full market price of the service.

4.2. Legal Issues

A well-defined legal system is *sine qua non* for privatization. Thomas (1987) argues that to protect all the concerned parties, the rules and procedures for privatization must be embedded in the legal system. He considers the legal issues in two types of privatization actions, namely, management contracts and divestitures. In the former, government is contracting to a private vendor and the applicable rules are those relating to service or management. In divestitures, the emphasis is on securities law and the regulations relating to stock transactions. General legal issues covering both methods include several important considerations. First, the basic authority to privatize should be vested in government. Second, privatization is legally unusual in the sense that it is a transaction between a sovereign entity and private individuals (human and corporate). While a government possesses sovereign immunity, this very quality can impede a transaction if the authorities are perceived as not having a genuine interest. Third, contractual restrictions with international lenders can hasten or delay privatization arrangements since in many legal systems these agreements have the force of law. Fourth, dispute-settlement clauses should convince foreign participants that their grievances will be resolved fairly. Fifth, the legal status of current and potential employees of any affected bodies should be always examined. Sixth, it is essential to ensure that the privatization arrangement does not result in a government monopoly being replaced by a private monopoly. Seventh, legal, financial and economic issues are intertwined in privatization arrangements.

Management contracts are generally associated with cost savings, since the public sector typically lacks the flexibility to respond efficiently to changes in work requirements. Legal ramifications permeate all aspects of the arrangement, including the planning process, the bid process, evaluation and selection, monitoring and followup, as well as settlement of disputes. Legal issues in divestitures are more involved. First, the form of ownership—wholly owned, majority holdings, or joint holdings—affects the ease with which the entity can be floated. Second, structuring the organization includes decisions on the type of share structure, degree of capitalization, government seed capital, and guarantees of revenue. Third, the use of an underwriter or advisor has legal ramifications. If the action is a floatation requiring substantial research and dealing with the investing public, the agent acts directly on behalf of the government. However, if the action is a placement, the agent is an intermediary between the buyer and government whose exposure is more direct. Fourth, the nature of the offering—stock, long-term bond, short-term debt, or convertible security—should be investigated from financial and marketing perspectives and legal sufficiency. Finally, there may be special considerations that have legal implications. For example, the government may need to require an undertaking not to increase its shareholdings above an upper bound. In some cases, determining the priority of claimants on the income stream or assets of the corporate entity is a legal concern.

4.3. Financing Issues

Castillo (1987) notes that the process of privatization has two distinct phases of financing. The first phase involves the transfer of ownership and the second relates to operations of the new corporate entity. The latter phase includes capital for modernization and investment, compensating for loss of government subsidies, guarantees, and government-backed lines of credit, as well as providing working capital. The transition in ownership structure is accompanied by shifts from sovereign risk to corporate risk.

Ownership transfer may be effected by public sale of equity shares, sale financed by a leveraged buyout, open auction, or negotiated sale of the enterprise. In some instances, the SOE may need to be prepared for the sale through restructuring—selling excess assets, sizing down the enterprise, infusing government funds, hiring private management, etc. Several factors affect the method of transfer and financing requirements:

- The overall quality and size of the business.
- The presence of a viable and regulated securities market is a facilitating influence. In addition to distributing ownership among the investing public, the securities market is an efficient source for the supply of private domestic capital and promoting a tradition of equity investment and risk taking.
- Political receptivity to permit the free flow of domestic and foreign capital.
- Integration of the country's capital markets with international capital markets. Even if full integration is not possible, the establishment of basic relationships promotes the country's creditworthiness and access to international capital markets.

4.4. Pricing Issues

Two common methods of privatization are tender offers and offers of sale. In a tender offer, prospective buyers bid for the shares available for purchase. This arrangement represents an equilibrium position between supply and demand that determines price and quantity of shares sold. In an offer of sale, the government determines the sale price and prospective buyers indicate the number of shares they would accept. In this instance, correct pricing is crucial. If the price is set too high, the sale does not go through. On the other hand, if the price is set too low, the government does not get a fair price and investors reap a windfall. However, more widespread ownership is likely with an offer of sale. While theoretical models of valuation are available, they are not always applicable, as the necessary information may be lacking. The value is determined by heuristic methods with reference to recent earnings or future earnings potential, dividend-paying capacity, adjusted value of assets, or some combination of these variables. If liquidation of the enterprise is a practical alternative, this value is also used.

Several nations have established mandatory rules on valuation. In France, value is determined by the Privatization Commission as a weighted function of the market value of securities, value of assets, earnings records, subsidiaries, and prospects for performance. Similar procedures are adopted in Senegal and Tunisia. On the other hand, in the Philippines, standard formulae are used to produce a range of values including estimates of appraised value of assets, replication cost, capitalized earnings, and other methods.

Other factors that affect pricing include potential market response, investor interest, availability of financial resources, limitations on foreign holdings or on given groups of investors. In addition, there may be interrelationships between the procedure adopted and price.

4.5. Costs of Privatization

Costs of privatization fall under two broad categories. The first is transaction cost or the expense incurred in carrying out a privatization transaction. The second is the residual cost, which includes budgetary burden related to liabilities that remain after the transaction.[11]

Transaction cost includes administrative costs, financial restructuring, physical rehabilitation and settlement of employee claims. Administrative costs include advisory services as well as brokerage and underwriting commissions in public and private sales. Financial restructuring costs include settlement or assumption of loans and other liabilities, conversion of government-held loan into equity, and recapitalization of SOEs prior to sale. In some cases, SOEs may have tax arrears that the government may have to forego. Interim physical maintenance is again a cost for the government to incur. Settlement of employee claims include severance pay, pension-plan funding, and possible retraining expenses. Discount in offerings for sale as well as interest rate concessions are also transaction costs.

Residual costs vary a great deal from large capital gains to assumption of liabilities and their servicing.[12] In a sale of shares, the purchaser assumes the related liabilities as well, but in the case of sale of assets, the purchaser may not cover the liabilities. The size of residual costs does not carry implications for the desirability of the transaction. It may still be more beneficial to sell the enterprise than to retain it.

5. TECHNIQUES OF PRIVATIZATION

There are several methods of disposing of SOEs available to governments. Each case needs to be considered on its own merits and in the context of the national environment. The fact that a particular technique gained success in a particular instance does not make it an automatic candidate for every other situation. The choice of the particular method is determined by several considerations, such as objectives of the government, current organizational form and sector of activity of the SOE, ability to mobilize private-sector resources, degree of development of capital markets, and sociopolitical factors. Commonly used methods of privatization are listed and discussed in detail below.[13]

- Public offering of shares
- Private sale of shares
- Sale of government or SOE assets
- Reorganization into component parts
- Management/employee buyout
- Lease and management contract

5.1. Public Offering of Shares

The government sells its full or part shareholdings in an enterprise in which it has full or part ownership. The enterprise is assumed to be a going concern established as a public limited company. The sale provides for redistribution of shares. Obviously, in instances where the government sells part of its holdings, there results a joint state–private-owned enterprise in which the private ownership has increased. This method may be adopted to continue the government's presence in the activity or as a first step towards privatization. The procedure followed is similar to that in any other new issue of shares. A prospectus is prepared and, in most cases, the services of an advisor are engaged. In some instances, the advisor may also perform the functions of an underwriter. The shares may be offered either on a fixed-price basis or as a tender offer. Finally, to be eligible for a public offering, the enterprise must comply with certain legal, financial, and disclosure requirements. In some instances, the enterprise may need time to meet those requirements.

The principal advantage of this technique is that the arrangement is open and transparent to public scrutiny and promotes widespread share ownership.

5.2. Private Sale of Shares

In this arrangement the government sells all or part of its shareholdings in a wholly or part-owned SOE to a preidentified single buyer or group of purchasers.

The identification of the buyer could be through a competitive process or individual negotiations. Sale of shares usually implies that the enterprise would be sold as a going concern with its entire assets and related liabilities. In some instances, it may be necessary to prepare the enterprise for the sale by restructuring its liability structure. In the absence of well-functioning equity markets, this arrangement may be the only feasible alternative. Its principal advantage is that the prospective buyer is identified in advance. Furthermore, the private sale is a simpler arrangement in terms of disclosure and other legal requirements. Of course, the disadvantage is that the selection of the buyer almost always draws criticism.

5.3. Sale of Government or Enterprise Assets

The transaction in this instance involves the sale of real assets rather than financial assets—shares in an enterprise. The assets may be sold individually or as a collection of related assets to private buyers. In some instances, the collection of assets may be sold as a new corporate entity. Shares in the spun-off corporation may be placed privately or sold publicly. In other cases, the assets may be offered to a corporate entity and in return the government receives equivalent shares. These shares are then disposed of by the government. Direct sale of the assets may be through competitive bidding or through auction. In cases where it is difficult to sell the enterprise as an ongoing concern, sale of assets may be the only available alternative. The treatment of liabilities and laid-off personnel needs to be handled on a case-by-case basis.

5.4. Reorganization into Component Parts

This method involves breaking up or reorganizing an SOE into separate entities or into a holding company and several subsidiaries.[14] The advantage of this technique is that it permits piecemeal privatization. Different methods of privatization are applied to different component parts, maximizing the gains from the overall process. If an SOE has developed into a conglomerate with several lines of activities, the whole enterprise may not be attractive to potential buyers. But fragmentation would be a viable alternative if the individual components were attractive to investors. In some instances, an SOE may be a monopoly firm and breaking it up would promote competition among the component firms.

5.5. Management/Employee Buyouts

This method refers to a situation in which controlling interest in a firm is obtained by management or management with employees. In a leveraged management buyout, outside investors provide a large proportion of the funds and take a very small equity position, whereas the management group takes the majority equity position while providing a small fraction of the funds. The advantage of this technique is that it provides a means of transferring ownership to the management group who are endowed with human capital but little monetary capital. A side benefit is that it promotes productivity. This technique may be the solution to employment issues when the only other alternative is shutting down the enterprise. A necessary condition is competent management, a stable workforce, and potential for cash flow from operations to service debt.

5.6. Leases and Management Contracts

These are arrangements in which private-sector management, technology, and skills are made available under contract to an SOE for a given period and compensation. There is no transfer of ownership or divestiture of assets. These arrangements may be used to prepare an SOE for its eventual divestiture by improving its operations.

In a lease arrangement, a private operator leases assets or facilities and conducts business in return for a payment to the state and per other conditions imposed by the agreement. The lessee assumes full commercial risk associated with managing the operations. All operating decisions, including employment and management of the assets, rest with the lessee.

A management contractor assumes total responsibility for management of an enterprise in exchange for compensation. In contrast to a lease contract, in which the lessee makes the payment to the state for the use of the assets, the management contractor is compensated for its skills in managing the assets on behalf of the state. The SOE bears all commercial risks and is responsible for all debt payments.

6. STRATEGIES FOR PRIVATIZATION

It is accepted that, in general, if the private sector can supply a given quantity and quality of goods more efficiently than a public enterprise, then the private sector should be employed. This decision is based on economic efficiency but has implications for equity as well. If such an arrangement results in lower income-groups being unable to consume adequate quantities and qualities of goods and services, then a decision can be taken on the method and level of public assistance to these groups. This is a decision based on political considerations. The choice between private and public assistance to facilitate consumption by lower-income groups is separable from the choice between private and public supply of goods and services. The issues relating to private and public supply can be considered independently of the methods used to finance the desired supply.[15]

Hanke (1987) notes that there are two elements to a strategy to implement privatization policies. The technocratic element would require bureaucrats to apply techniques that promote efficiency in the private sector. However, since there are no incentives for bureaucrats to pursue policies that adversely affect their job security and personal influence, it is to be expected that such techniques would not be applied.[16] This necessitates the second element of the strategy, namely, the political approach. Prices should be determined by supply and demand for the effective private provision of goods and services. Deregulation is, therefore, an important element of any privatization strategy.

Specific elements of a privatization strategy should address barriers to privatization and their elimination as well as mobilization of private resources.

6.1. Barriers to Privatization[17]

6.1.1. Inaccurate Cost Information. The cost advantage of the private sector argument is countered by the claim of equally cost-efficient provision of services by SOEs. However, the costs of state provision are understated in the following manner. First, when comparing prices from the two sources of services, the fact that the firm must price to cover its costs, while the SOE is usually subsidized is ignored. Second, while overhead costs of the private provider are covered explicitly in the price charged, the overheads of the SOE are diffused in the government budget. Third, private firms provide employee retirement services that are part of their overall costs, whereas those of the SOE may be integrated in the government budget. Fourth, in some cases, the lack of audited financial statements from SOEs make comparisions difficult. Nevertheless, any strategy for privatization should take these factors into account.

6.1.2. Job Losses and Unemployment. SOEs tend to be overstaffed. The fear of creating short-term unemployment is a significant political barrier when privatization is proposed. Strategies to deal with this problem include the following. First, in the event of privatization, the state can mandate that displaced government workers will have preference in future employment. Where feasible, privatization can be introduced gradually on a geographical basis. Public employees displaced by a privatization arrangement can be transferred to other districts to fill up vacancies arising from normal attrition. Second, government employees in an enterprise marked for privatization should be given the option of forming a company and submitting competitive bids for the service. The important element of these strategies is that the affected parties are given a stake in the privatization.

6.1.3. Fear of Corruption. When a government agency privatizes a service by contracting-out to private companies, a danger is that a particular firm may secure the contract for illegal considerations. Such practices tend to discredit privatization. A viable strategy calls for open bidding procedures and objective selection criteria. Corruption is much less when the state ceases to provide a service in favor of leaving it to the marketplace. Poole (1987) aptly observes, "The only way a firm can use bribery to increase its share of business in a competitive marketplace is to 'bribe' potential customers with lower prices or better service."[18]

6.1.4. Legal Prohibitions. There may be explicit legal restrictions requiring governments to provide a specific service. The administrative law may be ambiguous in many cases, and the strategy requires the legislative reform to researched, drafted, and enacted. Private-sector firms desiring to enter specific fields may be required to take the strategic initiative to develop administrative or legislative provisions to remove barriers to privatization. In the United States, this has been the case with the provision of correctional facilities.

6.1.5. Regulatory Reforms. An adverse climate of government regulation is a potential barrier to privatization. The strategy involves convincing legislators and public officials that competition is an alternative to state-imposed regulations and price controls. Where there are multiple suppliers, there is no need for price controls. It is recognized that this strategy runs against the very grain of an entrenched bureaucracy, but unnecessary regulation is not an alternative.

6.1.6. Inadequate Legal Structures. The willingness of entrepreneurs to take risks and invest in private-sector activities depends on the legal environment. There needs to be strong protection for private property rights and sanctity of contracts. Where legal protection is inadequate, it is likely to be channelized into informal sectors. The strategy, therefore, calls for instituting better access to courts, stronger legal protections and a tax code that does not penalize investments. It is recognized that this strategy, albeit with a long-term payoff, is nevertheless essential.

6.2. Political Feasibility, Constituencies, and Speed of Reforms

The biggest obstacles to economic transitions are political in nature. Furthermore, far-reaching economic transitions are confronted by unsurmountable (or seemingly so!) political constraints. Roland (1993) stresses two elements of strategy in the implementation of privatization programs. The first is the building of constituencies to ensure the political feasibility of the program. The second element relates to the tradeoff between the speed of reform and its budgetary impacts.

Political Feasibility and Building Constituencies. Consider a situation in which two reforms need to be implemented. The first reform is expected to have a positive outcome, whereas the second is expected to have a negative outcome. Both reforms are expected to occur in an environment of uncertainty. There are two approaches available towards the implementation of the reforms. One can either take the "big bang" approach—implement both reforms simultaneously (in parallel)—or implement the reforms sequentially (in series). Given the uncertainties, convincing the affected groups of the need for reforms is a daunting task. Resistance to the reforms can be countered by a "reversal option,"—reversal of the reforms if the outcomes are adverse—but if reversals are costly, the option is not favored. The second approach calls for sequential or gradualistic implementation—implement the first reform, await its outcome, and then implement the second reform. Even if the first outcome is unfavorable, it is easier to convince affected groups that partial reform is unstable and that the second reform should follow. On the other hand, if the first reform is successful and the second is expected to have negative results, it is easier convincing the affected groups that the second should follow so that the benefits of the first reform will not be dissipated. Accumulating support or "building constituencies" for the reforms among the affected groups is an important element in the implementation. It is easier to embark on the reforms and makes unpalatable future reforms more acceptable.

As privatization gains strength, there are accompanying efficiency gains. One may argue that there are increasing economies associated with the level of privatization. Such economies result from a greater number of private firms dealing with each other in a more competitive environment, information spillovers, and better management. Thus, there is a critical mass for privatization and efficiency gains result if the level of privatization is greater than this lower bound. In such circumstances, the scope for policy reversals is virtually nonexistent. On the other hand, if the level of privatization is less than the critical mass, efficiency gains are lower and the probability of a policy reversal increases. One may counter this argument by noting that dynamic efficiency gains are not contemporaneous but lagged over several periods. Even if the critical mass is achieved, there may be initial welfare losses, which should not be the reasons for policy reversals.

Speed of Reforms and Budgetary Impacts. The greater the rate of privatization, higher the allocative efficiencies that are usually accompanied by large-scale layoffs. To the extent that these workers are compensated with unemployment benefits and exit bonuses, such payments have budgetary implications. Thus, with no external aid and absence of large domestic savings, an argument can be made for gradual privatization to ensure macroeconomic stability and to recognize fiscal limitations in dealing with the budgetary burden.

6.3. Mobilization of Private Sources of Finance[19]

Strategies to promote the availability of finance, which has been a constraint in developing nations, are important to the success of privatization programs. This section presents some strategies in this direction.

6.3.1. Private Resources and Domestic Financial Markets. The specific method of privatization is determined by the level of development and liquidity of domestic financial markets. Development of financial markets refers to the extent of access the general investing public or other investors have to finance privatization. These channels, in turn, depend on intermediaries for share distribution and other financial services, sophistication of potential investors, and liquidity of the investing market. In the absence of an organized capital market or local financial intermediation, a public offering is made difficult. However, the experiences of several countries indicate that even in the absence of organized

capital markets, the process of generating funds for privatization identifies un-official financial markets and an incentive is created to promote official markets. The strategy should particularly focus on the creation of secondary equity markets, which provide liquidity to the securities issued in the primary markets.

6.3.2. Acceptance of Payment Terms. Payment terms for the purchase of SOE shares or assets in public offerings as well as private sales are becoming in-creasingly popular. Strategies for financing privatization, specially large-scale arrangements, should recognize this possibility.

6.3.3. Direct Borrowing. The availability of credit may be a determining factor for a transaction to proceed. Such assistance may facilitate some public offerings, private sale of shares or assets, investment in new equity or a leveraged management–employee buyout. Strategies to encourage the banking sector to finance such activities, for example through rediscounting loans, need to be promoted. Similar strategies extend to financing new equity issues of SOEs either to the general investing public or workers.

6.3.4. Debt–Equity Swaps. While debt–equity swaps are designed as debt-relief mechanisms, they facilitate privatization transactions. Specific rules and provisions govern the transactions and, in some instances, specify the eligible debt, conversion procedures, and eligible investments. Remittances of capital and earnings may be limited. The rules specify priority applications—highest priorities and therefore highest redemption prices are available to buyers of privatized state-owned enterprises. Strategies employing debt–equity swaps to finance em-ployee buyouts facilitate privatization programs.

6.3.5. Instsitutional Investors. Strategic decisions to permit pension funds, insurance companies, and other institutional investors to take equity positions in SOEs accelerates privatization. Shares of such mutual funds sold to the investing public provides them indirect ownership in privatized SOEs.

6.3.6. Tax Incentives. In some nations, strategies to finance privatization in-clude tax incentives. Such schemes include reduction of taxable income of in-vestors as well as tax-free dividends of selected shares.

Perotti and Guney (1993) suggest that governments undertaking privatization programs are required to build credibility of their sustained commitment to these programs. The question remains in the minds of new investors is whether they will be exposed to "adverse policy changes" resulting in renationalization. Such ap-prenhensions may be genuine when firms being privatized are monopolies. The government needs to structure the sales of firms so as to build its credibility. The authors suggest this goal may be accomplished by the government retaining a stake in the firm while relinquishing managerial control, thus demonstrating its willingness to bear the partial financial costs of policy changes. A second strategic measure is the underpricing of shares. The authors extend this credibility-buildup hypthesis to explain the data on privatization programs as a counter to the limited market-capacity argument. However, they conclude that the data exhibit support for both hypotheses.

Credibility buildup need not be a compelling requirement for all governments undertaking privatization programs. For example, such a requirement would not be imposed on a government led by the Conservative party in the UK during the 1980s! But a demonstration of commitment might be required of a goverment of one of the erstwhile socialistic states in Eastern Europe. Or such a requirement may be imposed on a country with a historic commitment to a dominant public sector. Such credibility buildup may be a strategy designed more to attract foreign investors rather than domestic investors.

It is clear from the foregoing discussion that there are several strategic considerations in the overall privatization process. These include examining the relative importance of privatization objectives, establishing the legislative and organizational framework, creating a ranking system, preparing an inventory of SOEs, and, finally, selecting the specific enterprises to privatize. Given the economic, legal and political ramifications of privatization and the competing interests the process generates, a clear-cut strategy is critical to ensure the program's success.

7. EVALUATION, IMPACTS, AND IMPLICATIONS

The correct pricing of securities in the sale of a public firm is a crucial aspect of the transaction. Underpricing implies undesirable wealth distribution. The use of market forces in setting the price—as in tender arrangements—assists in getting the price right. Through correctly priced transactions, privatizations improve both economic efficiency as well as public finances. Finally, privatization in a developing nation is a mechanism to generate and promote interest in equity investments.

7.1. Lessons from the British Experiences

Under the Thatcher government in the 1980s Britain acquired extensive experience in privatization. The main lesson from the British experience has been that sales under privatization have been generally underpriced. The degree of undervaluation depends on the method of sale of the issue. Vickers and Yarrow (1989, p. 178) report that the average price change for offer of sale was 21.1% but −1.9% in the case of a tender offer. The tender offer is likely to be priced more correctly, since supply and demand directly interact. The underpricing was highest in companies that were new to the market, as there were no similar companies against which comparisions could be made. In offers for sale, government officials have incentives to set prices low. The advantages of this strategy are several. It encourages widespread ownership and, at the same time, avoids political embarrassment. It minimizes the probability of capital losses by individual investors who are also voters. The real beneficiaries are the financial intermediaries.

7.2. Implications for Wealth Distribution

What are the possible implications of underpricing for wealth distribution? There are shifts in the distribution of wealth consequent to the sale of public assets. The gainers are, of course, the successful applicants for shares and the financial services industry. As a direct result of the underpricing, government has lost funds that can be made up only by taxation. Those individuals who otherwise would have enjoyed lower taxation are the obvious losers. The distribution of income and wealth is affected in other ways, namely, the changes in prices, output, and employment decisions of the firm.

There are undesirable features of this wealth distribution.[20] The gainers have reaped considerable rewards inconsistent with the negligible risks involved. To some extent, this possibility encourages unproductive wealth-seeking activity. Much of the windfall profits have been gained by overseas investors.[21] Finally, it should be noted that the cost to the economy of underpricing is greater than the amount of equivalent tax revenue. The cost of raising $1 in tax revenue is greater than $1, due to the costs of tax collection and implicit cost of distortion to efficient resource allocation caused by additional taxation.

7.3. Alternate Approaches to Implementing Privatization Programs

Vickers and Yarrow (1989, p. 184) observe that there could be improvements in the British government's approaches to privatization. First, the better use of market forces suggests tender offers as the preferred alternative to offers for sale. Even in offers for sale, it would be advantageous to have syndicates bid for the sale. Second, rather than sell the shares in one lump sum, it may be advantageous to sell them in stages. It is likely that after the first lot, the market establishes the price and subsequent lots then may be sold at the prevailing market price. Third, in many instances, the costs of the arrangements were increased by the government directly underwriting the privatizations. Finally, the authors suggest that a simple alternative to the various arrangements is to distribute equal shares to each member of the adult population.[22] The advantage of this proposal is that it is a fair method of asset disposal. Each member has after privatization what he/she ostensibly had before privatization. The opportunity to vary ownership of the company is possible through sales and purchases. There are no arbitrary redistributions of wealth nor windfall profits. There need not be any concerns with correct pricing or aspects of underwriting. This method promotes widespread ownership of shares, in fact across the entire population. The disadvantage is the need to raise compensating funds from other sources and to cope with the distortions caused by tax and debt burdens.

7.4. Privatization and Public Finance

Privatization has an overall impact on public finance of the nation. The government would need to issue bonds to finance an SOE. In privatizing the enterprise, the government issues equity in place of bonds. The only difference is that, in the first case, the enterprise is still in the public sector, whereas in the second case it has been taken off the government's hands. Nevertheless, the transaction has macroeconomic impacts. Let us define the net worth of the government as the aggregate net worth of all its SOEs. Assume that the privatization of the enterprise does not alter its performance. Further, assume the firm is sold at its correct value and there are no transactions costs to be incurred. The government is selling the enterprise at its market value—measured by its discounted stream of future dividends. In this instance, the net worth of the government has not been altered by the transaction, as it receives in cash payments the market value of the enterprise whose ownership it has relinquished. There is only a redistribution of assets in the balance sheet of the government. If however the enterprise is underpriced and the government incurs large transactions costs (promotional expenses, professional fees, underwriting, etc.), the government's net worth actually declines by this arrangement. The government may be better off financing the enterprise with bonds that are relatively less expensive in terms of underpricing and transactions costs.

Let us relax the first assumption and recognize that privatization can increase the efficiency of the firm. The government then sells a more valuable income stream than it would have received under its ownership of the firm. As to whether the government's net worth increases or decreases depends on whether the increase in value of the firm compensates for the underpricing and transactions costs. It is important to note that any increase in value is not determined by the transfer of ownership per se, but by the potential for more efficient operations. If there is an increase in value and there are no significant transactions costs, it can be concluded that privatization improves both economic efficiency and public finances.[23]

7.5. Privatization and Broader Share Ownership

The introduction to this chapter referred to "peoples' capitalism" which is a goal of privatization. If privatization influences a large number of individuals to hold and invest in corporate shares, then it would have accomplished its goal. If a greater proportion of the population is convinced that corporate equity stock are good long term investments, then the conversion to a "property-owning democracy" would have been effected. How does privatization attain its goal of broader share ownership? Privatization is usually accompanied by measures to provide information about the available investments in equity shares. Further, there are additional incentives to hold these investments in privatized companies. Both the available information and incentives in the case of privatized companies are different from regular equity investments. For example, privatization arrangements are usually accompanied by intense advertising campaigns promoting the availability of shares. Incentives to buy shares in privatized companies are greater due to the potential for quick capital gains in the initial stages. The possibilities of vouchers and stock dividends (bonus shares) accruing to long-term holders of shares enhance these incentives.[24] The promotion of wider and deeper share ownership requires the elimination of disincentives, if any, in the form of selective, expropriatory taxation on capital gains or dividend income. In conclusion, privatization in a developing country is a useful mechanism to generate and promote interest in equity investments.

8. CONCLUSION

The essence of privatization is competition among firms and broad capital ownership among the general public. Ownership of a home, business or place of employment generates far greater loyalty than distant ownership of a public enterprise, which in turn generates greater loyalty than no ownership at all. It is relevant to recall Schumpeter's observation that not all property rights are equivalent in their abilities to generate loyalties and political support[25] So much for the case for privatization.

It is useful to end this chapter with some precautions. The behavior of corporate managers depends not only on ownership incentives, including shareholder monitoring and threats of takeovers and bankruptcy, but on market forces and regulation. Competition improves allocative and operating efficiencies by eliminating asymmetries of information between managers and owners. Hence, the conclusion that private ownership and privatization are most suitable in conditions where competition exists. However, in situations where monopoly is dominant, the case for private ownership substituting for public ownership is weaker. Private profit-seeking behavior will not lead to socially efficient results. The scope for competitive forces should be expanded by eliminating barriers to entry and restructuring the monopoly. Hence rapid privatization and broadened share ownership without adequate measures to improve competitive structures are prescriptions for inefficiencies.

NOTES

1. See "A Survey of Third World Finance," *The Economist*, October 1, 1993, p. 16.
2. See *Biennial Report 1985–87*, p. 4.
3. Since we are concerned with ongoing firms, we do not consider constraints imposed on management by creditors in this discussion.
4. While not all stockholders may share this homogeneous interest—some shareholders

may be consumers of the firm's products—it is a safe assumption that all stockholders are interested in the financial welfare of the enterprise.

5. See Alchian (1977a, 1977b), Furobotn and Pejovich (1972), and Demsetz (1964, 1966, 1967).

6. For example, a chemical engineer with specialized knowledge of chemical processes can exploit this comparative advantage with appropriate entrepreneurial activities. Similarly, a physicist with patent rights over specialized processes can capitalize on this comparative advantage.

7. On grounds of internal efficiency, a private monopolist may still be preferable to a public-sector monopoly. See the discussion in subsection 3.1.3.

8. See Vickers and Yarrow (1989), pp. 39–43, and the references cited therein.

9. See Vickers and Yarrow (1989), p. 48, for a simple model and for references to more detailed treatments of this problem.

10. See Millward (1982), Yarrow (1986), and Fitch (1988).

11. See Vuylsteke (1988), p. 139.

12. Ibid., pp. 139–40.

13. See Vuylsteke (1988) for a detailed discussion of these methods.

14. Vuylsteke (1988) points out that this technique can be considered to be a form of restructuring prior to privatization. Since it has been popular in many developing nations, it is treated as a separate form of privatization.

15. See Hanke (1987), p. 78.

16. Both the public bureaucrat and the corporate manager are similar in the sense that both are agents. Shareholders of the corporation are clearly identified as the principals of the corporate manager. However, the identity of the principal of the public bureaucrat is less clear. Suitable incentive structures can be designed for corporate managers but are more difficult in the case of the public bureaucrat, as market mechanisms are absent.

17. See Poole (1987) for a more complete discussion.

18. Ibid., p. 41.

19. For a more complete discussion, see Vuylsteke (1988), II(7).

20. See Vikers and Yarrow (1989), p. 180.

21. With the increased globalization and integration of markets, this possibility will only increase in the future.

22. This proposal is similar to the voucher scheme proposed in Poland and other Eastern European nations.

23. It should be noted that there is a potential tradeoff between economic efficiency and financial gains. If the firm is privatized in an environment of low regulation and a sheltered market, financial gains will be clearly high at the cost of ecomomic efficiency. On the other hand, if the firm is privatized in a competitive environment, economic efficiency will be attained at the cost of financial gains. The situation may also be described as a tradeoff between consumer and producer surpluses. High economic efficiency is consistent with consumer surplus, whereas larger financial gains from a sheltered market are consistent with producer surplus.

24. Vickers and Yarrow (1989) report that while wider shareholdings had been achieved in Britain, they lacked depth, i.e., there were more shareholders but per capita shareholdings were low.

25. See Schumpeter (1950).

8

Internal Sources of
Development Finance

1. INTRODUCTION

In this final chapter we first review the major policy and strategic considerations in developing the internal sources of finance. Necessary reforms of the financial sector, specifically financial liberalization, are discussed in the third section. This discussion stresses a stable macroeconomic climate as a prerequisite for these reforms. Further, exchange-rate adjustments, trade and public enterprise policy reforms preferably should precede financial liberalization. A comprehensive legal and regulatory system is a substitute for direct intervention in financial markets by the government. The chapter concludes by drawing attention to the role of government. In this context, government's operations are limited to oversight, supervision, and ensuring that markets function effectively. Government has a greater, not diminished, role in the development of internal finance.

2. INTERNAL SOURCES OF DEVELOPMENT FINANCE

This section summarizes the principal policy and strategic considerations in developing the internal sources.

2.1. Tax Policy

Tax policy is an integral element of the financing process through its linkage with savings. Development requires increasing rates of savings and investments to expand output and enhance social investments in health, education and welfare. Through taxation, the government finances its capital construction and other developmental projects. Tax policies have several objectives: to correct market failure, reduce the foreign-exchange gap, encourage intermediation through financial markets and institutions, influence changes in factor proportions through incentives, etc. There are some necessary conditions for tax policies to succeed in their objectives. They should have limited goals. Further, tax policies should be as broad-based as possible. It is essential that the administrative capacity to implement the schemes be available. Finally, tax programs assume that individual behavior is price responsive. But if behavior is affected by other factors and noneconomic considerations, then tax policies are undermined. Tax reform has to be accompanied by a combination of expenditure reform, state enterprise pricing reform, as well as macroeconomic policy reform regarding exchange rates, interest rates, and wage rates.

2.2. Capital Markets

Financial intermediation through securities markets has been gaining importance for several reasons. These markets facilitate varying levels of direct investments by savers, thus providing portfolio diversification. On the other hand, corporate users of these funds can pool investments from a large body of individuals. An active secondary market for securities provides liquidity, which is enhanced by the presence of institutional investors.

Certain essential "infrastructure" is needed to promote securities markets. A basic prerequisite is a legal framework within which contracts can be designed, implemented, and enforced. Accounting information needs to be standardized and brought into conformance with accepted international standards. Modern communications and computing technologies are essential. An efficient banking system promotes the smooth flow of transactions. The legal framework should provide a regulatory environment that promotes free and fair price formation. There needs to be full and reliable disclosure of information with adequate safeguards and protection for investors. These requirements, along with rigorous listing standards, ensure open, free, and fair price formation. Finally, institutions such as mutual funds, unit trusts, and pension funds broaden securities markets through their trading activities. These elements of "infrastructure" enable securities markets to supply development finance efficiently.

2.3. Development Finance Institutions

Financial intermediation through development banks focuses on their specific abilities to identify, select, finance, and monitor the performances of entrepreneurs and their projects. As these institutions assist entrepreneurs in selecting technology and disseminating technical knowledge, they create and promote human capital. Given the competitive environments of the 1990s for developing nations, three goals are identified for development banks. First, they should be self-supporting, i.e., capable of raising funds in domestic and foreign markets at reasonable costs and in amounts adequate to maintain an acceptable scale of operations. Second, quality of development bank operations should ensure profitability with diversified financial services. Finally, these institutions need to accumulate human capital with organizational and management strengths to broaden the scope of their services and to ensure that they develop independently.

Specific strategies are identified to ensure the achievement of these goals. First, development banks should improve their profitability and flexibility over the business cycle through diversification into activities such as leasing, provision of working capital, and trade finance. Consultancy services complementary to the existing term-finance business of the development bank, such as product identification, selection of appropriate technology, and marketing, will provide diversification. These activities capitalize on the accumulated experience of the staff and on established client relationships. Second, in most developing nations, financial markets for nondepository instruments, such as money market instruments, debentures, long-term bonds, and equity shares are underdeveloped. The development bank can assist these financial markets by expanding into investment and merchant banking activities. As a result of their long term association with firms, development banks can "certify" issue prices as reflecting future prospects of these firms. Finally, development banks can assist in creating the financial infrastruture which facilitates transactions. Such activities include promoting accounting and auditing standards and the legal framework to enforce contracts. Communications technology, that permits quick transfer and uniform accessibility of information is essential for modern financial transactions. Development banks can assume a catalytic role in introducing such technology.

2.4. Privatization of the Public Sector

The movement towards privatization had gained impetus in the 1980s in developed, developing, and the erstwhile socialist nations. Privatization has become the medium for raising development finance and for allocating resources according to market priorities based on a redefinition of the role of government. Since privatization involves the sale of firms to large numbers of individual shareholders, it is said to promote "peoples' capitalism." The operating motives for privatization extend from reducing the financial drain on government, releasing capital from nonproductive government investments, attracting new capital through growth of domestic capital markets and broadened base of domestic equity ownerships, creating growth-oriented jobs, and to enable government to focus on policy. The empirical evidence generally indicates that privately owned firms tend to have greater internal efficiency than publicly owned firms when product markets are competitive.

Correct market-determined prices are essential for the private supply of goods and services and, hence, deregulation is an important element in any privatization strategy. Obviously, such a strategy needs to be directed at eliminating barriers to privatization, which stem from apprehensions regarding job losses and unemployment or unbridled corruption. On the other hand, strategies to promote the supply of finance are important to the success of privatization programs. Even in the absence of organized capital markets, steps to identify unofficial financial markets

and incentives to promote official markets are in the right direction. Other strategies directed at encouraging the banking sector to finance privatization by rediscounting loans, debt–equity swaps to finance employee buyouts, investments
by institutional investors, and tax incentives are useful in mobilizing resources.
Broader share ownership in the privatized firms can be accomplished by suitable
advertising campaigns, potential distribution of vouchers and stock dividends, and
elimination of taxes on capital gains or dividends.

However, in extending the case for private ownership and privatization, it
should be noted that a necessary condition is a competitive environment. Eliminating barriers to entry and diluting monopolistic power are essential to reduce
inefficiencies and to ensure success of privatization programs.

3. REFORM OF THE FINANCIAL SECTOR

During the 1980s many developing nations emphasized incentives for private-
sector activities and initiated free-market-oriented policies. This thrust was cen-
tered on appropriate tax policies, capital-market development, new orientations for
financial institutions, and privatization of public-sector activities. This focus emphasized reform of the financial sector. The *World Development Report, 1989*
documents several case studies of efforts at financial-sector reform. Some broad
conclusions emerge from these experiences. First, a prerequisite to financial-sector
reforms is a stable macroeconomic environment. Reforms in an unstable macroeconomic climate only tend to compound the instability. Such reforms result in
high real interest rates, volatile real exchange rates and insolvencies among firms
and banks. Second, in situations where protection and controls have distorted
prices, financial liberalization may not result in improved resource allocation.
Deregulation may cause the financial system to respond more flexibly to bad
signals. Exchange-rate readjustments and reforms in trade and public-enterprise
policy should at least be simultaneous with, if they do not precede, financial
liberalization. Chile's experience in the early 1980s is worth noting in this respect.
Third, efforts to establish a comprehensive legal and regulatory system should
replace efforts to intervene directly in the existing financial markets and institutions. For example, inadequate prudential regulation and bank supervision was the
cause of financial insolvency in the Southern Cone countries, Philippines, and
Turkey. Regulation and supervision by management of financial institutions, by
market forces and by public authorities are necessary to instill discipline in
entrepreneurs and corporate managers. Fourth, reforms undoubtedly affect relative
prices, which have differential impacts on various groups of individuals. Thus,
reforms have distributional implications. For example, the beneficiaries of interest
rate liberalization are creditors, whereas debtors bear the increased burden. Financial institutions with imbalances in the maturity structures of their assets and
liabilities—long-term loans and short term deposits—can be similarly affected.
Firms employing foreign exchange debt can be exposed to arbitrary losses when

currency is devalued. It may become necessary to provide assistance to groups most affected by the liberalization programs to weather the transitions.

Given the necessity of financial sector reform in developing nations, is there a particular sequence for the process? The *World Development Report, 1989* suggests there are three distinct stages. The first step is to get the fiscal deficit under control and establish macroeconomic stability. At the same time, the authorities should improve the financial "infrastructure"—accounting standards and legal stystems, procedures for the enforcement of contracts, disclosure requirements, and bases for prudential regulation and supervision. Further, the authorities should reduce or eliminate directed credit programs and permit interest rates to reach their natural levels, reflecting inflation as well as other market forces. At the micro level, managerial autonomy in financial institutions should be encouraged. If required, some financial institutions may be restructured. Liberal policies in trade and industry are necessary to improve efficiency in the real sector. The second step promotes the creation of a variety of markets and institutions to foster competition. Deposit and lending rates should be effective over broad ranges. The final step includes complete liberalization of interest rates, total elimination of directed-credit programs, relaxation of capital controls, and removal of restrictions on foreign institutions. Trade transactions should be liberalized first, followed by capital movements, since capital markets adjust faster than the goods markets. An inflow of capital results in an appreciation of the exchange rate, which vitiates trade liberalization. Each step should be implemented expeditiously, allowing for appropriate adjustments between steps.

The four sources of internal finance considered here are not substitutes nor are they mutually exclusive. But complementarities exist among them. Public deficits can be reduced by taxation or by borrowing. Borrowing from the central bank increases inflation, whereas borrowings from the banking system through high reserve and liquidity requirements is less inflationary but carries the price of reduced bank profitability, distorted interest rates, and crowded-out private-sector borrowers. A hierarchy exists in the methods of financing public-sector debt. Borrowing from a securities market is preferable to forced borrowing from financial institutions, which is preferable to borrowing from the central bank. If the government agrees to pay market interest rates, then a market trading in short-term government bills can be created. Such a market would have the advantage of reducing inflation as well as providing the government with a method to engage in open-market operations. Eventually, this market for short-term government bills can lead to a corporate securities market.

The reform of the banking sector should not be the only goal of liberalization, which should also cover a broadly based financial system including financial markets and nonbank intermediaries. Experiences in countries such as Malaysia and Philippines indicate that liberalization of commercial banking will not add to the supply of long-term credit and equity capital. In contrast, the growth of Korean capital markets and development of nonbank financial institutions there promoted the supply of long-term credit, despite the limited liberalization of the banking sector.[1]

In most developing nations, unhealthy financial institutions are in the public sector. One way of improving their efficiency would be to privatize them. This line of action can be followed only after the quality of their portfolios and the regulatory framework have been improved. In some developing nations, thin security markets prevent the widespread distribution of shares of the privatized institutions. This sale would transfer the ownership from the government to large private groups. Such a move would result in concentrated ownership and undermine sound banking. In such situations, the alternative to privatization would be to improve efficiency through autonomous management and strict supervision.

4. CONCLUSION

It is appropriate that any study of the financing of development end on a note of caution. Previous chapters have not stressed adequately the difficulties or impediments in implementing the necessary reforms. First, common-interest groups will combine to oppose policies that are not in their interests even if these policies are in the national interest. Furthermore, efforts to develop these internal sources will not bear results immediately. Consumers and entrepreneurs will be slow to recognize and react to the benefits of these efforts. However, the biggest advantage is the demonstration effect that success of these reforms in a particular group of nations has for other groups.

In this overall scheme, government has an important role. It provides oversight and prudent supervision to ensure that financial markets and institutions function effectively. To the extent that these intermediaries function effectively, the role of government is minimal. But when the functioning of markets and institutions is impaired, government will be required to intervene to rectify the situation. Financial liberalization calls for an enhanced, not lessened, role for government.

We started this study by drawing attention to the financing constraints in developing nations. This impediment has been a source of concern. Given the increased competition for external finance, developing nations have to rely increasingly on internal sources. Financial liberalization and reforms have become major elements in their overall schemes. A welcome consequence of these internal reforms is the increasing flow of external capital. A clear conclusion is that there are no alternative strategies to promoting the internal sources of development finance.

NOTE

1. See *World Development Report, 1989*, p. 130.

Bibliography

Abramovitz, M. 1956. "Resources and Output Trends in the United States since 1870." *American Economic Review, 43*, pp. 5–23.

———. 1979. "Rapid Growth Potential and its Realization: The Experience of Capitalist Economies in the Post-War Period." In Malinvaud, E. (Ed.), *Economic Growth and Resources*. New York: St. Martins.

Adelman, I. 1975. "Development Economics: A Reassessment of Goals." *American Economic Review, 65*, 302–09.

———, et al. 1979. "A Comparison of Two Models for Income Distribution Planning." *Journal Of Policy Modeling, 1*(1), pp. 37–82.

Alchian, A. A. 1969. "Corporate Management and Property Rights." In Manne, H. (Ed.), *Economic Policy and the Regulation of Corporate Securities*, pp. 337–60. Washington, DC: American Enterprise Institute. Also reprinted in Alchian (1977a).

———. 1977a. *Economic Forces at Work*. Deerfield Beach, FL: Liberty Press.

———. 1977b. "Some Economics of Property Rights." In Alchian, A. A. *Economic Forces at Work*. Deerfield Beach, FL: Liberty Press.

Ames, E. and N. Rosenberg. 1963. "Changing Technological Leadership and Industrial Growth." *Economic Journal, 73*, 13–31.

Arrow, K. J. 1962. "The Economic Implications of Learning by Doing." *Review of Economic Studies, 29*, 155–173.

"A Survey of Third World Finance." *The Economist*, October 1, 1993, p. 16.

Atkinson, A. 1987. "The Theory of Tax Design for Developing Countries." in Newbery, D. and N. Stern (Eds.), *The Theory of Taxation for Developing Countries*, pp. 387–406. New York: Oxford University Press.

——— and J. E. Stiglitz. 1980. *Lectures on Public Economics*. New York: McGraw Hill.

Auerbach, A. J. and M. Feldstein. (Eds.). 1985. *Handbook of Public Economics*, Vols. 1 & 2. Amsterdam: North-Holland.

Balassa, B. 1978. "Exports and Economic Growth: Further Evidence." *Journal of Development Economics, 5*, 181–89.

Balogh, T. 1963. *Unequal Partners*. Oxford: Blackwell.

Baltenspreger, E. 1980. "Alternate Approaches to the Theory of the Banking Firm." *Journal of Monetary Economics, 6*, 1–37.

Bardhan, P. 1988. "Alternative Approaches to Development." In Chenery, H. B. and T. N. Srinivasan (Eds.), *Handbook of Development Economics*, Vol. 1, pp. 40–71. New York: Elsevier.

Barletta, N. A. "Preface." In Hanke, S. H. (Ed.), *Privatization and Development*, pp. ix–x. Washington, DC: International Center for Economic Growth.

Barnea, A., R. A. Haugen, and L. W. Senbeb. 1985. *Agency Problems and Financial Contracting*. Englewood Cliffs, NJ: Prentice-Hall.

Bauer, P. T. and B. S. Yamey. 1957. *The Economics of Underdeveloped Countries*. Cambridge: Cambridge University Press.

Becker, R. and E. Burmeister (Eds.). 1991. *Growth Theory*, Volumes 1–3. Brookfield, VT: Edward Elgar Publishing Company.

Beckerman, W. 1962. "Projecting Europe's Growth." *Economic Journal, 72*, 912–27.

Benston, G. J. and C. W. Smith, Jr. 1976. "A Transactions Cost Approach to the Theory of Financial Intermediation." *Journal of Finance, 31*, 215–31.

Biennial Report 1985–1987. 1987. Washington, DC: Center for Privatization.

Black, F., M. C. Jensen and M. Scholes. 1972. "The Capital Asset Pricing Model: Some Empirical Tests." In Jensen, M. C. (Ed.), *Studies in the Theory of Capital Markets*. New York: Praeger.

Black, J. 1970. "Trade and the Natural Growth." *Oxford Economic Papers, 22*, 13–23.

Bond, M. E. 1987. "An Econometric Study of Primary Product Exports from Developing Country Regions to the World." *IMF Staff Papers, 32*(2), 191–227.

Bosworth, B. P. 1984. *Tax Incentives and Economic Growth*. Washington, DC: The Brookings Institution.

Boyd, J. H. and E. C. Prescott. 1986. "Financial Intermediary Coalitions." *Journal of Economic Theory, 38*, 211–32.

Britto, R. 1973. "Some Recent Developments in the Theory of Economic Growth: An Interpretation." *Journal of Economic Literature, 11,* 1343–66.

Bruck, N. 1991. *Lecture Notes on Development Banking*. Washington, DC: Economic Development Institute, The World Bank.

Buffie, E. F. 1984. "Financial Repression, the New Structuralists, and Stabilization Policy in Semi-industrialized Economies." *Journal of Development Economics, 14*, 305–22.

Burmeister, E. and A. R. Dobell. 1970. *Mathematical Theories of Economic Growth*. New York: Macmillan.

Cameron, R. (Ed.). 1972. *Banking and Economic Development: Some Lessons of History*. Oxford: Oxford University Press.

———, O. Crisp, H. T. Patrick, and R. Tilly. 1967. *Banking in the Early Stages of Industrialization: A Study in Comparative Economic History*. Oxford: Oxford University Press.

Campbell, T. and M. Kracaw. 1980. "Information Production, Market Signalling, and the Theory of Financial Intermediation." *Journal of Finance, 35*, 863–82.

Candoy-Sekse, R. 1988. *Techniques of Privatization of State-Owned Enterprises*, Volume III, *Inventory of Country Experience and Reference Materials*, Technical Paper No. 90. Washington, DC: The World Bank.

Canto, V. A., D. H. Joines, A. B. Laffer, P. Evans, M. A. Miles and R. I. Webb. 1983.

Foundations of Supply-side Economics: Theory and Evidence. New York: Academic Press.

Castillo, R. J. "Financing Privatization." In Hanke, S. H. (Ed.), *Privatization and Development*, pp. 119–26. Washington, DC: International Center for Economic Growth.

Caves, R. E. 1966. "Vent for Surplus Models of Trade and Growth." In *Trade, Growth and Balance of Payments*. Chicago: Rand McNally.

———. 1970. "Export-Led Growth—The Post War Industrial Setting." In Eltis, W. A., M. F. Scott, and J. Wolfe (Eds.), *Induction, Growth and Trade*. Oxford: Clarendon Press.

———. 1971. "Export-led Growth and the New Economic History." In Bhagwati, J. N., R. W. Jones, R. A. Mundeu, and J. Vaner (Eds.), *Trade, Balance of Payments, and Growth*. Amsterdam: North-Holland.

Chakravarty, S. 1987. "The State of Development Economics." *The Manchester School of Economics and Social Studies, 66*(2), 125–43.

Chan, Y. S. 1983. "On the Positive Role of Financial Intermediation in Allocation of Venture Capital in a Market with Improper Information." *Journal of Finance, 38*, 1543–68.

Chandavarkar, A. 1992. "Of Finance and Development: Neglected and Unsettled Questions." *World Development, 20*(1), 133–42.

Chelliah, R., H. J. Bass, and M. R. Kelly. 1975. "Tax Ratios and Tax Effort in Developing Countries, 1969–71." *International Monetary Fund Papers, 22*(1), 187–205.

Chenery, H. 1957. "The Interdependence of Investment Decisions." In Abramovitz, A. (Ed.). *The Allocation of Economic Resources*. Stanford: Stanford University Press.

———. 1983. "Interaction between Theory and Observation in Development." *World Development, 11*(10), 853–861.

——— and M. Bruno. 1962. "Development Alternatives in an Open Economy." *Economic Journal, 72*, 79–103.

———, et al. 1974. *Redistribution with Growth*. New York: Oxford University Press.

——— and T. N. Srinivasan (Eds.). 1988. *Handbook of Development Economics*, Vols. 1 & 2. New York: Elsevier.

——— and M. Syrquin. 1975. *Patterns of Development: 1950–70*. New York: Oxford University Press.

Cho, Y. J. 1986. "Inefficiencies from Financial Liberalization in the Absence of Well-Functioning Equity Markets." *Journal of Money, Credit and Banking, 18*(2), 191–99.

Choi, K. 1983. *Theories Of comparative Economic Growth*. Ames: Iowa State University Press.

Cutler, D. M., J. M. Poterba and L. Summers. 1988. "What Moves Stock Prices?" National Bureau of Economic Research Working Paper No. 2538.

DeLong, J. B., A. Shleifer and L. M. Summers. 1989. "The Size and Incidence of the Losses from Noise Trading." *Journal of Finance, 44*, 681–96.

DeMeza, D. and D. Webb. 1987. "Too Much Investment: A Problem of Asymmetric Information." *Quarterly Journal of Economics, 102*, 281–92.

Demsetz, H. 1964. "The Exchange and Enforcement of Property Rights." *Journal of Law and Economics, 7*, 11–26.

———. 1966. "Some Aspects of Property Rights." *Journal of Law and Economics, 9*, 61–70.

———. 1967. "Toward a Theory of Property Rights." *American Economic Review, 57*(2), 347–73.

———. 1970. "The Private Provision of Public Goods." *Journal of Law and Economics, 13*, 293–306.

———. 1983. "The Structure of Ownership and the Theory of the Firm." *Journal of Law and Economics, 26*, 373–90.

Denison, E. F. 1962. *The Sources of Economic Growth in the United States and the Alternatives before Us*. Washington, DC: Committee for Economic Development.

Diamond, D. 1984. "Financial Intermediation and Delegated Monitoring." *Review of Economic Studies, 51*, 393–414.

——— and P. Dybvig. 1983. "Bank Runs, Insurance and Liquidity." *Journal of Political Economy, 85*, 191–206.

Diamond, W. and V. S. Raghavan (Eds.). 1982. *Aspects of Development Bank Management*. Baltimore: Johns Hopkins University Press.

Diaz-Alejandro, C. 1985. "Good-bye Financial Repression, Hello Financial Crash." *Journal of Development Economics, 19*, 1–24.

Dixit, A. 1976. *The Theory of Equilibrium Growth*. New York: Oxford University Press.

Domar, E. D. 1946. "Capital Expansion, Rate of Growth, and Employment." *Econometrica, 14*, 137–47.

———. 1947. "Expansion and Employment." *American Economic Review, 37*, 34–55.

———. 1957. *Essays in the Theory of Economic Growth*. Oxford: Oxford University Press.

Dorfman, R. 1967. *Prices and Markets*. Englewood Cliffs, NJ: Prentice-Hall.

Ebrill, L. P. 1987a. "Are Labor Supply, Savings, and Investment Price-Sensitive in Developing Countries? A Survey of the Empirical Literature." In Gandhi, V. (Ed.), *Supply-Side Tax Policy: Its Relevance to Developing Countries*, pp. 60–90. Washington, DC: International Monetary Fund.

———. 1987b. "Optimal Taxation of Financial Savings in Developing Countries: Relevance of Supply-Side Tax Policies." In Gandhi, V. (Ed.), *Supply-Side Tax Policy: Its Relevance to Developing Countries*, pp. 91–114. Washington, DC: International Monetary Fund.

———. 1987c. "Income Taxes and Development: Some Empirical Relationships for Developing Countries." In Gandhi, V. (Ed.), *Supply-Side Tax Policy: Its Relevance to Developing Countries*, pp. 115–139. Washington, DC: International Monetary Fund.

———. 1987d. "Evidence on the Laffer Curve: The Cases of Jamaica and India." In Gandhi, V. (Ed.), *Supply-Side Tax Policy: Its Relevance to Developing Countries*, pp. 175–197. Washington, DC: International Monetary Fund.

Elicker, P. H. 1987. *Some Political Aspects of Privatization*. Washington, DC: Center for Privatization.

Eltis, W. A. 1973. *Growth and Distribution*. New York: Wiley.

———. 1984. *The Classical Theory of Economic Growth*. New York: Macmillan.

Evans, M. K. 1983. *The Truth about Supply-side Economics*. New York: Basic Books.

Fei, J. C. H. and G. Ranis. 1965. *Development of the Labor Surplus Economy: Theory and Policy*. Homewood, IL: Irwin.

Fink, R. H. 1982. "Economic Growth and Market Processes." In Fink, R. H. (Ed.), *Supply-Side Economics*, pp. 372–94. Lanham, MD: University Publications of America.

Fitch, L. C. 1988. "The Rocky Road to Privatization." *American Journal of Economics and Sociology, 47*(1), 1–14.

Friedman, M. and A. J. Schwartz. 1963. *A Monetary History of the United States 1867–1960*. Princeton: Princeton University Press (for National Bureau of Economic Research).

Fry, M. J. 1978. "Money and Capital or Financial Deepening in Economic Development?" *Journal of Money, Credit and Banking, 10*(4), 464–75.

———. 1980. "Saving, Investment, Growth and the Cost of Financial Repression." *World Development, 8*(4), 317–27.

———. 1981. "Inflation and Economic Growth in Pacific Basin Developing Economies." *Federal Reserve Bank of San Fransisco Economic Review*, Fall, 8–18.

———. 1988. *Money, Interest, and Banking in Economic Development*. The Johns Hopkins University Press.

Furobotn, E. G. and S. Pejovich. 1972. "Property Rights and Economic Theory: A Survey of the Recent Literature." *Journal of Economic Literature, 10(4)*, 1137–62.

Galbis, V. 1977. "Financial Intermediation and Economic Growth in Less Developed Countries: A Theoretical Approach." *Journal of Development Studies, 13*(2), 58–72.

Gandhi, V. (Ed.). 1987a. *Supply-Side Tax Policy: Its Relevance to Developing Countries*. Washington, DC: International Monetary Fund.

———. 1987b. "Relevance of Supply-Side Tax Policy to Developing Countries: A Summary," In Gandhi, V. (Ed.), *Supply-Side Tax Policy: Its Relevance to Developing Countries*, pp. 3–44. Washington, DC: International Monetary Fund.

———. 1987c. "Tax Structure for Efficiency and Supply-Side Economics in Developing Countries," In Gandhi, V. (Ed.), *Supply-Side Tax Policy: Its Relevance to Developing Countries*, pp. 225–49. Washington, DC: International Monetary Fund.

Gemmell, N. 1987. *Surveys in Development Economics*. Oxford: Basil Blackwell.

Gerschenkron, A. 1962. *Economic Backwardness in a Historical Perspective*. Cambridge, MA: Harvard University Press.

———. 1968. *Continuity in History and Other Essays*. Cambridge, MA: Harvard University Press.

Gersowitz, M., C. F. Diaz-Alejandro, G. Ranis, and M. R. Rosenzweig. (Eds.). 1982. *The Theory and Experience of Economic Development*. London: Allen and Unwin.

Ghosh, P. K. (Ed.). 1984. *Third World Development: A Basic Needs Approach*. Westport CT: Greenwood Press.

Gilder, G. 1982. "The Supply-Side." In Fink, R. H., *Supply-Side Economics*, pp. 14–32. Lanham, MD: University Publications of America.

Goldsmith, R. W. 1969. *Financial Structure and Development*. New Haven: Yale University Press.

———. 1983. *The Financial Development of India, Japan and the United States*. New Haven: Yale University Press.

———. 1985. *Comparative National Balance Sheets*. Chicago: The University of Chicago Press.

Goode, R. 1984. *Government Finance in Developing Countries*. Washington, DC: The Brookings Institution.

Gordon, D. 1983. "Development Finance Companies, State and Privately Owned: A Review." World Bank Staff Working Papers No. 578. Washington, DC: The World Bank.

Greenhut, M. L. 1983. *From Basic Economics to Supply-side Economics*. Lanham, MD: University Press of America.

Greenwald, B., J. E. Stiglitz and A. Weiss. 1984. "Informational Imperfections in the Capital Market and Macroeconomic Fluctuations." *American Economic Review, 74*(2), 194–9.

Grilli, E. R. and M. C. Yang. 1988. "Primary Commodity Prices, Manufactured Goods Prices and the Terms of Trade of Developing Countries: What the Long-run Shows." *World Bank Economic Review, 2*(1), 1–48.

Gurley, J. G. and E. S. Shaw. 1955. "Financial Aspects of Economic Development." *American Economic Review, 45*(4), 515–37.

———. 1956. "Financial Intermediaries and the Saving-Investment Process." *Journal of Finance, 11*(2), 364–81.

———. 1960. *Money in a Theory of Finance*. Washington, DC: Brookings Institution.

———. 1967. "Financial Structure and Economic Development." *Economic Development and Cultural Change, 15*(3), pp. 257–68.

Haache, G. 1979. *The Theory of Economic Growth: An Introduction*, New York: Macmillan.

Haberler, G. 1961. *A Survey of International Trade Theory*. Princeton Special Papers in International Economics.

Hahn, F. H. and R. C. O. Mathews. 1964. "The Theory of Economic Growth: A Survey." *Economic Journal, 74*, 779–902.

Hailstones, T. J. 1982. *A Guide to Supply-side Economics*. Houston: Robert F. Dame.

Hamberg, D. 1971. *Models of Economic Growth*. New York: Harper and Row.

Hanke, S. H. (Ed.). 1987. *Privatization and Development*. Washington, DC: International Center for Economic Growth.

Hansen, B. 1958. *The Economic Theory of Fiscal Policy*, Cambridge, MA: Harvard University Press.

Harrod, R. F. 1939. "An Essay in Dynamic Theory." *Economic Journal, 49*, March, 14–33.

———. 1948. *Towards a Dynamic Economics*. New York: Macmillan.

Hart, O. D. and D. M. Jaffee. 1974. "On the Application of Portfolio Theory to Depository Financial Intermediaries." *Review of Economic Studies, 41*, 129–47.

Hazlett, T. W. 1982. "The Supply-Side's Weak Side: An Austrian's Critique." In Fink, R. H. (Ed.), *Supply-Side Economics*. Lanham, MD: University Publications of America.

Henriot, P. J. A. 1981. "Development Alternatives: Problems, Strategies, and Values." In Callaghan, D. and P. G. Clark (Eds.), *Ethical Issues of Population Aid: Culture, Economics and International Assistance*, pp. 207–238. New York: Irvington.

Hicks, J. R. 1965. *Capital And Growth*. New York: Oxford University Press.

Hinrichs, H. H. 1966. "A General Theory of Tax Structure Change during Economic Development." Cambridge, MA: Harvard University Law School.

Hirschman, A. O. 1958. *The Strategy of Economic Development*. New Haven: Yale University Press.

———. 1982. "The Rise and Decline of Development Economics." In Gersowitz, M., C. F. Dias-Alejandro, G. Ranis, and M. R. Rosenzweig (Eds.), *The Theory and Experience of Economic Development*. London: Allen and Unwin.

Hyman, D. 1972. "A Behavioral Model for Financial Intermediation." *Economic and Business Bulletin, 24*, 9–17.

Jao, Y. C. 1985. "Financial Deepening and Economic Growth: Theory, Evidence and Policy." *Greek Economic Review, 7*(3), 187–225.

Jensen, M. C. and W. H. Meckling. 1976. "Theory of the Firm: Managerial Behavior,

Agency Costs and Ownership Structure." *Journal of Financial Economics, 3*, 305–60.

John, K. and L. Senbet. 1988. "Limited Liability, Corporate Leverage and Public Policy." Unpublished manuscript.

Jorgensen, D. W. and Z. Griliches. 1967. "The Explanation of Productivity Change." *Review of Economic Studies, 34*, January, 249–84.

———. 1972. "Issues in Growth Accounting: Reply to Denison." *Survey of Current Business*, 65–94.

Kaldor, N. 1961. "Capital Accumulation and Economic Growth." In Lutz, F. A. and D. C. Heath (Eds.), *The Theory of Capital*. New York: Macmillan.

———. 1978. *Further Essays in Applied Economics*. New York: Holmes and Meier.

Kapur, B. K. 1975. "Money as a Medium of Exchange and Monetary Growth in an Under-development Context," *Journal of Development Economics, 2*(1), 33–48.

———. 1976a. "Alternative Stabilization Policies for Less Developed Countries," *Journal of Political Economy, 84*(4), 777–95.

———. 1976b. "Two Approaches to Ending Inflation," in R. I. McKinnon (Ed), *Money and Finance in Economic Growth and Development: Essays in Honor of Edward S. Shaw*, pp. 199–221. New York: Marcel Dekker.

———. 1992. "Formal and Informal Financial Markets, and the Neo-Structuralist Critique of the Financial Liberalization Strategy in Less Developed Countries." *Journal of Development Economics, 38*(1), January, 63–77.

Kennedy, K. A. 1971. *Productivity and Industrial Growth—The Irish Experience*. Oxford: Clarendon Press

Khatkhate, D. and K. W. Richel. 1980. "Multipurpose Banking: Its Nature, Scope and Relevance for Less Developed Countries." *International Monetary Fund Staff Papers, 27*(3), 478–516.

Kindleberger, C. P. 1962. *Foreign Trade and the National Economy*. New Haven: Yale University Press.

———. 1964. *Economic Growth in France and Britain, 1851–1950*. Cambridge, MA: Harvard University Press.

———. 1967. *Europe's Post War Growth: The Role of Labor Supply*. Cambridge, MA: Harvard University Press.

Klein, M. 1971. "A Theory of the Banking Firm." *Journal of Money, Credit and Banking, 3*(2), 205–218.

Krugman, P. R. 1987. "Is Free Trade Passé?" *The Journal of Economic Perspectives, 1*(2), 131–44.

Kumar, P. C. and G. Tsetsekos. 1989. "The Agent–Common Interest Group Nexus: Towards a Theory of Economic Organizations." *Proceedings*, Washington Consortium Schools of Business Research Forum.

———. 1992. "Security Market Development and Economic Growth." In Fischer, K. P. and G. J. Papaioannou (Eds.). *Business Finance in Less-Developed Capital Markets*. Westport, CT: Greenwood Press.

Kuznets, S. 1966. *Economic Growth and Structure*, London: Heinemann.

———. 1967. "Quantitative Aspects of the Economic Growth of Nations: Level and Structure of Foreign Trade: Long Term Trends." *Economic Development and Cultural Change, 15*(2) 1–140.

Lal, D. 1985. *The Poverty of Development Economics*. Cambridge, MA: Harvard University Press.

Leland, H. and D. H. Pyle. 1977. "Informational Asymmetries, Financial Structure, and Financial Intermediation." *Journal of Finance, 32*, 371–87.

Leontieff, W. et al. 1977. *The Future of the World Economy.* New York: Oxford University Press.

LeRoy, S. and R. Porter. 1981. "The Present-Value Relation: Tests Based on Implied Variance Bounds." *Econometrica, 49*, 555–74.

Levine, R. 1990a. "Stock Markets, Growth and Policy." Washington, DC: Country Economics Department, The World Bank, WPS 484.

————. 1990b. "Financial Structure and Economic Development." Washington, DC: International Finance Discussion Paper No. 381, Board of Governors of the Federal Reserve System.

Lewis, W. A. 1954. "Economic Development with Unlimited Supplies of Labor." *Manchester School Economics and Social Studies, 20*, 139–92.

————. 1984. "The State of Development Theory." *American Economic Review, 74*(1), 1–10.

Lintner, J. 1965. "Security Prices, Risk and Maximal Gains from Diversification." *Journal of Finance, 20*, 587–616.

Little, I. M. 1982. *Economic Development.* New York: Basic Books.

Lubitz, R. 1973. "Export-led Growth in the Industrial Economies." *Kyklos, 26*, 301–21.

Lucas, R. J. 1988. "On the Mechanics of Economic Development." *Journal of Monetary Economics, 22*, 3–42.

MacKenzie, G. A. 1987. "A Simple Model of Income Tax Reductions on Economic Growth and Aggregate Supply," in Gandhi, V. (Ed.). *Supply-Side Tax Policy: Its Relevance to Developing Countries,* pp. 45–59. Washington, DC: International Monetary Fund, 1987.

Maslow, A. H. 1970. *Motivation and Personality.* New York: Harper and Row.

Mathieson, D. J. 1979. "Financial Reform and Capital Flows in a Developing Economy." *International Monetary Fund Staff Papers, 26*(3), 450–89.

————. 1980. "Financial Reform and Stabilization Policy in a Developing Economy." *Journal of Developing Economics, 7*(3), 359–95.

Mayer, C. 1989. "Myths of the West: Lessons from Developed Countries for Development Finance." Washington, DC: Development Economics Department, The World Bank, WPS 301.

McKinnon, R. I. 1973. *Money and Capital in Economic Devlopment.* Washington, DC: Brookings Institution.

———— (Ed.). 1976. *Money and Finance in Economic Growth and Development: Essays in Honor of Edward S. Shaw.* New York: Marcel Dekker.

————. 1986. "Financial Liberalization in Retrospect: Interest Rate Policies in LDCs." Stanford: Stanford University, Center for Economic Policy Research, No. 74.

McNamara, R. S. 1973. "Address to the Board of Governors." *World Bank Report*, pp. 10–11.

Meade, J. E. 1961. *A Neoclassical Theory of Economic Growth.* London: Allen and Unwin.

Meier, G. M. (Ed.). 1983. *Pricing Policy for Development Management.* Baltimore: Johns Hopkins Unversity Press.

Melitz, J. and M. Pardue. 1973. "The Demand and Supply of Commercial Bank Loans." *Journal of Money, Credit and Banking, 3*(2), 669–92.

Meyer, L. H. (Ed.). 1981. *The Supply-side Effects of Economic Policy.* Boston: Kluwer-Nijhoff.

Millward, R. 1982. "The Comparative Performance of Public and Private Ownership." In Roll, E. (Ed.), *The Mixed Economy*, New York: Macmillan.

Morris, C. T. 1984. "The Measurement of Economic Development: Quo Vadis?" In Ranis, G., R. L. West, M. W. Liserson, and C. T. Morris (Eds.). *Comparative Development Perspectives: Essays in the Honor of Lloyd C. Reynolds*. Boulder, CO: Westview Press.

Mossin, J. 1966. "Equilibrium in a Capital Asset Market." *Econometrica, 34*, 768–83.

Musgrave, P. 1959. *The Theory of Public Finance, A Study in Public Economics*. NY: McGraw-Hill.

Musgrave, R. A. 1969. *Fiscal Systems*. Yale University Press.

———. 1987. "Tax Reform in Developing Countries," in Newbery, D. and N. Stern (Eds.). *The Theory of Taxation for Developing Countries*, pp. 242–63. New York: Oxford University Press.

Myers, S. C. and N. S. Majluf. 1984. "Corporate Financing and Investment Decisions When Firms Have Information that Investors Do Not Have." *Journal of Financial Economics, 13*, 187–221.

Myrdal, G. 1958. *Economic Theory and Underdeveloped Regions*. Bombay: Vora and Company.

Nankani, H. 1988. *Techniques of Privatization of State-Owned Enterprises*. Volume II (Selected Country Case Studies), Technical Paper No. 89. Washington, DC: World Bank.

Newbery, D. 1987. "Taxation and Development," in Newbery, D. and N. Stern (Eds.). *The Theory of Taxation for Developing Countries*, pp. 165–204. New York: Oxford University Press.

——— and N. Stern (Eds.). 1987. *The Theory of Taxation for Developing Countries*. New York: Oxford University Press.

Niskanen, N. 1971. *Bureaucracy and Representative Government*. Chicago, IL: Aldine, Atherton.

North, D. C. 1987. "Institutions, Transactions Costs and Economic Growth." *Economic Inquiry*. 25(3), 419–28.

Nurske, R. 1953. *Problems of Capital Formation in Underdeveloped Countries*. Oxford: Oxford University Press.

———. 1961. *Equilibrium and Growth in the World Economy*. Cambridge, MA: Cambridge, MA: Harvard University Press.

Olson, M. 1971. *The Logic of Collective Action*. Cambridge, MA: Harvard University Press.

———. 1982. *The Rise and Decline of Nations*. New Haven: Yale University Press.

Pack, H. 1988. "Industrialization and Trade." In Chenery, H. B. and T. N. Srinivasan (Eds.). *Handbook of Development Economics*, Vol. 1, pp. 334–80. New York: Elsevier.

Papanek, G. 1972. " The Effects of Aid and Other Resource Transfers on Savings and Growth in Less Developed Countries." *Economic Journal, 82*, September, 934–50.

———. 1977. "Economic Theory: The Earnest Search for a Mirage." In Manning, N. (Ed.). *Essays in Economic Development and Cultural Change*, pp. 270–81. Chicago: University of Chicago Press.

Parkin, M. 1970. "Discount House Portfolio and Debt Selection." *Review of Economic Studies, 37*, 469–97.

Parvin, M. 1975. "Technological Adaptation, Optimum Level of Backwardness, and the

Rate of Per Capita Income Growth: An Econometric Approach." *American Economic Review, 19*, 23–31.

Patrick, H. J. 1966. "Financial Development and Economic Growth in Underdeveloped Countries." *Economic Development and Cultural Change, 14*(2), 174–89.

———. 1967. "Japan 1868–1914." In Cameron. R. et al (Eds.). *Banking in the Early Stages of Industrialization: A Study in Comparative Economic History*. New York: Oxford University Press.

Perotti, E. C. and S. E. Guney. 1993. "The Structure of Privatization Plans." *Financial Management, 22*(1), pp. 84–98.

Pesek, B. 1970. "Bank's Supply Function and the Equilibrium Quantity of Money." *Canadian Journal of Economics, 13*, 357–85.

Pesmazoglu, J. 1972. "Growth, Investments and the Savings Ratio: Some Long Term Associations by Groups of Countries." *Bulletin of the Oxford University Institute of Economics and Statistics, 34*, 309–28.

Poole, R. 1987. "The Political Obstacles to Privatization." In Hanke, S. H. (Ed.). *Privatization and Development*. Washington, DC: International Center for Economic Growth.

Prebisch, R. 1950. *The Economic Development of Latin America and Its Principal Problems*. New York: United Nations.

Pyle, D. H. 1971. "On the Theory of Financial Intermediation." *Journal of Finance, 26*, 737–47.

Reilly, F. K. 1989. *Investment Analysis and Portfolio Management*, 3rd ed. Homewood, IL: The Dryden Press.

——— and E. F. Drzycimski. 1981. "An Analysis of a Multi-Tiered Stock Market." *Journal of Financial and Quantitative Analysis, 16*(4), 559–75.

——— and J. M. Wachowicz. 1979. "How Institutional Trading Reduces Market Volatility." *Journal of Portfolio Management, 5*(2), 11–17.

——— and D. J. Wright. 1984. "Block Trades and Aggregate Stock Price Volatility." *Financial Analysts Journal, 40*(2), 54–60.

Roberts, P. C. 1982. "The Breakdown of the Keynesian Model." In Fink, R. H. *Supply-Side Economics*, pp. 1–13. Lanham, MD: University Publications of America.

Robinson, S. 1971. "Sources of Growth in Less-Developed Countries: A Cross-Section Study." *Quarterly Journal of Economics, 85*, 391–408.

Roland, G. 1993. "The Political Economy of Restructuring and Privatization in Eastern Europe." *European Economic Review, 37*, 533–40.

Roll, R. 1977. "A Critique of the Asset Pricing Theory." *Journal of Financial Economics, 4*(2), 129–76.

Romer, P. 1986. "Increasing Returns and Long Run Growth." *Journal of Political Economy, 94*, 1002–37.

———. 1990. "Endogenous Technological Change." *Journal of Political Economy*.

Rosenstein-Rodan, P. N. 1943. "Problems of Industrialization of Eastern and South-Eastern Europe." *Economic Journal*, June-September, 202–99.

Ross, S. A. 1976. "The Arbitrage Theory of Capital Asset Pricing." *Journal of Economic Theory, 13*(2), 341–61.

Rostow, W. W. 1960. *The Stages of Economic Growth: A Non-Communist Manifesto*. Cambridge: Cambridge University Press.

Sametz, A. W. 1981. "The Capital Market." In Polakoff, M. E. and T. A. Durkin (Eds.), *Financial Institutions and Markets*. Boston: Houghton Mifflin Company.

Sanchez-Ugarte, F. 1987. "Rationality of Income Tax Incentives in Developing Countries: A Supply-Side Look." In Gandhi, V. (Ed.). *Supply-Side Tax Policy. Its Relevance to Developing Countries*, pp. 250–78. Washington, DC: International Monetary Fund.

———— and J. R. Modi. 1987. "Are Export Duties Optimal in Developing Countries? Some Supply-Side Considerations." In Gandhi, V. (Ed.), *Supply-Side Tax Policy: Its Relevance to Developing Countries*, pp. 279–320. Washington, DC: International Monetary Fund, 1987.

Sandmo, A. 1985. "The Effect of Taxation on Savings and Risk Taking." In Auerbach, A. J. and M. Feldstein (Eds.), *Handbook of Public Economics*, Vols. 1 & 2, pp. 265–311. Amsterdam, North-Holland.

Schmookler, J. 1966. *Invention and Economic Growth*, Cambridge, MA: Harvard University Press.

Schultz, T. 1964. *Transforming Traditional Agriculture*. New Haven: Yale University Press.

Schumpeter, J. A. 1911/1935. *Theory of Economic Development*. Cambridge, MA: Harvard University Press.

————. 1950. *Capitalism, Socialism and Democracy*. New York: Harper, 1950.

Scott, M. F. 1989. *A New View of Economic Growth*. Oxford: Clarendon Press.

Sen, A. 1988. "The Concept of Development." In Chenery, H. B. and T. N. Srinivasan (Eds.), *Handbook of Development Economics*, Vol. 1, pp. 10–26. New York: Elsevier.

————. 1983. "Development: Which Way Now?" *Economic Journal, 93*, 745–62.

Sharpe, W. F. 1964. "Capital Asset Prices: A Theory of Market Equilibrium under Conditions of Risk." *Journal of Finance, 19*, pp. 425–42.

Shaw, E. S. 1973. *Financial Deepening in Economic Development*. New York: Oxford University Press.

Shiller, R. L. 1982. "Do Stock Prices Move Too Much to be Justified by Subsequent Changes in Dividends?" *American Economic Review, 71*, 421–36.

Shome, P. 1987. "Limitations of the Role of Tax Policy in Economic Development," In Gandhi, V. (Ed.). *Supply-Side Tax Policy: Its Relevance to Developing Countries*, pp. 321–36. Washington, DC: International Monetary Fund.

Singer, H. 1950. "The Distribution of Gains Between Borrowing and Investing Countries." *American Economic Review, 40*(2), 473–86.

Solow, R. M. 1956. "A Contribution to the Theory of Economic Growth." *Quarterly Journal Of Economics, 70*, 65–94.

————. 1957. "Technical Change and the Aggregate Production Function." *Review of Economics and Statistics, 39*, 312–20.

————. 1960. "Investment and Technical Progress." In Arrow, K. J., S. Karlin, and P. Suppes (Eds.), *Mathematical Models in the Social Sciences*. Stanford: Stanford University Press.

————. 1970. *Growth Theory: An Exposition*. Oxford: Clarendon Press.

Squire, L. 1981. *Employment Policies in Developing Countries*. New York: Oxford University Press.

Srinivasan, T. N. 1977. "Development, Poverty, and Basic Human Needs: Some Issues." *Food Research Institute Studies, XVI*(2), 11–28.

Stern, N. 1989. "The Economics of Development: A Survey." *The Economic Journal, 99*, 597–685.

Streeten, P. 1972. *The Frontiers of Development Studies*. New York: Macmillan.
———. 1977. "The Distinctive Features of a Basic Needs Approach to Development." *International Development Review, 3*, 8–16.
———. 1979. "Basic Needs: Premises and Promises." *Journal Of Policy Modeling, 1*, 136–46.
——— and S. J. Burki. 1978. "Basic Needs: Some Issues." *World Development, 6*(3), 411–21.
Stewart, F. 1985. *Basic Needs in Developing Countries*. Baltimore: Johns Hopkins University Press.
Stiglitz, J. E. and H. Uzawa. 1969. *Readings in the Modern Theory of Economic Growth*. Cambridge, MA: MIT Press.
——— and A. Weiss. 1981. "Credit Rationing in Markets with Imperfect Information." *American Economic Review, 71*, 393–410.
Swan, T. W. 1956. "Economic Growth and Capital Accumulation." *Economic Review, 32*, 334–61.
Tait, A. A., W. L. M. Gratz, and B. J. Eichengreen. 1979. "International Comparisons of Taxation for Selected Developing Countries, 1972–76." *International Monetary Fund Staff Papers, 26*, March, 123–56.
Tanzi, V. 1983. *Tax Systems and Policy Objectives in Developing Countries: General Principles and Diagnostic Tests*. Washington, DC: International Monetary Fund.
———. 1987. "Quantitative Characteristics of the Tax Systems of Developing Countries." In Newbery, D. and N. Stern (Eds.). *The Theory of Tax Design for Developing Countries*. New York: Oxford University Press.
Taylor, L. 1979. *Macro Models for Developing Countries*. McGraw-Hill.
———. 1983. *Structuralist Macroeconomics: Applicable Models for the Third World*. New York: Basic Books.
Thirlwall, A. P. 1974. *Inflation, Savings and Growth in Developing Countries*. New York: St. Martins Press.
Thomas, P. 1987. "The Legal and Tax Considerations of Privatization." In Hanke, S. H. (Ed.). *Privatization and Development*. Washington, DC: International Center for Economic Growth.
Tobin, J. 1984. "On the Efficiency of the Financial System." *Lloyds Bank Review, 153*, July, 1–15.
Todaro, M. P. 1985. *Economic Development in the Third World*, 3rd ed. New York: Longmans.
Towey, R. E. 1974. "Money Creation and the Theory of the Banking Firm." *Journal of Finance, 29*, pp. 57–72.
Townsend, R. M. 1979. "Optimal Contracts and Competitive Markets with Costly State Verification." *Journal of Economic Theory, 21*, 265–93.
Ture, N. B. 1982. "The Economic Effects of Tax Changes: A Neoclassical Analysis." In Fink, R. H. (Ed.), *Supply-Side Economics*, pp. 33–69. Lanham, MD: University Publications of America.
Uzawa, H. 1965. "Optimum Technical Change in an Aggregative Model of Economic Growth." *International Economic Review, 6*(1), 18–31.
Van Wijnbergen, S. 1982. "Stagflationary Effects of Monetary Stabilization Policies: A Quantitative Analysis of South Korea." *Journal of Development Economics, 10*(2), 133–69.

————. 1983a. "Interest Management in LDCs." *Journal of Monetary Economics, 12*(3), 433–52.

————. 1983b. "Credit Policy, Inflation and Growth in a Financially Repressed Economy." *Journal of Development Economics, 13*(1–2), 45–65.

————. 1985. "Macro-economic Effects of Changes in Bank Interest Rates: Simulation Results for South Korea." *Journal of Development Economics, 18*(2–3), 541–54.

Verdoorn, P. J. 1949. "Factors that Determine the Growth of Labor Productivity." (Translated). *L'Industria, 1,* 3–11.

Vickers, J. and G. Yarrow. 1989. *Privatization: An Economic Analysis.* Cambridge, MA: The MIT Press.

Viner, J. 1953. *International Trade and Economic Development.* Oxford: Oxford University Press.

Voivodas, C. S. 1973. "Exports, Foreign Capital Inflow, and Economic Growth." *Journal of International Economics, 3*(3) 37–49.

Vuylsteke, C. 1988. *Techniques of Privatization of State-Owned Enterprises, Volume I (Methods and Implementation).* Technical Paper No. 88, Washington, DC: World Bank.

Watson, C. G., G. R. Kincaid, C. Atkinson, E. Kalter, and D. Folkerts-Landau. 1986. *International Capital Markets: Developments and Prospects.* Washington, DC: International Monetary Fund: World Economic and Financial Surveys.

Williamson, S. D. 1986. "Costly Monitoring, Financial Intermediation, and Equilibrium Credit Rationing." *Journal of Monetary Economics, 18,* 159–79.

————. 1987. "Recent Developments in Modeling Financial Intermediation." *Federal Reserve Bank of Minneapolis Quarterly Review,* Summer, 19–29.

Wolfson, D. J. 1979. *Public Finance and Development Strategy.* Baltimore: Johns Hopkins University Press.

World Development Report, 1989. Washington, DC: World Bank.

World Institute for Development Economics Research (WIDER), The United Nations University. 1990. "Foreign Portfolio Investment in Emerging Equity Markets." Study Group Series No. 5.

Yarrow, G. K. 1986. "Privatization in Theory and Practice." *Economic Policy, 1*(2), 323–77.

Author Index

Subject Index

ABOUT THE AUTHOR

P. C. KUMAR is Associate Professor at the Kogod College of Business Administration, The American University, Washington, D.C. His research interests are in the transfer of finance theories to developing nations. His articles have appeared in the *Journal of Finance, Journal of Financial and Quantitative Analysis, Decision Science,* and other leading journals.

ISBN 0-89930-461-3

9 780899 304618

90000>

HARDCOVER BAR CODE